Classified
Woman

Classified Woman

THE SIBEL EDMONDS STORY

A MEMOIR

SIBEL EDMONDS

Published by Sibel Edmonds, Alexandria, Virginia

ISBN-13: 978-0615602226

ISBN-10: 0615602223

On Sibel Edmonds

"We have been doing national security litigation for more than 30 years, and in our view, this is the most egregious misuse of the classification authority we've seen."

—Michael Kirkpatrick, *Washington Times*

"Having lived under tyranny in Iran and elsewhere, Edmonds knows what it looks like. In her case, and in many other recent cases, tyranny comes in the form of the state secrets privilege, a foolproof mechanism of the federal government to hide executive branch corruption, incompetence, and illegal activity. This is a practice more at home with czars and nabobs, and should have no place in the United States. But Edmonds gave the government something it never expected—a no-holds-barred battle. She hoisted the black flag and went on the attack by forming the National Security Whistleblowers Coalition, an organization dedicated to changing the law, exposing government misdeeds, and giving hell to those who richly deserve it."

—Professor William Weaver, University of Texas

"She's a First Amendment cannonball. She speaks up for what she believes in. She's a leader. The fact that she, not only, was a strong advocate for her own case, but she became a strong advocate for the public policy, for the greater good."

—Congresswoman Carolyn Maloney (D-New York)

"She had the intuition, the courage, and the backbone to stand up and do it. And we are very grateful to her. And the PEN Award is significant in that regard. Tell the public what happened—Sibel Edmonds was a heroine in this."

—Senator Frank Lautenberg (D-New Jersey)

"Sibel Edmonds is certainly one of my heroes and I'm glad to have heard of her effort. I admire what she is doing very much. I think she's serving the country very well."

—Daniel Ellsberg, "Democracy Now"

"Sibel Edmonds' Kafkaesque ordeal underscores how easily government powers, especially powers wielded in the name of national security, can be abused to keep the public in the dark about official failings. PEN is deeply troubled by Sibel Edmonds' story and by the growing number of reports of efforts by the administration to silence government employees."

—Larry Siems, PEN American Center

"Sibel Edmonds is an American Patriot. She has a classic story to tell—which is the story of an immigrant, who came here seeking more freedom, and seeking a real democracy—and was unfortunately shut down when she tried to exercise her rights under the First Amendment."

—Ann Beeson, American Civil Liberties Union

"For nearly a decade, Sibel Edmonds has fought against excessive government secrecy, built up an organization of more than one hundred national security whistleblowers, and exposed government attempts to cover up abuses."

—James Bamford, bestselling author and award-winning journalist

"The silencing of Edmonds has been remarkably silent. Which is probably just what the FBI was counting on in the first place."

—Clay Risen, *The New Republic*

To Ela & F.R. Deniz

Contents

Introduction

ome say life is a journey. I agree. My life has been three major journeys, each marked by a distinctive set of events that defined and shaped who and where I am today.

The first journey of my life took me to Iran. It was marked by witnessing my father subjected to arrest, interrogation and, of course, torture, a common practice in the reign of Shah Reza Pahlavi, Iran's king. My father—a doctor, a surgeon—believed in democracy and liberal values; he advocated collective bargaining for the working class to achieve health care benefits and wages that would enable them to survive. For this he was marked as a Communist and imprisoned. For doing right by others he was tortured. In spite of it all, and against ardent protestations of his family, he continued to fight for his country's freedoms; to help where he could, to ease suffering. His were deeply held beliefs. His journey became mine, at a very early age. We were bonded.

That first journey too was marked by revolution: I watched it unfold and witnessed oppression, persecution, and merciless injustice. Overnight, fundamental values were forced on me: how I should be dressed, how I should cover every strand of hair, how precisely and how many times I must pray. I had no choice in the matter of where I lived; we don't get to choose where we are born or taken by our parents. While this bumpy road ended as tumultuously as it started, I carry its scars with me. They are permanent. My disdain for any form of religious fundamentalism, aversion to even the word *monarchy*, and hatred for any despotic practice, all were acquired during this time and will stay with me forever.

The second journey began on my return to Turkey. This one was marked by censorship: my fellow Turks and I were forced to swallow words and black out any sentence forbidden by those who ruled. Punishment for violators was cruel and severe, as happened to many authors and reporters I admired: all of them locked up for expressing opinions that many shared but few dared even to acknowledge. Here it was in black and white: when freedom of the press and expression are taken away, the suffering and ill consequences are not limited to only those few who write and report. All of my father's resolve, for instance, all his hard work and support, were not adequate to prevent censorship from affecting what I was taught in school, what I yearned to learn and what I longed to express. These were forbidden.

The iron force of the Turkish state marked my second journey with its mass killing of its minorities, mass detention of its dissidents, and mass corruption among its ruling parties. This journey too was one by default; I played no role in starting it. I did, however, conclude it by making the decision to leave it behind and choosing the next path myself. These experiences too, for as long as I live, are engraved in my conscience and soul. My passionate love for freedom of speech and of the press, my dedication to the protection of due process, and my endless quest for government held accountable—gained in the void of their absence—always will remain an inseparable part of me.

The most important of my three journeys is the third. This is the one chosen freely: coming to the United States of America. This journey started as love at first sight. Its beginning was marked by living with the kind of freedom and rights that had existed only in books and my fantasies. This road became a highway as I began to know the Constitution my new country theoretically upheld, the separation of powers it said it exercised, and a fairly new concept of equality it tried to nurture. I chose this country, and I wanted to immerse myself in its culture; to meld with it, blend into it; become inseparable, so that all those things I admired and longed for would apply to me; would envelop me. I rushed through its steps until I reached the top, where I would declare my oath to my newfound land, and dedicate myself not only to cherish but also to protect it for as long as I chose to live in it. The strength and fidelity of this union didn't lessen over time. Each passing year, of education in its laws and history, of visits to any of the diverse cultures it contained, left a lovely mark in me to hold on to, show, and treasure.

Until, that is, the chosen road changed shape and took me in a blind direction, leading me into dark, cold places I never thought existed. Just like the dark side of the moon, here was the dark side of my precious third journey—a side not many talked of or wrote about; an ugly side that may have shown up here and there, once in a while, throughout its history, like a child's "bad monster" popping up in the night, then retreating into shadows, never lingering long enough to be seen or figured out, or ever exposed in the light.

Prologue

I threw my carry-on into the backseat. Once behind the wheel, I paused to take a mental inventory of what I would need: passport, *check*; traveler's checks, *check*; cash in dollars and Turkish lira, *check* . . .

I looked at my watch: half past three. I gazed on our townhouse, reflecting; the third Christmas in a row with no jolly wreath on our door or festive lights decorating the trim. I had a little less than two and a half hours to get to the airport, which was less than fifteen minutes away, to purchase my tickets to JFK with a continuing flight to Istanbul, get on the plane, and take off. I couldn't procrastinate any longer, so I started the engine, pulled out of our driveway, and headed north toward Reagan National Airport.

The gray, windy December day promised a heavy downpour, precisely mirroring my mood. I tightened my grip on the wheel to steady my shaking hands. I'd left a short note for my husband telling him it was time for me to go and face whatever awaited me there. I was not going to miss the chance to see my grandmother one last time. I would not let them erase me from my family's map.

Until a few years earlier, before the dark journey began, we frequent-ed the country at least once a year, and my family paid us annual visits. Then came the nightmare; changing everything, turning our life upside down.

I had plotted the trip in secrecy, something I had never done in all our years of marriage. I knew he would do everything he could to stop me from taking this trip. It was, after all, a matter of life and death.

I turned right at the airport entrance and squinted to make out the signs to long-term parking. My vision blurred, and I knew at once it was not poor visibility but tears. My determination, my will, began to melt with each passing second. I drove past the parking entrance and con-tinued on. I made two more turns around the airport, tears still falling, before I took the exit. Now I was crying out loud, sobbing. The pangs, pain, fear, rage and everything else I had bottled up in me for the past four years began to pour out; a floodtide of grief.

Yes, this was true acceptance, full acknowledgment. I could never ever go back. I would never see my extended family again. My past, my ties, my bonds and heritage all had been wiped out—completely and for-ever.

In my country of origin I have been branded as a spy for the United States of America. There I have been characterized as a "traitor against the country" and named as "the enemy of the state."

According to Turkish government insiders, there exists an outstand-ing warrant for my arrest and incarceration. The moment I set foot in that country, I'll be arrested and jailed under its so-called State Treason Laws, and be prosecuted in a military tribunal without access to outside representation. This is only if I'm lucky, since the likely fate that awaits me is to be taken—disappeared—and added to the list of tens of thou-sands of "unexplained" missing persons.

I am no longer able to visit Turkey or any of my family there, includ-ing my beloved grandmother. The ties that connect me to my past have been permanently severed. My family members have been warned and threatened to cease all contacts with me. The bonds that connect me to my friends as well, even those from childhood, no longer exist.

Instead of driving directly back home, I exited left, to the quiet Potowmack Landing, a sailboat marina in a quaint little harbor on the Potomac River facing the airport's runways. The place seemed deserted. Considering the now steady rain, I wasn't surprised.

I parked in an isolated, gravelly space, pulled up the zipper on my gray fleece jacket and tucked in my knitted scarf before stepping out. I walked to the pier, ignoring the razorlike wind and rain striking me in the face.

The view was beautiful, soft and melancholy. The masts on many of the boats were strung with multicolored lights, but the cheery decorations only darkened my mood.

Across the river, despite the poor visibility and encroaching night, I could make out the famous landmarks of Washington, DC; of its past, its government. The Jefferson Memorial, Washington Monument, the Capitol . . . I smiled bleak and bitterly, for once upon a time I'd seen them with different eyes and marveled at all they represented. They served as reminders of our democracy, the Bill of Rights and a government of the people, by the people, for the people. They used to fill me with a sense of pride and contentment. Now they carried an awful, different meaning; one that evoked in me fear, disappointment, distrust, rage and sadness. These feelings were mingled with futility, a sense of desperation that things would never be fixed, and pessimism too—about the chances of ever recovering what was lost, or even if that were possible.

I felt deep pangs when I thought about this government, this monstrous new entity, taking over. I felt all the wounds, inflicted on me directly; they began to ooze and bleed. I couldn't go back to where I came from, but I didn't want to stay here either. I was too tired to fight. I had battled for four long years nonstop and been defeated in every single one. They had taken nearly everything from me, everything I was. Here I was now, a woman excluded from her nation's laws, protections and rights; a woman whose very existence has been attacked; a woman who has been shut up by the government she so once admired.

By the media and the public, I'm commonly referred to as the State Secrets Case, the Gagged Woman or the Classified Whistleblower.

Among legal experts I'm cited as "the most egregious case of unjustified secrecy and classification"; "the most gagged woman in the known history of the States"; and "the unprecedented case in application of State Secrets Privilege."

Many of my old friends and associates consider me "too dangerous to associate with," "too risky to get close to," and "a reason to land us on a government watch list."

The United States government has declared me "a woman who knows too many sensitive secrets," "a woman who should remain gagged," and "a person who should be classified at every level and in every aspect."

The United States government has officially declared my birthplace, my heritage, as Top Secret Classified Information containing State Secrets.

My birth date has been designated classified, and its divulgence a serious threat to the United States' sensitive diplomatic relations. The United States judicial system has agreed with this designation and ruled for its enforcement.

I am forbidden to reveal my mother tongue; all languages I speak have been banned from being officially stated. Per the government's demand, the federal courts have ruled against those who tried to ask me what languages in which I'm fluent.

My employment history has been classified as top secret. Those who have requested this information have been prevented by court orders.

My education background, including college degrees and areas of study, are designated as classified and covered by the State Secrets Privilege. The government has claimed that divulgence of my education pedigree would jeopardize our nation's security and sensitive secrets.

The First Amendment right has been officially and formally taken away from me. I am excluded from the protection of freedom of speech guaranteed by the Constitution.

The Fourth Amendment does not apply to me. My right to due process and access to the courts has been officially taken away. In 2002, the Department of Justice invoked the State Secrets Privilege, barring my cases from moving forward in the courts. The United States federal courts have obliged.

The U.S. Congress is forbidden to discuss my case or refer to me. The Justice Department has issued a formal gag order to Congress with regard to my case. My right to petition Congress has been taken away.

I looked up at another plane that had just taken off, blinking away raindrops as I followed it across the sky. I wondered if it was the plane I had planned to be on, now taking off without me as I sat there in the rain, pondering how I'd come to this point. With my family taken from me, my past erased, my voice gagged, and most of my identity classified, I felt incapable of taking charge of my life or whatever was left of it. What had gotten me here was a set of turning points imposed on me, all beyond my control. For four years I'd been gripping a steering wheel that simply was not connected. I knew what I wanted: an untraveled road, a different car, a brand-new start; but I didn't know how. All I knew at this time was that I had to step out of this person I'd become—no, actually *been molded into*—during those past four years: the whistleblower and the gagged woman; the Classified Woman.

I

CALL TO DUTY

1

How It All Began

The beautiful sunny Friday afternoon on September 14, 2001, did not reflect our grim mood, as my husband and I sat across from each other in a deserted restaurant in Eden Center, often referred to as Little Vietnam, in Arlington, Virginia.

The small technology business we had started two years earlier had come under a tremendous amount of pressure due to the recently collapsed Dot Com industry. We had to let go of several employees and were in the midst of turning the company into a small consulting firm with less than a handful of people. I had switched from part-time to full-time status at George Washington University, where I was pursuing double majors in criminal justice and psychology, registered for a fifteen-credit course load, and determined to wrap up all my graduation requirements in less than fifteen months.

The clear, pleasant day certainly did not reflect the country's mood either. Only three days past, the United States was attacked within its borders—not by a nation or government but supposedly by stateless invisible enemies scattered around the globe. Without any prior warnings from our own government or from any national or international entities—including the media—we all were caught off guard.

As we sat on 9/11 watching footage of buildings getting hit and collapsing, I could scarcely believe that the carnage, bloodbaths and wars I had witnessed as a child, when I lived thousands of miles from here, had found their way into my chosen country, the United States of America.

I remembered the period of anarchy in Turkey in the 1970s. My early childhood there was marked by bomb explosions and shootings in unexpected public places. Whether densely populated universities or overcrowded bazaars, all were considered highly probable targets; no place was considered safe.

I recalled an incident in Iran I had witnessed a few years later, when I was eight years old. I was in a minivan with six other girls, on my way home from school. We'd heard an explosion. Traffic stopped and we saw thick smoke rising in a column only a few yards away. Our driver got out and started talking with other drivers. I rolled down the window to hear one man explain, ". . . either a big fire or a bomb explosion in a building, probably the movie theater on the circle. I heard there were many people trapped inside . . ." As we passed the building, I leaned out the window and looked. The rescue teams, together with civilian volunteers, were removing charred bodies and stumps, dropping them on the sidewalk in front of the building. The driver, recovering as though from a trance, turned around and yelled, "Get down on the floor! You shouldn't be looking at this!"

It was too late. That scene—the smell and horror of what I witnessed then—remains with me forever.

I had seen it too in hospitals during the Iran-Iraq war, where my father spent most of his time tending to badly burned bodies, amputating arms and limbs. I remember him showing me holes drilled in the molten faces of babies to act as air conduits so they could breathe. While certainly traumatic for a child, such a lesson was, in my father's eyes, needed for life to teach what war is and what it does to its victims. My conscience thus was molded at an early age.

The 9/11 attack had brought back viscerally all that horror and trauma. Another casualty of that day was my newly shattered sense of security and optimism about a country I believed would never experience such horrors.

As depressing as things felt, we knew that together we would make it in the end. Our marriage, our true partnership for the past ten years, had made it through other difficult times and crises, the last being my father's sudden death a year earlier; it would also make it through this one, I was sure.

After finishing our comfort soup and ordering our customary Vietnamese coffee, Matthew used his cell to check voice mail at home, jotting down the messages on a napkin. He slid it toward me and pointed to one. Someone from FBI Headquarters had left his number, urging me to call him back as soon as possible.

I wondered what this was about. The only connection I had with the FBI had to do with my application for a temporary part-time intern position I had sent them four years earlier, in 1997. I was interested in their department that dealt with crimes against children, having worked as a trained and certified advocate for the Alexandria Juvenile Court, where I investigated and represented child abuse cases for over two years. I had sent them my application for an internship (summer or a part-time position) relevant to the degree I was pursuing in criminal justice.

After reviewing my application, someone at the bureau evidently found my linguistic abilities of interest and asked me to take proficiency tests in those languages and in English. At first I was put off by the prospect of working as a translator but on second thought decided it could be a stepping-stone to where I wanted to be until I completed my degrees. I went ahead and took the intense and excruciating proficiency tests in the summer of 1997. Afterwards they said that all language specialists, whether full-time or contract, were required to obtain top-secret clearance (TSC), since they would be dealing with sensitive and classified intelligence and documents. The process of background checks and issuance of TSC could take anywhere from nine to fifteen months, I was told. They would then notify me and offer me options, such as contract or full-time employment.

Nine months passed; then another nine, and another. In 2000, I called FBI Headquarters to inquire about the status of the position I had applied for nearly four years earlier. Toward the end of that year I finally received a call from a woman from FBI Headquarters who told me with much sincerity and apologies that in 1999 the bureau had lost my entire information package and test results, together with those of over 150 other applicants. That package contained my bank account information, tax records, Social Security and private medical and family-related information. "What?!" I asked, incredulous. ". . . Do you realize what people can do with that information?"

She apologized again and said the bureau would conduct expedited background investigations and have the position ready for me in a year. "If you change your mind and decide to go ahead with it," she told me, "the position will be ready and available for you." That was the last I'd heard from the FBI—until then.

I grabbed the napkin and stepped outside to make the call. The HQ man came on and thanked me profusely for returning his call. He then went on to explain how badly the bureau was in need of translators in Middle Eastern and certain Asian languages: Farsi, Turkish, Arabic, Pashtun, Urdu, Uzbek, and so on. The bureau had tens of thousands of leads and evidence waiting to be translated into English before the agents could take any further action. They had thousands of pieces of raw intelligence pouring in daily, but they all were in foreign languages and could not be processed or assessed until translated. "Ms. Edmonds," he concluded his pitch, "we need your skills badly. Your TS clearance came in last week and we would like you to start working for us immediately."

I told him about my course load at school, our business, and that circumstances had changed.

"We are willing to accommodate your schedule and workload," he appealed. "You can work for us as a contract linguist; determine the hours you can contribute each week . . . as much as you want, or as little as you can. Even if you could spare ten hours a week . . . We are at war, Ms. Edmonds; the FBI needs your skills badly. . . . You can serve your country . . ."

I remembered images, of young children not even six, hurling stones at monstrous tanks in the street. Tiny kids, against powerful war machines, but instead of running away they chose to stand their ground and fight, however insignificant their weapon—however small the force of their skinny arms.

I felt like those kids. I didn't want to run and hide. I had to stand and fight, but I couldn't find so much as a rock, and I couldn't see the enemy. I hated feeling helpless. Now, only three days after the attack, the Federal Bureau of Investigation was imploring me that I in fact possessed a rock, several, in fact: my language skills. Our country could use my help. How could I say no?

"All right," I said, one hundred percent confident. "I will. When can I start?"

I was told to stand by for another call in a minute or so. He would have an administrative supervisor at the FBI's Washington field office call immediately and give me instructions. The supervisor's name was Mike Feghali, and I would be assigned to his unit in that Washington office. I jotted down the name and waited for the call.

In less than two minutes, as promised, Mike Feghali called and briefly introduced himself as an administrative supervisor in charge of Farsi and a few other Language units. From his accent I could tell he was Middle Eastern, most likely Lebanese. He congratulated me on my decision to join and asked how soon I could start.

"How soon *can* I start?"

"Immediately; early next week," he replied. I would first be briefed by a security agent on security and classification issues, asked to sign certain papers, and receive my entry and identification badge. I was told to come down Saturday; that time is of the essence. I could start the following week.

I wrote down his information and told him I would be there on Tuesday. Then we hung up.

I realized I had been out of the restaurant for at least twenty minutes.

Matthew was curious. I told him I would be working for the FBI starting Tuesday, as a contract language specialist.

He looked concerned. I was only just recovering from the major blow of my father's death, and with the school load and our business he didn't believe I could handle that much at once. I tried—unsuccessfully—to assure him I could; he suggested I choose between school and the bureau, that it was not too late to drop some of my courses. I shook my head and told him I could handle it.

That night I lay awake thinking about the call: to duty. I spent hours unable to sleep; my mind wandering through twists and turns in my life.

The course of one's life is shaped by turning points: many for some, a few for others—mine being a nonstop roller coaster ride. The arrest and torture of my father, for instance, for advocating and fighting for human rights and civil liberties, was a blow to my family and an early one for me at three years old. Our life turned upside down. Within months, my family packed up and returned to Turkey, where they had to rebuild from scratch. That was a turning point.

Within three years, when I was six, we found ourselves in the midst of daily terrorist attacks and the start of a period of anarchy in Turkey. There was an attack on a passenger bus in which innocent riders were senselessly gunned down—another turning point. We packed our bags and left the country, this time to Iran, where followed further hardships.

Four years later, we found ourselves in the middle of what came to be known as the Islamic Revolution that initially started with people from different backgrounds and political views coming together to depose the Shah and bring in a democratically elected government. The goal was to end monarchy. Yet within two years, fanatic Islamist dictators took over the country and began to implement fundamentalist laws that dictated not only how we were to dress and speak but what we were permitted to talk about. Ultimately, methods of harsh repression and certainty of punishment if their rules and restrictions were not obeyed came to govern how we were to think and act toward one another. Where control is total, we are told how to feel and what to believe.

The last straw for me, the turning point that led me to a life-changing decision, involved an essay I wrote for an inter-high school competition. My chosen subject was Turkey's censorship laws, and why it was wrong to ban books and jail dissident writers. The school principal was outraged and asked my father to get me to write something else. He believed the essay would land me in jail and subject me to the torture reserved for political activists. My father refused, but the incident caused a crisis in my family; he was the only one who supported what I had done. For nearly eighteen years I had been subjected to constant upheavals that threatened my family's survival; I was affected by their decisions. Now, for the first time, I would be the sole decision maker based on an experience that targeted me directly. This was to be my own turning point. A few months later, I was on a plane on my way to the United States.

As I lay awake that night, less than twelve hours from officially becoming a contract language specialist with the FBI, thinking on these pivotal points in my life, I could sense another one nearing: some major change, a turning point. I just didn't know how, in what way, or what direction.

The next day, at ten on Saturday morning, I arrived at the Washington field office, where I was met by a female agent, very pregnant and blond, who then escorted me to a small meeting room on the entry floor. She seemed hassled and had a cool, dry attitude. She spent almost an hour going over Top Secret (TS) classification rules. She then placed a stack of papers in front of me and asked me to read and sign each document; I could ask for clarification if needed. They were filled with references to byzantine laws indicated only by their numbers, all in fine print and hard to read.

I asked whether we were expected to know these laws by heart, and wondered why they were cited without descriptions. "If we included the actual laws," she said, "you'd have hundreds of boxes of documents to read and sign; as you see, the stack is already large enough." Then she crisply added, "No, nobody knows these laws; people just sign them. This is the FBI, after all!"

I shrugged and went back to reading, doing my best to try to understand what I was being asked to sign. (I was taught never to sign anything I didn't first read or fully understand.) Then again, as the agent said, this is the Federal Bureau of Investigation. I signed all the papers.

My badge and ID would be ready in a few days. I could start on Tuesday. In the meantime, other employees could escort me to and from the unit and the building's security gates. With that said, she escorted me out.

As soon as I got to my car, I called Matthew to let him know I was on my way home. He asked me how it went. "I think I signed away my entire life to the Federal Bureau of Investigation; but hey, if you have to sign your life over to someone or some organization, wouldn't you rather it be them?"

2

Washington Field Office

On Tuesday morning, a few days after I received the call to duty, I showed up for my first workday at the FBI's Washington field office, located on Fourth Street between E and F Street in Washington, DC. Since my badge and identification card had not yet been issued, I had to check in at security and wait for my unit supervisor, Mike Feghali, to send someone down to escort me upstairs.

That morning I had taken extra time to prepare. I was going to work for the Federal Bureau of Investigation and my attire had to reflect that— an assumption proven wrong within the first few days. I had chosen a black light wool pantsuit with a long-sleeved parliament blue shirt, black pumps, and a black suede briefcase; classic.

A few minutes later, I noticed a short man bustling toward me. He was bald and overweight by at least fifty pounds and clad in a shiny-gray polyester suit. His dark olive complexion glistened with oil and perspiration. He greeted me with a big forced smile and introduced himself as Mike Feghali. After checking the status of my entry card and ID badge (another two days for both), we took the elevator to the fourth floor, which housed the FBI's largest and most important Language unit.

Here were dozens of cubicles and over one hundred agents. Feghali pointed out different areas, identifying the Counterterrorism division, private offices of Supervisory Special Agents (SSAs) and their bosses, Special Agents in Charge (SACs), then he turned right toward a set of wide double glass doors. He touched his entry card to the black square reader. "We are entering one of the most sensitive, most secured units in the entire building ... we, and everyone else in the unit, can walk over to any of those Counterterrorism, Criminal, or Counterintelligence units. But those guys, all those agents, cannot enter this unit—the Language unit. If they want to see us or meet with us, they have to call in advance and have someone from our unit escort them inside . . . their entry cards won't work over here; ours work everywhere." This evidently pleased him.

As we entered this "most sensitive, most secured unit," I found myself in the middle of a square open area filled with over a dozen cubicles only barely separated by chest-high dividers. There were a dozen or more people, each behind a computer screen. Some wore headphones, others were typing; three were gathered around one cubicle deep in discussion, in Arabic.

Feghali pointed. "This is our Arabic unit, now considered the most important language unit within our division. In a few weeks we expect it to double in size and in less than a year it will be quadrupled." He pointed to the group of three. "That woman on the right is my wife. She works for NSA as a translator, but I arranged for her to be transferred here for a few months on loan. I'll introduce you to all these people later." He led and I followed.

The Arabic unit section narrowed into a dark hallway. On the left was a small conference room, and next to it was reception, where sat the administrative secretary, Liz. On the right were three small offices. In the last, the third, someone had squeezed in a tiny round table with three chairs. Feghali pointed to the rooms. "These are LS supervisors' offices. I am one of the supervisors; the third office is mine. We have three more supervisors. Each supervisor has several language units under him or her, depending on the size of the unit. For example, I have Farsi, Turkish, Pashtun, Urdu, and Vietnamese. Stephanie has Spanish, Russian, and a few others. Same with the other two supervisors; we all used to be Language Specialists." He turned again and walked forward.

The hallway opened to a huge L-shaped room. Here were a hundred or more cubicles (or rather, modular desks, since they had no real dividers) clustered around the room. Translators sat shoulder to shoulder in front of their monitors, some dressed in jeans and sweatshirts, others with headscarves and saris; almost no one wore a suit.

Back in his office, Feghali explained the difference between three types of people I would report to and have ongoing working relationships with. He was one: an administrative supervisor who handled paperwork, scheduling and assignments; he would not know anything about the content of what I would translate or any other related information. The second group consisted of special agents from the Washington field office (WFO) involved in my long-term and ongoing counterintelligence projects in Turkish, Farsi, or both. The third category was comprised of special agents from FBI field offices all over the country, who would send our unit (since it was the largest) their documents or audio related to their investigations—mainly counterterrorism, with some counterintelligence and occasional criminal operations.

I was to provide translation and interpretation in both Turkish and Farsi. Feghali asked if I had a preference. "Turkish," I answered, "that's my primary language." He nodded. "We don't have a single Turkish language specialist . . . In the past, we assigned Turkish tasks to some Persian, Iranian, translators who claimed they understood the language; we later found out that they didn't."

I was surprised. Considering Turkey's geopolitical significance, its well-known involvement in narcotics, money laundering, and illegal arms sales—including the nuclear black market—I found it hard to believe that the FBI did not have a Turkish unit, or even a single translator, for its counterintelligence and counterterrorism operations.

Surprising too was that this would be on-the-job training, or "learn as you go," as Feghali explained it.

"Are there any documents, manuals, or booklets I can read for training purposes in addition to 'following' the translators and watching them translate?"

No. I found that interesting too. He took me out again to introduce me to those I would "follow" and those with whom I'd be working.

First I was introduced to Muala, an Iranian translator in her late forties who had been with the Farsi unit for over twelve years. A few years back, she had secured positions in the same department for her two younger sisters, Ayla and Suheyla. The three worked side by side as Farsi translators, somewhat removed from the other Iranian translators clustered a few feet away. By way of introduction, Feghali mentioned that these three also translated Turkish intelligence as extra assignments for overtime pay. I paid a compliment to Muala in Turkish; she made a sour face and didn't acknowledge what I'd said. At the time, I shrugged it off.

Afterwards, Feghali walked me over to another Iranian group and introduced me to a delicately built man in his mid-to-late sixties, Behrooz Sarshar, a Farsi translator who had been with the bureau for almost ten years. His eyes showed intelligence and wisdom, reflecting a kind nature and mild temperament. Unlike Muala, he greeted and welcomed me warmly.

Feghali then had one of the more senior supervisors, Larry, set up my access code, password, and username for the unit's LAN-based computer system. He also showed me the unit's central filing cabinet, organized by language, where archived copies of everything that had been translated in the past five years were kept. That was about it. He left me with Muala and went back to his office.

Muala didn't seem too happy. I didn't blame her; I assumed she had a lot to do and considered this a distraction. She directed me to the archived cabinet where I was to begin reading files at random: that way I would become familiar with how translation documents were titled, formatted and written. I started with Turkish and Farsi files, filled with hundreds of pages. Translations were performed in two ways: verbatim (from foreign to English, word by word, phrase by phrase); and summary (translate only a summary of what you heard or read).

In a couple of hours, I finished my review. I had a good grasp of the format and general flow, but reading the English translation without hearing actual audio in the target language gave me only half the picture. I decided to review an archived translation and listen to the audio in Farsi or Turkish simultaneously.

As I plugged in my headset, Muala came over and asked me what I was doing. When I explained my idea of listening and reviewing the translations simultaneously, she seemed panicky and started going through the files I had selected, a mixture of Farsi and Turkish archived translations. She grabbed the stack of Turkish files and said, "Hmmm, I think it is better to do it for Farsi for right now." Then she walked away with all the Turkish files. Though I found this a little peculiar, again I shrugged it off.

Around three, Sarshar stopped by my desk and invited me to join him for a cup of tea in the little kitchen area. He asked me about my background, and when I told him about my father's position in the Shah's Hospital in Tehran, he asked for his name. To my utter surprise, he not only told me the name of my father's high school but he actually knew my father, having attended the same. *What a small world!* I thought. From that day on, Sarshar became my closest colleague at the unit.

He pointed toward the door. "Be careful of the three devils," he said in a close whisper. "They are a little odd and more than a little devious. The rest of us Farsi translators don't speak more than a word—*hello* or *bye*—to them. Muala is not happy to have you here; she's threatened."

I was surprised. "But why?"

"You'll find out more, later . . . The problem they've got is this: they are not even a little bit proficient in Turkish. Their mother's ancestors were from Turkey, but the women never lived there, never attended school . . . they simply don't have any proficiency. . . . The special agent in charge of Turkey will tell you about the entire fiasco; he's a nice guy, his name is Saccher or something like that."

My jaw dropped. I didn't believe him. How could that be? The FBI wouldn't allow people to "claim" proficiency; they had tests for that—didn't they? This was impossible. Then I remembered the response Muala had given me—the face she pulled—and her later panic at the idea of me going over Turkish files and listening to their sources at once. I decided not to dwell on office gossip but to focus instead on actual work.

My first two days were spent reviewing archived translated files and listening to or reading their original sources. The rest of the time was spent learning the ropes. Sarshar was very helpful; he would take time with a question and show me how to do certain things.

In a few days I would meet Special Agent Dennis Saccher, in charge of my newly assigned unit, Turkish Counterintelligence, and he would go over my primary and permanent projects.

On my third day, Friday, Feghali came by and told me to go home and pack for a two-day trip, a very important counterterrorism assignment.

"What trip?"

"First to Wilmington, then to Philadelphia, and maybe afterwards to New Jersey."

I thought he was joking. "I'm not trained yet; I still have a long way to go."

Feghali laughed and patted me on the shoulder. "Woman, they badly need a Turkish interpreter; you're all we got; you are it, baby. Consider it your *baptism by fire!*"

I pressed him for details, but he didn't know much. Something about agents holding Turkish-speaking detainees related to 9/11. He gave me a piece of paper with the address of the Wilmington field office and a phone number for the agent in charge of the investigation. They would wait for my arrival that same night.

When I got home, I headed directly to our bedroom and started packing an overnight bag. I explained the assignment to Matthew as I packed and changed into my jeans and T-shirt. His reaction was exactly like mine. "But honey, you're not ready. . . . They can't send you on an assignment like this." I shrugged and told him they "can and did," assuring him I would be OK.

By the time I pulled up in front of the FBI Wilmington field office's nondescript brick building it was almost eleven.

I went inside and gave the receptionist my name and that of the agent given to me by Feghali. Less than two minutes later, a man in his mid thirties, dressed in wrinkled khakis and looking exhausted, came to get me. On the way to what he referred to as "the interrogation room," he explained that they had detained two men under suspicious circumstances; they were here illegally and did not speak any English.

Inside the room, under harsh fluorescent lights, men were seated around a gray aluminum desk. It was easy to identify the two detainees: each was chained to a chair by his wrists and ankles. The older, in his late thirties, had a dark olive complexion and black mustache; the other, in his late twenties, had fair skin and honey brown hair. Three agents sat across from them; no one was speaking. They all looked exhausted. I was thanked for getting there on such short notice, offered the desk and chair, and given a yellow legal notepad and an FBI pen.

The session started immediately. An older agent, who seemed to be in charge, asked me to interpret his questions and translate their responses into English. His questions were straightforward, and the men's answers were mostly "yes," "no," and "I don't understand," with a few that were a bit longer.

The session lasted almost two hours, during which one of the detainees requested a bathroom. One of the agents removed his cuffs and walked him there. I was impressed with the level of respect with which the FBI agents treated both men, and their professional and courteous manner. It was 1 A.M. by the time the session ended. The agent in charge asked me to walk out with him, and after we left the room, asked me what I thought of the men's answers and their attitudes in general. I gave him my assessment: one seemed a bit more evasive than the other; one was from a particular region known for nationalism but not religious fanaticism; the other seemed of Kurdish descent from that particular region with the following characteristics . . . The agent listened carefully. Would I come to the Philadelphia field office and do the same thing there? I said I could. I was to meet them in front of the building at eight o'clock, less than seven hours away!

We were joined in Philadelphia by several other men, some of them from the Immigration and Naturalization Service (INS), others from the FBI Philadelphia and New Jersey field offices. From their looks and what they talked, about I could tell they had been working around the clock since 9/11. They seemed exhausted yet eager to get things done, to accomplish something. Their dedication was worthy of respect.

"What we want to do is this: question, interrogate these guys, check out their background, and decide whether they are keepers or not," one of the younger agents told me. "If not, let them go, and go back and chase the real bad guys until we get 'em." He shook his head in disgust. "The jerks at HQ have issued an order for us to go and round up as many people as we can; chain 'em, lock 'em up, and send HQ the count. The larger the number the better; they've set a quota. They're not after the bad guys, they just want to show the press and the Hill this number, to be able to say, today we arrested this many; yesterday we arrested that many ..."

That surprised me.

The other agent added, "We get these guys on a simple INS violation. What do we do? We have to arrest 'em, sit around and baby-sit 'em while they're interrogated and locked up, instead of being out there and doing what we're good at doing."

This interrogation lasted three hours. Before they began the questioning, the agents first asked me to interpret the detainees' Miranda rights. One of the detainees shook his head. "How can that be?" he said, confused. "If we don't have money, they—the government—will assign a government attorney for us; but that doesn't make sense! If they are government attorneys, they will always represent the government and try to set us up and screw us over! Is this a trap?"

I understood only too well. In countries like Turkey, Miranda rights, due process, or court-appointed attorneys at no cost simply don't exist. This was a thought-provoking dilemma, similar to a "diminished capacity" or "mental defect" case: having grown up with oppression and become accustomed to it, they could not comprehend or believe the rights being explained to them. In this case, the two waived their rights for exactly this reason.

Almost three hours later, after the session was over, the agent in charge suggested to the others that they have a briefing session with me and discuss my impression and analysis based on the cultural, geographical and education background of these detainees. All agreed.

I then went over each of the three detainees, describing the environment each grew up in, that area's culture and religious outlook, level of education based on language skills and degree of articulation, and anything else to help these agents assess the level of risk.

At first it felt preposterous for me, a novice, to be providing these experts with my analysis, yet within minutes their willingness to truly listen, their eagerness to find out, and their subsequent to-the-point questions put me at ease. I was impressed with these field agents.

When I finished in Philadelphia it was almost four o'clock. Once on the highway I called Feghali's office, telling him I was on my way back.

"What!" he screamed. "No—turn around and go back!"

"What? Why? I'm finished."

He replied without a pause, "Because we already approved the hotel and meal budget for your trip until Sunday—go back, check into a hotel, order yourself a nice dinner, sleep late and drive back tomorrow. Then of course send us the bill."

I tried to reason with him. The job was over; I could be home by eight. Why waste the money?

He continued in a more irritated tone. "Don't you understand? Each supervisor has a budget for his translators, for his unit. The larger that budget the more important the unit. I want you to *spend* your budget: hotel, meals, and everything. Consider it your mini rest day; we are not in the business of saving the FBI money, my friend. The motto here is, the more your department spends, the more your department is loved."

I was getting really annoyed. "Well, I'm halfway there already. I have a paper due on Monday. I'm heading back. I'll see you next week." With that I hung up.

This budget quota business didn't make sense; in fact I hated the whole idea. I told myself to stop thinking about Feghali and be happy for a job well done. Soon I would be home.

———————————————

The following week, on my first day at work since the trip to Wilmington and Philadelphia, Feghali told me to call Special Agent Dennis Saccher, to whom I now was formally assigned. I could detect coolness toward me; Feghali was still upset with me for not staying the extra night.

I called Saccher's extension and was asked to go up one floor. Saccher, in his late thirties, stood around five foot ten, stocky but not fat, light brown hair and fair complexion. After shaking hands, we walked through a maze of halls to his cubicle.

Saccher was friendly but to the point. After chatting a few minutes, we talked about political and other important aspects in the target country. He was surprised by how up to date I was. We discussed major criminal activities and entities within and outside Turkey, and their overlapping partnerships with other foreign criminal networks.

He covered the importance of counterintelligence and his areas of investigation. He went over what was considered significant: exchange of money; information exchange involving intelligence, technology and financial activities; activities involving penetration of government; narcotics (particularly heroin); financial and political institutions and organizations; and other areas significant to FBI counterintelligence and counterterrorism operations and national security.

Saccher briefly explained the foreign targets of FBI operations and their possible counterparts in the United States. There were many, divided into primary, secondary, and "not significant" categories. We discussed a bit more, after which he praised my familiarity with the subject area and said he looked forward to my feedback and analysis.

On the way to the elevator he remarked, "I've been bugging HQ to hire a real translator, someone competent. I'm sure you've already met the three sisters from hell down there. These crooks claimed proficiency in Turkish and talked the administrators into assigning them overtime projects in the language. It didn't take me long to realize the shoddy work they produced, so I reported it to HQ and asked them to administer proficiency exams . . . HQ sends them notification asking them to go to HQ and submit to these tests, right? Guess what these crooks did? First they dragged their feet, and then they simply refused to take the test. Of course, they knew the uproar that would occur if they did! Can you believe this went on for two years? Man, am I glad you're here."

I was flabbergasted. How could HQ not be able to demand that they take the tests and allow them to continue for two more years?

He shook his head. "Just wait. There is so much shit going on down there; you'll get to know all about it in no time. . . . Just watch your back and don't get close to or involved with these people; keep your head down and keep your distance."

He asked me to call any time and to shoot for briefing sessions every few days at a minimum. I rode the elevator down with my head spinning.

In the following weeks I had several counterterrorism assignments from different field offices, including New York, New Jersey, Los Angeles, Detroit and others. These were top priority cases with direct relevance to the 9/11 attacks. The FBI had a huge backlog of untranslated e-mails, tapes, letters and other documents. Part of my job involved going over these and related materials—some collected long before 9/11—to connect certain dots and possibly find more clues. Counterterrorism agents from around the country began to call me directly, begging me to expedite their projects: they depended on the translated documents and audios to make a case or drop it, to arrest or release a suspect.

During this hectic period I also worked on my permanent counterintelligence projects involving Turkish targets in Saccher's unit. Here I had to divide my time between new and real-time intelligence and those not yet translated from years earlier, some dating back to 1996. The LA field office also sent me several CDs of intelligence they wanted me to review.

At once I began to realize the critical role played by language specialists in these investigations. In fact, I had come to see translators as the most important players. So much for boring clerical administrative work!

Field agents, analysts, and other decision makers in FBI offices and HQ depend on translators for their investigations of foreign targets—which means that they need to be able to trust that the translated foreign intelligence received is thorough, accurate and unbiased. They have no way to double-check or assess information given to them by translators, and so must use it as a basis for taking action or not.

If processed and transmitted in time, even one sentence of an intercepted communication can save thousands of lives. A piece of competently translated and analyzed intelligence can, for instance, lead to dismantling a network of deadly criminals.

Imagine, for a moment, that a language specialist is listening to a verbal communication between two targets of an FBI investigation. She or he first must determine whether this bit of intelligence is worthy of being translated, processed and sent to the agent or analyst in charge. If the specialist determines that the information is not significant, she or he stamps it *Not Pertinent* and there it ends. No one—no agent or analyst—ever sees, reads or knows about this particular piece of intelligence.

Now imagine that the specialist indeed has determined that this bit of intelligence is worthy of being translated and processed. The translator now must make a critical decision: Is this important enough to be translated *verbatim*, or can it be translated in *summary*—that is, condensed into a short paragraph or two without details or quotes. Note too that this summary also will deprive any analyst or agent in charge of the operation from seeing and analyzing the entire picture. If the translator isn't well trained or competent, then she or he may fail to understand the significance of this communication, or pieces thereof, and again the decision makers and action takers will have lost that opportunity.

Anyone determined to penetrate and throw off our intelligence agencies would most likely choose the Language unit—at the heart of the intelligence-gathering mechanism—to block, alter or simply steal sensitive, highly classified intelligence. Think of translators as valves: just as valves in a water system allow water to flow, be blocked or diverted, translators control the transmission of information from its first entry point, the frontlines, to the ultimate action takers, the special agents.

Considering the importance of translators and what they do, the agencies must perform a careful investigation into the background of candidates—including detailed interviews and in-person assessments to determine whether these individuals' loyalties, ideology, or personality may be in conflict with tasks they will be called on to perform. The agencies also should have a mechanism in place to spot-check, review and audit the work performed by each translator.

Right away I understood the potential for disaster if the job was not done properly. Feeling the weight of my position not only raised my level of awareness and diligence but also made me alert to that of others as well. Very soon I would begin to witness mind-boggling and appalling incidents within the FBI Washington Field Office Language unit that would impact directly on the bureau's ongoing investigations and, thus, on our national security.

Heeding Dennis Saccher and his warnings, I began to pay attention to my surroundings. My exposure to the routine and daily doings within the department was limited, however; I was still part-time.

I told Sarshar, my colleague, about Saccher's cautions. He thereupon provided me with an in-depth, detailed account of the crisis. Things were far worse than I imagined.

I was told of frequent internecine sabotage: between the Hebrew division and Muslim Arab-origin translators; between the Indian and Pakistani Muslim translators—all were at war with one another, and it sometimes erupted in actual bloodshed. People were accusing one another of being spies: of spies spying on each other. Classified files were stolen, documents went missing, locks were tampered with. Rearranging how these groups were clustered within the unit seemed to be the only departmental response; that and tepid reassurances.

Soon I began to witness such incidents. I recall one particularly irate Hebrew translator red-faced and screaming that his locked cabinet had been broken into and highly classified information stolen. On his way to the supervisors' offices, Feghali intercepted him. This was not the first time, the translator raved. He was determined to take this to HQ. I didn't blame him—I'd have done the same thing myself! Other supervisors crowded around, and he finally followed one of them into her office. That was the last we heard.

Later, during my now customary Persian tea break with Sarshar and his buddy Amin, who had just returned from Afghanistan, two Arabic translators walked in. One of them excitedly recounted the episode and asked what we all thought. I didn't respond; Amin and Sarshar mumbled something. One of the Arabic translators said, "After all, it is about Israel . . . He is an Israeli spy. Why do you think he keeps going back there? Sarshar, you know that; he's been to Israel at least three times in the last year or so."

With Amin's help, Sarshar tried to change the topic. Neither one wanted to get into the middle of an Arab-Israeli war. I remembered what

Saccher had warned me about and kept my mouth shut.

What I couldn't understand is why, if we were all supposed to keep our sensitive and top-secret files inside the unit's Sensitive Compartmented Information Facility (SCIF) and not in our file cabinets, I hadn't yet seen anyone doing so.

"Because they're lazy," Amin responded. "That would mean, if observed, that every time you go to the bathroom, every day when you come in and leave, the supervisor has to handle those documents for you—in and out of the SCIF. With this many translators, that would mean a lot of walking in and out of the SCIF; too much hassle for the supervisors."

The more I thought about the problem—sabotage and stealing top-secret documents—the more troubled I became. Not only does it put our national security and intelligence at risk, it also jeopardizes the target countries' intelligence and secrets. What if terrorists got hold of these? What if those acting as middlemen got this information and sold it to whoever was willing to pay? What if one or more of these translators, with this extraordinary, unchecked access, became that middleman? What if some of these translators were in fact moles?

In addition to sabotage and stolen documents, laptops disappeared with alarming frequency, many of them loaded with sensitive case data related to open counterterrorism and criminal investigations. Once every few weeks we would receive e-mails from the supervisors alerting us to missing laptops and asking us for help to establish chain of custody in the event that they were recovered.

These laptops were supposed to be kept in a secured and locked facility. No translator should have been able to access them without first going through supervisors, and then being accompanied by the special agents who were allowed to carry and use these computers during travel assignments or court hearings. Detailed procedures, such as who possessed the key and access to the facility, how to sign the laptop checkout sheet in the presence of a witness, and how and where to maintain these laptops during use, apparently existed only in writing. The supervisors and those in charge evidently didn't bother to keep the facility locked. The e-mail alerts continued.

I worked for the bureau twenty-five hours a week on average; school took a lot of time and energy. I tried hard to spend every working minute on top priority and urgent tasks and assignments. If I got an urgent call from an agent begging me to get something done, I would stay late until I could complete that project.

One day in early October, I received such a call from a New Jersey field agent. I could hear his desperation. He suggested that to save time I should have the results faxed to him over an FBI-secured fax line immediately after I was finished. (Ordinarily, completed assignments from field offices had to be sent to HQ in hard copy; the administrators then would send it via secure mail to the requesting field agents. That slowed everything. Our Language unit could not or would not send anything electronically.)

I worked quickly until I finished the agent's documents. Since I was not familiar with the secure fax, I went to Feghali's office and asked him for instructions. He asked me to sit down. Feghali had something to tell me.

"I see you are working very hard and fast. That's very good but you need to slow down a bit and take breaks during your work. You don't want to burn out or collapse in exhaustion. We wouldn't want that for you either; you have already become a very popular translator. Look what I have for you."

He handed me a two-page document. It was from the special agent from Baltimore who had supervised my interrogation translation. The commendation letter praised my work, professional conduct, and insightful feedback I'd given them.

"He says he will request you in particular for anything else they may have in the future that deals with Farsi or Turkish. You see, you don't have to kill yourself, work too hard, to be liked and admired."

I assured him that I knew my limitations and wouldn't exhaust myself.

Grinning and nodding to show that he understood, Feghali nevertheless went on to emphasize that it is not helpful to work fast; that doing so may in fact "end up hurting the department."

I was baffled. I had no idea what he was getting at. Had someone complained?

"What do you mean?"

"Look," he began (never a good sign), "for years and years the bureau, all these agents, treated us, the translators, as second-class citizens. . . . Now, thanks to the 9/11 terrorist attack, all that has changed; the terrorists and what they did put us translators on the map." Feghali continued, "That's why I say sometimes good things come out of bad things. Some may consider what happened on 9/11 terrible, but we, the translators, see it as a cause to celebrate. Look at these date cookies my wife baked yesterday: see, we are still celebrating the attack; this is our customary celebration cookie. Have some." He extended the cookie bowl toward me.

I was sick to my stomach. I shook my head and refused. Perhaps I misunderstood; could he have possibly meant that the attack finally opened people's eyes to the threats we all face? Could that have been it?

Yet Feghali continued in this same disgusting vein. "This is the time for us, for our department to flourish. . . . This November the FBI is going to present its budget request for our department, and to make the case, they have to show this huge backlog of untranslated material: the bigger the backlog, the more money and more translators for this department. Do you get the picture?"

"But we already have a huge backlog; hundreds of thousands of hours and pages, if you count all the languages."

"I know, I know," he said dismissively, "but still . . . for instance, you worked so hard and too fast to translate this agent's document, and want to go the extra mile . . . You say this guy is desperate; well, some-times desperation is a good thing. Better to have this guy complain to and pressure his bosses and HQ for not getting his translated documents than to make him satisfied and happy . . . and have him forget about it later. All I'm asking you is to be a better friend to your colleagues: ac-company them to lunches and coffee breaks, take regular breaks, and do not work this fast, that's all."

This was hateful. I had to get out of his office, right away. I started out when he called me back. Now he held the cookie bowl only inches from my face. "Have a cookie. Don't refuse my wife's famous cookies." I grabbed one and left.

As soon as I found my way clear of his office, I dumped the cookie in the nearest trashcan. Not on my life would I ever eat anything baked to celebrate 9/11. My first order of business was to fax this document to the agent in New Jersey. (I did, with Amin's help.) What happened in Feghali's office was sickening. I well knew this was the second time I had defied him; I prayed it would be the last.

The next day I started experiencing problems with saved documents in my computer. The problem continued for days. Typically, I would work on a document for hours, translating it verbatim—which is tedious and time-consuming—and then save it at the end of the day. When I opened that document the following workday, the page would appear but with paragraphs deleted and sentences cut in half, with the other halves missing. I would have to start from scratch. It was driving me nuts. What ordinarily took me two days to finish was dragging into five. To make matters worse, this particular translation was urgent business.

I had never before experienced anything like this. I called Amin, since he was the most technologically savvy in the unit.

Amin checked and tried everything. Nothing worked. Then he had an idea. "How many people know your password?"

"No one, except for supervisors—they have a key password for all our computers."

This interested him. "Maybe someone who doesn't like you stood behind you and stole it. I know the three sisters don't care for you at all. Maybe it was one of them."

I told him I didn't think so.

"There is only one way to find out. We'll report it to the computer and database department downstairs. They can print out the records of all log-in and logout sessions into your computer. Match that against the hours you worked and *bam!* we'll know if anyone logged in to your system when you were not here. If it was one of the supervisors, it'll show that it was from another computer and will tell you whose computer it was from."

Brilliant. How does one go about reporting this to the database department downstairs? Amin said the best and fastest way is to inform my supervisor and have him report it and request the data. So I went to Feghali's office and explained the problem, asking him to do exactly that.

"That's interesting," he said. I urged that we find out right away.

"I don't think it is a good idea for you to report this. Let it slide one more time. We don't want this to turn into a major incident."

"It *is* a major incident. Whoever did this should be reprimanded, fired. This is sick!"

Feghali replied a little more sharply, "No. I won't report it this time. If it happens again, I will. Maybe you should consider it a lesson. Maybe you were working too fast and someone decided to warn you, to teach you a lesson."

It suddenly sank in. My own supervisor had done this—right after I had defied him and sent the expedited translation to New Jersey. The man would halt urgent counterterrorism investigations for a budget increase. If I had any doubts before, I now believed I was on his wrong side—permanently.

In mid October, another Turkish translator, Kevin Taskesen, entered the department. Feghali brought Kevin to my desk, and after a short introduction asked me to train and supervise him. Kevin was in his mid-forties, overweight and dark with a thick black mustache and a noticeable limp. He was hired as a "monitor." The bureau divides translators into two ranking groups. The language specialists are those with high scores in both the target language and English: they perform all types of translations (verbatim, interviews, live interpretations) and supervise monitors. The monitors are those with low scores in either English or the target language. Technically (that is, as presented in FBI rulebooks and classification manuals), monitors are only allowed to perform summary translations; they are not to translate verbatim or interpret for court cases or live interviews, and they must submit their final product to their assigned language specialist for approval. In actuality, things never worked that way.

Kevin seemed timid and not very social. He spoke only in Turkish, with me. I tried my best to explain things to him, to demonstrate by having him sit next to me and watch. Saccher also helped and had a briefing session with Kevin in my presence.

In less than a week, Feghali had Kevin performing summary translations of our ongoing counterintelligence project. Kevin didn't know how to use a computer; he had never typed a word in his life on a word processor. Feghali asked Amin to show him how.

On his first real workday, Kevin stopped by and asked me the English translation for three common words. Thirty minutes later, he came to me with a list of seven or eight words, again, all very simple. Then he was back again. That did it. I asked him to take a coffee break with me.

"You don't speak much English, do you?"

He shook his head no.

I asked him what he would do when they found out, to which he replied, "They already know."

"Who is *they*?"

"Feghali, HQ."

He then began telling the story very matter-of-factly. He was working as a cook in a restaurant in Istanbul when he met his American wife, Cynthia, an English instructor. The couple married and moved to California, where Kevin got a job as a busboy and kitchen helper in a nearby restaurant in Malibu.

Cynthia later applied for a job as an administrator in FBI Headquarters. She got a position in the FBI's language department division and the family moved to DC. Kevin found another kitchen helper job in downtown DC and started work there for very little money. Here I interrupted him. "So that's how you got this job without speaking any English? Your wife—"

He asked that I let him continue. "Feghali became supervisor only seven or eight months ago. He talked my wife at HQ into fudging a few linguist candidates' applications and testing results as a favor. These people are all his family members and close friends. Look, half of the Arabic department is his tribe: two brothers, sister-in-law, his wife, his niece and several close friends. How do you think they got there? Many couldn't have if it weren't for Cynthia! Some had background check problems; others had proficiency shortcomings . . ."

As soon as we got back, I marched into Feghali's office. He listened and smiled. "Sibel—sweet, beautiful, tiny, skinny Sibel—Taskesen won't do any harm . . . Between you and me, we'll baby-sit and take care of him. I know it means more work for you, but people should help each other."

Then he turned the conversation around to me. "You're taking this huge load at school, and work here only twenty-five hours a week. I want you to come over here on weekends—Saturdays and Sundays—bring all your schoolbooks, punch in your time card and turn on your computer, then, sit and study your school work. You'll take care of your study assignments, and make over five hundred dollars per weekend, eh?"

I stared at him hard and cold. "That would be defrauding the bureau and the taxpayers. Are you asking me to commit fraud?"

He chuckled and went on to explain that "everybody does it here." He then launched into an exhausting personal history that involved what he called "perks" for him and his extended family, not to mention FBI coworkers and fellow employees: plane tickets, car rentals, hotel expenses, frequent trips, you name it, all on the taxpayers' dime. "That's an advantage of working for the government, among many others," he assured me, looking pleased.

I felt close to puking, I was that repulsed. I asked him point-blank, "Are you trying to bribe me?"

"That's an ugly word; we never use ugly words here. I am trying to *help* you, make your life easier, and increase your loyalty to the bureau. We are one big family here. I'd be more than happy to pay for you and your husband's next travel to Turkey. We have an office in Turkey, in Ankara; did you know that? Also, don't forget to check in on Saturdays and Sundays."

I turned around and walked out. There was no point in discussing Kevin Taskesen's case with this man or anyone else in this unit. Maybe Saccher would realize this and do something about it. Or maybe Feghali would have Kevin sit in a corner and do nothing for two years—just have him get paid, which would be better than having him actively destroy investigations or clues to possible future attacks.

This was wishful thinking. Kevin indeed was given important projects and sensitive documents and audio to translate—all ruined and destroyed, as expected. Not only that, a few months later Kevin came to me in tears to let me know that he had been assigned to Guantanamo Bay to translate detainee interviews for those inmates who spoke Turkish and Turkic languages. That includes prisoners from Turkey, Uzbekistan, Kyrgyzstan, Chechnya, Turkmenistan and others. He had begged Feghali not to send him; he felt utterly incompetent, but Feghali didn't want to lose this golden opportunity for his unit's budget and record of "important" assignments.

Kevin Taskesen was only one of many incompetent translators hired by the FBI after 9/11 who failed to possess the proficiency, knowledge, education or clearance needed to accomplish vital tasks to which they were assigned. Many counterterrorism and counterintelligence investigations and operations were irreparably damaged or destroyed as the result of deliberate or unintentional mistranslations and blockings by the translators involved.

3

Cover-Ups and Betrayals

I spent a lot of time on my permanent and ongoing counterintelligence projects under Dennis Saccher during my short tenure with the FBI. Despite some overlapping with terrorism-related intelligence involving Central Asian narcotics and money laundering, my first two months were spent mostly on counterterrorism investigations dealing with 9/11.

Reams of documents and audio files sent to the FBI Washington Field Office by field agents nationwide had been intercepted prior to 9/11—evidence that was never processed or translated until the attack. Now, after the fact, these files were being checked and reviewed for any possible connection. Some dated back to the late 1990s.

Certainly not every lead had been worth following up; but things were different now: old evidence carried new weight. Having originally overlooked pertinent and alarming intelligence may or may not be understandable, yet the bureau's response to such evidence *after* 9/11 was and remains reprehensible and inexcusable. The lengths to which the top tier went to ensure the covering up of these cases to prevent exposure and any investigation at all is almost incredible.

Many such cases were subsequently withheld from both the Independent Commission on 9/11 and its predecessor, the Joint Inquiry into 9/11 by the House and Senate Intelligence Committees. Other cases brought to the attention of these bodies, by whistleblowers or anonymous employees, were omitted from their final reports or outright buried. The public hadn't a clue.

One afternoon toward the end of October 2001, slightly over a month after I began working for the bureau, Mike Feghali stopped by my desk to hand me a box containing tapes and a thin file of paper documents. He said an agent from one of the Nevada field offices had sent them. The operation dated back to July and August 2001, and the contents initially had been translated by a language specialist in summary format.

In light of the events of September eleven, on a hunch the agent decided to send it to us for review: he believed something had been overlooked or not translated correctly, and if true, he wanted to be informed immediately and have everything translated verbatim. The agent also included in the package information obtained post-9/11, up to October 1, 2001.

"I'm sure everything was OK the first time around," Feghali commented. "Just go over these and see if anything significant was missed." With that he dropped the file and the accompanying tapes on my desk and walked away.

After a short lunch break, I switched gears. I put aside what I had been working on and started the new assignment. I decided to give a quick listen to the tapes and skim the package before typing, to see if anything grabbed me. Later, I would go back and start over again, if necessary, the tedious, slow translation.

For the first few minutes I was having a hard time staying focused; boredom had set in. The target was in jail, talking to someone in a remote and underdeveloped border region of Pakistan and Iran (I knew from the accent and dialect where they were from). They chatted about some real estate and bridge projects; all the requirements they had to meet and the schedule they had to maintain. The very short, less than three-sentence-long original translation basically said that the subject discussed inconsequential matters and talked about some real estate development. I thought it more or less sufficient and accurate. Feghali's observation seemed to be right—so far.

A few minutes passed before something made me sit up at once, with the force of an electric jolt. I thought I had heard something that didn't fit, something that was out of place. I wasn't sure what it was, but I felt spooked.

I rewound the tape and this time listened carefully. Oh my God—there it was! The target was going to send the blueprints and building composites for the project: those buildings had to be skyscrapers, a hundred floors or higher, to fit the specifications. I looked at the date: late July, 2001. The region to which these blueprints, building composites and bridge specifications were to be sent was as primitive as could be; they barely had mud huts. How could they be discussing the construction of skyscrapers in a nomadic village with huts? They specifically mentioned *skyscrapers*. Also, the blueprints and building composites were to be sent via human courier, not by mail, FedEx, or fax. Why would someone go to that much trouble to send simple blueprints, building and bridge plans and composites? Why was a "trusted source" to travel around the world to deliver it?

I believed the agent's hunch was right on target. September eleven attacks and skyscrapers; blueprints and building composites of skyscrapers hand delivered to Iran; the date preceding the attacks by approximately two months.

Now I was awake and alert. I decided to go over a little bit more before notifying Feghali and the agent who'd sent the assignment. I fast-forwarded the tape to the first recorded date after September 11, 2001, to 11 A.M. September 12, 2001. I pushed the Start button and went over it. Bingo! First, the target and recipient congratulated themselves for this precious *Eid*. (*Eid* is a religious holiday in the Muslim world.) I knew all the dates for *Eid* that year: there were no religious holidays in September. These congratulations were given one day after the 9/11 attacks. Were they celebrating a successful operation? I jotted that down too.

Within the same communication, on September 12, the target warned that "using men would be dangerous, not wise, after this. The next round had to be women, young women between the ages of eighteen and twenty-four." There also was a brief discussion of "channels to obtain visas in return for money," most of them in the United Arab Emirates. Their network included people with connections and contacts in U.S. embassies there.

I stopped everything. First, I went to Amin's station. He wasn't there, so I grabbed his Farsi dictionary and returned to my desk. Having little-to-no familiarity with construction lingo, I needed to track down the names of several minerals: metals and other building materials, to find their precise corollaries in English. I had to double-check the translations. Then I locked up the tape and the original file, grabbed my notepad with the important points jotted down in my indecipherable script, and headed—no, ran—to Feghali's office.

His door was half closed; I lightly tapped. He was on the phone, but he asked me to come in. I sat in the side chair and waited for him to wrap up his conversation in Arabic. My heart was pounding, and I loved that agent without ever meeting him or even knowing his name. The man had a good nose; he had smelled this one big time, and he was right. Catching this could help us uncover much more on the attacks and those behind them. Feghali's voice brought me back to the present.

"How is it going?"

I came straight to the point and told him about the discovery. Without so much as a pause to catch my breath, I concluded, "So we need to call this agent right away, let him know right now. Call him on the secure phone and read him my notes. Here," I handed him my notes. "Now I'll go back and start the verbatim translation. It will take me at least a couple of days. Maybe we should have Amin or Sarshar do it; they are stronger in Farsi language . . . meanwhile, the agent will know that he's on the right track."

Feghali paused. "So the original translation didn't have this information?"

I shook my head. "No, but I can see why. Without nine eleven I wouldn't have found it significant either. This may be one of those hindsight cases . . . I guess . . ."

"Very well. Go and start translating the whole thing. I will call the agent myself and will have him call your extension."

I left his office and returned to my desk. I spent the rest of the day on that project. I was almost halfway done. The agent didn't call.

I devoted my time exclusively to the translation. One more day and it would be finished; I needed only two or three hours more. The agent still hadn't called. Feghali was not in his office so I couldn't ask him about it.

On the third day, I arrived to find the file was gone—missing. I checked the second drawer for the tapes and they were gone too. I turned on my computer and clicked on my Blueprint translation document: still there. I checked my voice mail: no messages from the agent.

I walked over to Feghali's office. Without entering, from the door I asked, "What's up with the agent? He hasn't called me. Did you call him? Did you reassign the files to Sarshar or Amin? The tapes and files are missing, so I assumed you reassigned the case to them."

Feghali beckoned me in. "Close the door and have a seat."

I shut the door. "Why hasn't the agent called me? It's been almost a week!"

"I sent the agent the tapes and the original documents. It went out two days ago."

I was baffled. "But we haven't translated it yet. Did you tell him about the discovery? What was his reaction? Who is going to take care of the translation? Does he still have the suspect in custody?"

He sat silently for what felt like too long. "We sent him everything with a note stating that everything was checked, reviewed thoroughly, and no discrepancy was found."

Was he joking? He didn't appear to be. What in the world was going on? I couldn't find words to express my shock; neither could I sort through the questions I so badly wanted to fire at him.

I was only able to mumble, "I don't understand. This is one of the most damning pre-attack evidences I've come across here . . . But why?"

"How would you like it if the shoe was on the other foot? How would you have liked some translator coming after you, checking what you produced, and questioning its accuracy? What if you missed something explosive, something that may have—only *may* have—prevented thousands of deaths, and someone reported on you? You wouldn't have appreciated that kind of a backstabbing, Sibel, right?"

I thought I was daydreaming, imagining what he had just told me. "Mike, I don't even know the name of the original translator, I don't even know if he or she was from this office or another field location; it is all irrelevant. I told you he or she couldn't be blamed for this. Considering the fact that before nine eleven this might not have raised any eyebrows, why would it be blamed on the original translator?"

"It is not that simple. That translator would be made a target: they'd blame him for it whether right or wrong. As I have told you before—several times, in fact—we are like one big family here, we watch out for our own. We believe in one for all, all for one, as far as all our translator brothers and sisters are concerned. We don't rat each other out to get some credit or receive recognition."

I exploded. "*Screw* recognition or getting credit! Is that what you think this is all about? I even told you to assign it to more savvy Farsi translators! This is about the nine eleven terrorist attacks, Mike. This suspect may hold a big key to what occurred, how it was planned, and the ones behind its planning. There was discussion on future 'operators,' this time women, being sent; illegally obtained visas . . . this agent had already suspected that much. There is a reason he sent those for re-translation and review. You are obligated to report to him what we have found—now! You better call him or give me his number and let me call him now. This is not about some stupid office politics and bureaucracy, damn it!"

Feghali stared at me coldly. "The case is closed, forever. We, the FBI

Washington Field Office, thoroughly examined the document and found no discrepancy, period. I'll have the computer department remove your notes from your computer today. I should not have assigned that task to you. You haven't been here long enough to know how we operate in here." He took a deep breath and continued. "Now, go back to your regular assignments. As far as you know, everything has been taken care of."

I stood up, shaking with rage. "You are an administrative supervisor. You have no authority over the actual projects and their contents. This has to be dealt with by the agents and agents in charge, not you. If I have to report to the agent in charge in here, I will."

"I have the approval of everyone in charge here," he hissed. "Whatever we do here is sanctioned by the agent in charge of our unit. This conversation is over and I suggest you go and cool off; then, after coming to your senses, do what you are supposed to be doing: Do as you are told by me."

I stormed out. Once in the hall, I stopped to figure out what I would do next. Who should I see? I knew of only one special agent in charge, Bobby Wiggins, formally assigned to the Language department, who kept a small office here; yet he was almost always absent. Due to retire soon, he only showed up once a week, in silly clown-like golf attire to check messages and retrieve any memos. During my entire tenure, I only saw him inside the unit and among the translators once, at his own goodbye party. When I thought about what the agents in the field go through daily—putting their lives on the line—this manager's indifference made me cringe.

I thought of going to Dennis Saccher; but then I changed my mind. First, he was in charge of his unit only and had no authority over my department or the counterterrorism case involved. Second, doing so would be seen as going beyond the department's turf and result in disciplinary action against me.

Frustrated, angry, and feeling thwarted by not having the agent's contact information, I marched over to the Farsi translators' cluster, the unit's Iranian territory. Sarshar, Amin, and a few others looked up. "Any of you know about this project?" I named the file, field office and division involved. "Did anyone here originally translate this particular document?" The translators exchanged looks and shook their heads no.

Amin saw that I was shaking and brought me some hot tea. Sarshar rolled his chair over. "Do you want to tell us what happened to get you so very furious?"

I began slowly and told them everything, leaving nothing out. When I got to what Feghali had said to me, I started shaking all over again.

"Welcome to FBI-WFO Inferno department, Sibel," Amin said. "You have just begun to discover and understand how this department operates. My friend, you haven't seen anything yet, just wait."

"Don't repeat Feghali's lines to me," I lashed out. "I am not going to get used to this and shrug it off with a 'hey this is how things are, what you gonna do' attitude. I accepted this position only for one reason: nine eleven."

"Don't misunderstand ... All I am saying is that we all have big bags of fiascos, scandals, cover-ups and complaints. There is nowhere to go, no one to report to. We have seen and faced worse stuff—especially nine eleven-related ..."

Sarshar added, "Not only that, we're stuck with the worst guy among the supervisors: Feghali. Do you know how he became supervisor here? Let me tell you ..."

He then launched into the sordid history of a sordid man, a bureaucrat who clawed his way into his current position by using and stepping on people, committing fraud, abusing his authority (there were charges of sexual misconduct and other outstanding complaints against him), and threatening those who challenged him with phony discrimination lawsuits. Apparently, this last threat got the FBI's attention and he was left alone—to continue his abuses. The managers all were wary of him.

Disgusted with everything I heard, I was in no mood to talk about the past and told them so, adding only that I was concerned about this particular cover-up and damage to 9/11-related information and investigations.

"If you think this is bad," Amin replied, "then you haven't seen anything. This is nothing compared to some other cover-ups that had direct bearing on what happened here on September eleven!"

"Do you mean other nine eleven cases have been similarly destroyed, covered up?"

"I am saying that and ten times worse," he avowed. "Yours won't begin to measure up to what we have seen this agency cover up." He turned to Sarshar. "Do you want to tell her about our case or do you want me to?"

Sarshar got up and grabbed a file from his desk drawer, then came back and sat down. "Sit tight. What you will hear and see will blow your mind."

Sarshar then began to tell me about the Iranian informant.

The story began in the early 1990s. The bureau hired an Iranian man who had been the head of SAVAK (Iran's main intelligence agency) as a reliable source on its criminal, counterintelligence and counterterrorism operations and investigations. The man was very good at what he did and had established a large number of sources and informants in strategically important areas within Afghanistan, Pakistan and India. Notably, he managed intelligence-gathering operations in Sistan and Baluchistan, two semi-independent regions on the border with Afghanistan.

Once on the payroll, he began providing extremely useful and reliable information. The bureau was so pleased with his performance that it began using him both as an informant and as an asset. On a regular basis, almost monthly, agents from the FBI HQ and WFO would meet with him in a location outside the bureau to obtain information and intel on various ongoing operations and investigations.

The agents needed an interpreter for these regular monthly meetings, Sarshar explained, which is where he and Amin came in. "Around the end of April, two thousand one," he told me, "I was asked to accompany two special agents from the FBI-WFO . . . to a meeting arranged with this informant . . . We met in a park and spent nearly an hour discussing the case, asking detailed questions, and of course, with me translating back and forth. Once we were finished with the session and ready to head back to the WFO, the informant urged us to stay for a few minutes and listen to something very important and alarming he had recently received from his sources."

According to Sarshar, the informant then proceeded to tell them, "Listen, I was recently contacted by two extremely reliable and long-term sources, one in Afghanistan, the other in Pakistan's border region with Afghanistan. In the past, these guys had provided me with inside information and intelligence that was extremely hard to come by, considering the tightly based networks and groups they were able to enter and penetrate. They notified me that an active mujahideen group led by Bin Laden had issued an order to attack certain targets in the United States, and were planning the attack as we spoke." Here, Sarshar explained, the agents seemed very alarmed, since their main unit of operation was under the WFO Counterterrorism division. All of them took notes.

The informant continued, "According to my guys, Bin Laden's group is planning a massive terrorist attack in the United States. The order has been issued. They are targeting major cities, big metropolitan cities; they think four or five cities: New York City, Chicago, Washington, DC, and San Francisco; possibly Los Angeles or Las Vegas. They will use airplanes to carry out the attacks. They said that some of the individuals involved in carrying this out are already in the United States. They are here in the U.S., living among us, and I believe some in U.S. government already know about all of this."

The informant was asked about specific dates, and whether they would use airplanes, bombs or hijacking; did he know?

"No specific dates," came the reply, "not any that they were aware of. However, they said the general time frame was characterized as 'very soon.' They think within the next two or three months. . . . As far as how they are going to use the planes to attack, your guess is as good as mine. My bet, it will be bombs: planting bombs inside these planes, maybe the cargo, then have them blown up over the populated cities."

Sarshar took notes in Farsi and later translated them verbatim. The informant urged them to report and act on this immediately, adding that Bin Laden had backing and experts. "If I were you guys, I'd take this extremely seriously. If I had the same position I had in SAVAK, I'd put all my men on this around the clock. I can vouch for my sources, their reliability. Make sure you put this in the hands of the top guys in Counterterrorism."

The agents discussed the best person to whom they should submit this warning and decided on Special Agent in Charge Thomas Frields, who was in charge of the WFO Counterterrorism division.

Once back at the office, Sarshar completed his translation and the agents filled out the necessary 302 forms for their formal report. (The 302 forms are used to report information gathered from assets and informants.) Two sets of 302 forms were filed: one for the ongoing criminal case and the other on the warning, as information related to counterterrorism operations. Sarshar coordinated with the agents for the final report and kept his own set of records. They submitted the warning report to SAC Frields with a note on the top reading VERY URGENT.

Nobody heard back from Frields or the Counterterrorism division. No one asked for any follow-ups or additional information. Two months went by. Around the end of June 2001, Sarshar met with the agents and the Iranian informant again. When they had completed their business, the Iranian asked about the warning he had passed along to them, now two months old, whether it had been reported to the higher-ups. He was told it had been. The informant, now animated, explained that he'd heard back from his source, who "swore the attack was on its way; any time now, a month or two, max" and asked point-blank, "Are they going to do something about it?"

The agent's response was, "I know, I hear what you're saying, man, but doing something about this won't be up to us. Plus, we don't have enough information to take any action here. We don't know when, how, or exactly where. The only thing we have is: Bin Laden, five cities, and airplanes. That ain't enough."

The informant went on, "I've been thinking about this, trying to make more sense out of it myself. The source mumbled something about tall buildings. Maybe they will blow up the plane over some tall buildings? I don't know. . . . Maybe the FBI can get more specifics from the Pakistanis, ISI. Have they tried? After all, they are your guys; and they know all about this."

The agents, exasperated and impatient, told him they reported it and now it would be up to those in charge. When they were leaving, the informant yelled in Farsi, "Why don't you tell the CIA? Tell the White House! Don't let them sit on this until it is too late . . ."

Sarshar asked one of the agents if he thought sharing this with other agencies might be a good idea. As Sarshar described it, the agent rolled his eyes. "Not up to us, Behrooz. As far as the White House goes, the HQ guys will include it in their briefings; I'm sure they've already done so. Frields is obligated to submit what he got, everything he gets under Counterterrorism, to the HQ guys in charge of White House national security briefings. He always does. So, the White House and other agencies have already heard about this. Let's drop this, man, will ya?"

He told me, "That was the last time we ever discussed this case before the nine eleven attacks took place. The only other person I told this to and showed the 302 forms and the translation report to, before September eleven, was Amin here. Then, on that Tuesday morning on September eleven, everything came back to me and hit me on the head like several tons of bricks ... we were warned about this. We were told, very specifically."

Sarshar spoke of getting together with both agents a few days later to go over an assignment; Amin had been present when he brought up the topic. "They avoided eye contact with me. I asked them what they were going to do, if they'd already done something. At first they were evasive.

Then, after I insisted, one of them said, 'Listen, Frields called us into his office and gave us an order, an absolute order.' I asked them what the order was. He said, 'We never got any warnings. Those conversations never existed; it never happened, period. No one should ever mention a word about this, period. Never!' I almost went ballistic; Amin sat quietly with his head down."

He paused. "That was the end of it, Sibel. The top managers—those in charge you now want to inform—are the ones who are covering up reports and cases like this. And you want to go and take it up to them?"

I was mortified; shocked. When I finally found my voice, I asked, "What are you guys going to do with this? Are you going to obey Frields' order, for God's sake?"

Amin responded this time. "It's too late, Sibel. What was done was done. We cannot turn back the clock. Also, there is no place to go with this. They seemed to all be in this together: the CIA, the White House . . . That's how I view it."

I turned to Sarshar. He whispered, "I can't let this go. One way or another, this will get out. I made several copies of the documents; they are resting in very safe places." He handed me the file with the 302 forms.

They were right. In my case, however, here was the difference: a man was in U.S. custody; the agent in charge of his case was suspicious, but did not know to what degree his target related to the events surrounding 9/11. Even more importantly, the target had discussed plans about future "female operatives" and means to obtain visas for them illegally; to what ends, exactly?

I repeated what I thought, this time out loud, and went back to my desk to make sure that my documents and file—what was left of it—remained in more than one safe place.

About half an hour later, Sarshar, Amin, and Mariana, a French translator in her early thirties, stopped by my desk. "Mariana here also has an interesting nine eleven story, a major case," Sarshar began. "Come on, Marie, tell Sibel."

Mariana didn't seem too happy to be dragged into this. She rolled her eyes. "In late June—two thousand one, that is—the French Intelligence contacted us, the FBI, with a warning of upcoming attacks. They had intercepted intelligence that showed planning for attacks in the U.S. via airplanes. They also provided us with some names: suspects." She sighed. "The FBI took it seriously; they sent me to France with a couple of CT [counterterrorism] and CI [counterintelligence] agents . . . The French were sharing everything; they gave us everything they had. Trust me, this was specific information. Later, somehow, FBI HQ chose to do nothing about it. As far as I know, it went up to the White House. It made it into one of their national security advisor's briefings, but . . . nothing."

I looked at her, then to Sarshar and Amin. "So . . . what you are going to do about this? We need to do something!"

Mariana shrugged. "It's none of our business. I'm sorry I even talked about this case, I shouldn't have. Nine eleven freaked me out. I couldn't stop thinking about this." She turned around and mumbled, "Just leave me out of this. The bureau may have its own reasons to close this case permanently." Then she walked away.

These two major incidents were my first experiences with the FBI's intentional cover-up and blocking of 9/11-related information, evidence and cases. During the next four months, I would stumble on other cases that involved similar blockings and cover-ups.

One such case involved a foreign network—from a so-called allied country—in the United States that was under FBI counterintelligence surveillance. Those communications I translated involved the selling of U.S. nuclear information, obtained by extortion and bribery, to two foreign individuals from another ally country. I knew, from a previous case, that the two individuals purchasing this information and material had connections to a particular terrorist financial institution with direct ties to 9/11 and certain Saudis. As the translator in both cases, I knew something that the agents in each separate case couldn't possibly have seen. There was a connection they didn't know about.

Despite my attempt to notify the two FBI field offices and the agents involved in both operations, the bureau, under pressure from the Department of State, prevented this or any such notification from taking place. Furthermore, they shut down one of the two operations to protect the so-called ally country.

In the months and years following the 9/11 attacks, Congress and various commissions and investigative bodies blamed the "walls"—those laws separating counterintelligence and Foreign Intelligence Surveillance Act (FISA) operations from domestic investigations—for the lack of sharing and communication between FBI counterintelligence and terrorism units, and, thus, for the failures that led to 9/11.

Their conclusion, and what they did to fix this problem—the Patriot Act, I and II—was wrong on the face of it and ineffective to boot. Even after passage of both Acts, the sharing and transfer of FISA-related counterintelligence information was and continues to be prevented. Why?

In some cases, it is to protect and preserve certain diplomatic relations with specific ally countries. If the bureau receives information implicating particular foreign entities or government officials and they happen to be valued customers for our weapons and military technology (or, if their countries happen to be a highly prized energy source), then no matter how many unconscionable deeds are committed by these targets—no matter how much damning evidence is collected against them—they will not be touched, investigated or arrested. They will be free.

II

FBI PENETRATED

4

Dickersons

My second month at the bureau was frenzied. Not only was I translating current and past data for Dennis Saccher's unit, I was also setting aside extra time to provide him with analysis and additional notes, as well as taking part in frequent strategy meetings.

Around mid-November, another Turkish translator joined the FBI Washington Field Office language division. Just like Kevin Taskesen, the new translator, Melek Can Dickerson (referred to as "Jan") did not score sufficiently well on the English portion of the proficiency test and thus was assigned to the Turkish division as a monitor. Her English was not as bad as Kevin's; at least she could speak the language and knew how to use the dictionary and her computer. I now had two Turkish monitors to supervise.

Jan Dickerson was in her early thirties, nondescript, medium height, heavyset, short dark brown hair and brown eyes. She was not very talkative and mostly kept to herself. After two or three training sessions, my contact with her became limited to checking, approving and initialing her summary translations that involved mainly Turkish counterintelligence operations under Saccher's unit. The only person to whom she appeared close was Feghali. She frequently visited his office, and oddly enough, the open door policy of the division did not apply to their meetings, almost every one of which was held behind closed doors.

Dickerson and I only had a few brief exchanges during her first two weeks with the bureau. She told me that her husband was American and that he worked for the State Department and Pentagon with a unit that dealt with Turkey and Turkic-speaking Central Asian countries. The two had met in Ankara in 1992, while he was stationed there and worked with the U.S. military attaché. They were married in 1995 and, after some years in Germany, moved to the United States in 1999. After a year or two in Alabama, they settled in Washington, DC. She asked about my marital status and wanted to know if my husband too was American. She asked where we lived and was surprised to find that we both lived in Alexandria, less than two miles from each other. She inquired about my family's whereabouts as well, and I briefly told her about my younger sister, who lived with me while attending college, and my mother, who lived in Turkey with my other sister and who visited frequently. This was the extent of my social small talk and interaction with Melek Can "Jan" Dickerson—until the unplanned visit to my house, two weeks later.

On the first Saturday in December, Matthew and I spent the entire day preparing and decorating our house for Christmas. I was doing my best to recreate our traditional holiday mood, despite the sadness and melancholy; this would be the second Christmas without my father.

That evening, while I was busy making dinner, the phone rang. Matthew answered. "It's for you," he called from our upstairs office, "Jan Dickerson, from the FBI." I was surprised. A few days earlier she had asked for my number in case of a work-related emergency. I picked up.

Dickerson apologized for calling us on a Saturday evening and asked us to brunch the following day.

I thought a moment before responding. "I have to check with Matthew. We don't have any particular plans, but there are tons of things to do around the house and I have five final exams in less than two weeks."

"Even an hour would do," she insisted, and mentioned being homesick before breaking the news that she was pregnant. I congratulated her, after which she suggested, "How about this? We can come to your house and take care of the introductions there."

At first I was taken aback but recalled my manners. "Sure . . . in fact, I'll prepare some Turkish delicacies and tea; instead of going to brunch, we'll have something here." She sounded delighted, and said they would come by our house at eleven the following morning.

The Dickersons showed up right on time and Matthew went downstairs to greet them. By the time I came down, the first round of introductions had been made. Douglas Dickerson appeared to be in his late thirties or early forties. He was tall and wiry, with salt and pepper hair neatly cropped, and a pair of steely gray eyes framed by silver-rimmed glasses. He shook my hand and asked me to call him Doug, and his wife gave me an unexpected hug. We moved to the kitchen and I went to pour hot tea while they were being seated.

We sipped our drinks and made small talk for about fifteen minutes. "Doug" briefly talked about his background and current position with the U.S. Air Force and Defense Intelligence Agency, under the procurement logistics division at the Pentagon, which dealt with Turkey and Turkic-speaking Central Asian countries: Turkmenistan, Uzbekistan, Azerbaijan, Tajikistan, Kazakhstan and Kyrgyzstan. And, he casually added, he was part of a team at the Pentagon's Office of Special Plans overseeing Central Asian policies and operations.

I was surprised. His wife had told me he worked for the State Department, and that's what I'd said to my husband. Without missing a beat, Matthew went ahead and asked, "I thought you were with the State Department?" Dickerson chuckled and said it didn't make any difference which agency, since his activities involved the Pentagon, State Department, DIA, NATO and others. Well, it made sense.

I started serving the pie and cake while Matthew, always to the point, answered their questions about what kind of work he did. As we ate, the Dickersons talked about their life in Turkey and Germany, and their plan to retire in a few years and move to Turkey permanently, where they owned several properties. I thought Doug looked too young to re-tire anytime soon but attributed that to his joining the military at a very young age.

Doug asked whether we knew a lot of Turkish people, since so many of them lived in the Washington, DC, area. We didn't. I told him that except for two brothers I had met in college and their family, we didn't know any other Turkish people, and added that we visited Turkey at least once a year and that my family visited us here annually. He nodded and exchanged a look with his wife, who nodded back.

He followed that up with another question. "How about Turkish or-ganizations here in the States? There are many of them, some very in-fluential and powerful."

Matthew shook his head and said no.

"Oh come on, how could you not?" he chided. "Some of these orga-nizations are movers and shakers, both in the U.S. and Turkey. You mean you don't know the American Turkish Council, ATC? Or the Assembly of Turkish American Associations, ATAA?"

I readjusted myself in my chair uncomfortably; I didn't want to dis-cuss those organizations. Of course I knew who they were and what they did—too well. They constituted a big chunk of what I worked on and monitored for Saccher's department.

Matthew, oblivious to my evident discomfort and sudden silence, be-gan by answering, "I know what ATC is, but they're involved with com-panies and people who do business with Turkey or Turkish businesses that export to or work with the U.S." Then he turned to me. "Honey, isn't that right? In fact, when we had our business, we checked them out as a possible advertising venue for our IT services."

I specifically avoided answering and asked if anyone wanted more tea. My transparent attempt to change the subject was ignored. Doug pressed harder. "Matthew, ATC is one of the most powerful organiza-tions in the States. They have several hotshot lobbying firms working for them: the Livingston Group, run by the former Speaker of the House,

Bob Livingston; the Cohen Group, headed by the former secretary of defense, and others. They deal with the highest-level people in the Pentagon, State Department and the White House. They're able to secure hundreds of millions of dollars of U.S. government contracts for Turkish companies every year, many of them for stuff in Central Asia; they rule Congress. Turkish companies, through ATC and ATAA, get most of the contract grants reserved for Central Asian countries and do tons of work for us; Uzbekistan, Azerbaijan and the rest of them, those countries are our future bases and energy sources. Where have you been?"

Now it was Matthew's turn to feel baffled and confused. "Okay, right, but as I said, they deal with those companies that are involved in those particular business areas. They don't invite individuals, people like Sibel or me, to join. It's a membership-based organization for Turkish and American businesses."

Doug smiled and said, almost as though he were spelling out each word, "*Of course* they will accept you, Matthew. In fact, they would *love* to have you join them. They will take care of setting up a business for you." He extended his left arm forward and pointed his finger at me while he kept his eyes on Matthew. "All you have to do is tell them where Sibel works: what she does and who she listens to. You'll get in "—he snapped his fingers—"just like that. They'll make sure you're set; you can retire in a few years and settle in Turkey. They'll take care of everything. I can assure you. How do you think I'm retiring, my friend? I'm already set, ready to live the good life over there."

I felt as if I'd been hit by a truck. Initially I was unable to move my body, even my head. I couldn't swallow. I couldn't sort out what was swirling so horribly inside me. When I finally managed to move, I turned around to look at Jan Dickerson. Was it possible that her husband, Doug, had no idea what she and I were doing at the bureau? Could that be? Or was this some sort of test, to see how the enemy camp might recruit me? Were these people sent by the bureau?

Jan locked eyes with me and smiled—no, it was a smirk: a lopsided, crooked grin. I realized then; they were trying to recruit me! They were here in my house, trying to purchase us. I thought, *My God, this can't be happening. How can this be?* Matthew continued to listen to Doug's pitch without a clue as to what was taking place.

Doug now pointed to his wife. "My wife worked for them, you know. Jan worked for ATAA and ATC. Before we came to the States, while in Germany, she worked for their sister organization in Germany. There are several Turkish-German organizations like that over there. I am very active with them and their Pentagon arm."

I was seized by a panic attack. My heart was pounding; my hands were sweating and my mouth had gone dry. This was surreal. It couldn't be real; maybe I was hallucinating. In fact, this was impossible. Melek Can Dickerson had been hired by the FBI and granted Top Secret Clearance after a thorough background check. No way in hell the bureau would hire her and give her clearance knowing that she worked for those organizations: they were our targets, housing high-level operatives and criminals.

Doug looked me in the eye. "Sibel, I'll introduce you to our two best friends, our Turkish friends. One of them lives in McLean, Virginia. In fact, later today we'll visit them. We visit their house at least once a week. Do you know the Mediterranean Bakery on Van Dorn? Jan shops for them there. We get them bread and Middle Eastern baked goods from there." He paused and named the individual. "He is one of the key operators for the ATC, Colonel _____." Doug named one of the FBI's top counterintelligence targets; in fact, one of our top, primary targets.

He continued. "When Jan worked at ATAA and ATC, she was liaisoned to his office since we knew him from way back when, in Turkey and later in Germany. You guys would like him; we'll introduce you to him. Also . . ." He went on to name others, detailing where they lived and what they did—two out of three being the FBI's primary counterintelligence investigation targets. The names he dropped kept on, from Douglas Feith to Marc Grossman, from a division in the Pentagon to a special unit in the State Department.

I sprang to my feet and grabbed Matthew's teacup, my hands badly shaking. Jan extended her cup to me. "More tea for me also. Aren't you glad we finally got together?" I looked at her in disbelief and grabbed the teacup. I brought the refilled cups back to the table, and before sitting down said, "I have two term papers waiting for me. Sorry to cut this short." Doug looked down at his watch. "Oh, I can't believe we've been here for almost two hours." Then to his wife, "Honey, we need to go also." Jan dropped two sugar cubes into her cup and said, "I know; on the way we have to stop at the Mediterranean Bakery."

I started clearing the table. Matthew shot me a quizzical look, sensing something was wrong—he just had no idea *how* wrong. A few minutes later, Matthew walked them to the door. I mumbled a cool good-bye and stayed in the kitchen, not bothering to see them out.

Matthew rushed into the kitchen as soon as he shut the door. "What the heck was that all about?"

I continued to empty plates, without looking up. "I know he gave you his number, but I don't want you to ever call him, OK? If he calls, just hang up—OK? Let me know, but do not talk with either of them. They are dangerous; extremely dangerous."

He seemed baffled. I knew I had to report this bizarre incident to FBI security and Feghali. I expected they would follow up and might even launch an investigation into the Dickersons. They could well end up interviewing Matthew, so I added, "Matthew, I'm not allowed to discuss with you anything classified related to the FBI. That's why I don't talk about work-related stuff at home. But I have to report to the FBI what occurred here with the Dickersons. I'll do it first thing next week."

Matthew finally seemed to get it. I too began to get it more clearly. The meaning and implications of what had happened had begun to sink in.

That day I was not able to focus. I felt certain that I needed to report the incident, every single word; but to whom? Personnel security? I wasn't even sure. Was I supposed to go directly to my supervisor, Feghali? I decided to wait until Tuesday, my next working day. I took a notepad and wrote down the entire conversation.

That night I lay awake and stared at the ceiling. The more I thought, the louder the alarm went off in my head. Waiting until Tuesday already was beginning to feel like weeks.

I went over their visit, just what had taken place.

Melek Can Dickerson had worked for ATC, ATAA, and before that, with these organizations' counterpart in Germany. Individuals and entities within these organizations, including certain Americans, were directly involved in global criminal activities: nuclear black market, narcotics, and military and industrial espionage. These organizations and their players are not driven by any ideology or nationalistic objectives. To them this is business, and the highest bidder, regardless of nationality or ideology, gets the goods.

Douglas Dickerson was an air force major; he had above Top Secret Clearance. Was it possible he used his position and access to sensitive classified information in the Pentagon to provide criminal entities with desirable information, and in return got paid handsomely overseas and set himself up to retire to a lavish life?

In one visit, he had named at least three or four targets of FBI counterintelligence investigations as their "close friends and business associates." Considering the importance and role of Turkic-speaking Central Asian countries in illegal activities carried out by these Turkish networks—and Dickerson's position in a weapons procurement division of the Pentagon dealing specifically with Turkey and these countries—his value to these criminal entities would make perfect sense.

With her background and ongoing relationships with the primary targets, how did Jan Dickerson obtain Top Secret Clearance and get into the bureau's most sensitive unit dealing with Turkish counterintelligence? As a translator, she could act as a valve, block information and intelligence from transmission, and meanwhile alert those targeted and tip them off.

Yet, I kept asking myself, why would the Dickersons risk recruiting me before checking me out thoroughly? And why would they risk even more by doing it in front of a witness—my husband—so boldly and without finesse?

Tuesday could not come soon enough.

On the following Tuesday morning, I arrived at work a little after 9:30. The first thing I did, even before signing in, was to turn on my computer and type a half-page report on the Dickersons' visit. I would cover the details in person, with Feghali.

I knocked on his half-open door three times. "Oh," he said, looking up. "Long time no see, Ms. Perfectionist, Ms. Bossy. What's bringing you to my office today? What is it we're doing wrong—or not right enough for your taste?"

I rolled my eyes and handed him the sheet. "This is urgent, Mike. I need to report a serious incident to you. You know the paper we sign . . . the one that says if we come across anything suspicious, if anyone tries to recruit us, we need to immediately notify FBI security and management? Well I'm here to report an incident like that. Am I in the right place, or should I just go directly upstairs to the personnel security division?"

He had already begun skimming my summary report. He motioned me to sit down while he continued to read. Then he asked what this was about. Recounting the exchange, I mentioned also the primary Turkish targets under Saccher's CI unit (I wasn't allowed to tell him more).

Feghali listened; then leaned back in his chair. "I'm sure you're making a mountain out of a molehill," he finally said. "Think about it, Sibel. The FBI spent months, if not years, checking out Melek's background, her past, her previous employment, her family . . . if they—the experts, the investigators—have determined that she is fit to be cleared at Top Secret level, if they have decided that she is qualified to have clearance and work here, it means she is cleared and OK. You and I are no experts. Do you know how arrogant that sounds, questioning the experts' and investigators' judgment?"

Yes, perhaps; that was one of the questions I had been asking myself for the past two days: How could she get clearance and get in? "I know," I said. "Believe it or not, I agree with your assessment. But what do you make of this? I mean, how could she be listening to people she used to work with, work for, and whom she still associates and socializes with? Also, her husband works with the ATC and is getting paid to do things for them, using his access and high-level position at the Pentagon. That's odd; suspicious!"

"Look," Feghali said, "the FBI had to check out their tax records and financial background; they had to interview her previous employers. If they said she is cleared at Top Secret level, I'd say she is; I wouldn't question or doubt their word."

I thought for a second. "What if she's a mole for the FBI? What if she's an informant? What if she's a *spy*? That would explain why she'd be associating with the targets of our wiretap, right?"

Feghali shook his head. "This ain't the CIA. Sibel, the FBI doesn't operate that way. The informants are not allowed to work inside the agency, they're kept outside. Only agents work undercover, not administrative personnel, translators. . . . I think Melek Dickerson is a fine woman. I don't see any reason to suspect her or doubt her loyalties."

"So should I go upstairs and report this to the Security Division, maybe even Saccher?"

"Oh no, that's my job. I'll take care of it. I'll send a report to security, with a copy to Saccher's division. In fact, I don't want you to talk about this with anyone, including Saccher. I'll take care of it myself; I'll do it right away."

I was satisfied with his response. I had given him a written memo, provided all the details verbally, and he would send a formal report to the appropriate parties, including Saccher. I thanked Feghali and left his office.

Toward the middle of December, right before Dickerson left for Turkey (she and her husband were spending their holiday season there), I had stayed late at the office to wrap up a few projects. I was busy typing up translations when Amin stopped by, holding in his weary hand a thick folder stuffed with paperwork.

I raised my head and smiled. "What's up, Amin?"

He told me he was exhausted. (Amin was the most competent and savvy Farsi translator in the bureau; therefore, many high-level, demanding projects were assigned to him.) He had stayed late to scan paper-based work project orders and transmit them to HQ, a new procedure that still had more than a few glitches. Amin was the only person who was able to get it done right.

"The incompetent man, Feghali, gave me this thick folder with tons of documents and asked me to transmit them one by one to HQ," he began. "Going through them, I came across several of yours that I couldn't read or make out the handwriting in the sections you are supposed to fill out as the translator in charge of completing the project."

He removed a few stacks and placed them on my desk. "Please be a doll and look at them and let me know what the codes and numbers are. I usually don't have any problem reading yours, but somehow I couldn't make these out." He pointed to several documents.

I picked them up and started reading. I stopped short within the first few seconds. "Hey Amin, these are not mine. I have never seen them before. You must be mistaken."

He bent over and turned the page. "Here it is, your initial, S.E., your last name at the bottom, and it is for the Turkish department; you are the only one who can initial and sign these, since the other two are only monitors."

I grabbed the documents, pulled them out of his hand and started to read the forms. He was right. My initials and name were signed, yet neither was in my handwriting. "This is not my handwriting; someone forged my initials and signature on a document that was supposed to be translated by me, assigned to me. Oh shit!"

Amin too looked alarmed. "What were these about—the documents, the project?"

"I don't know. The actual work—the original document in Turkish and any translation corresponding to that—was already sent to the re-questing field office . . . let me look at it again."

I went over every page. "Judging from the file number, it's relevant to nine eleven operations. Also, the field filled out by the agent in charge indicates detainees of Turkish and Uzbek origin, that's all. Oh, let's see here . . . this was sent back to the requesting office together with the translation almost two weeks ago."

"Which one do you suspect, Kevin or Dickerson?"

I already knew which one had done this but I wanted to make sure and to have another set of eyes confirming it. We pulled out Dickerson's file, and checked the handwriting on the first document. Bingo!

"But it still doesn't explain why she would do such a thing. This is forgery, for God's sake; people go to jail for this."

Then it struck me. "Oh my God! What if someone guilty was released based on what she sent? What if someone who *should have been released* was sent to jail based on what she did? What if it's too late?"

There was nothing we could do at that late hour. I decided to wait until the following morning. Amin asked me to make sure to report the incident in writing.

The next morning I went directly to my desk, pulled out a copy of one of the forged signed documents and walked straight over to Dickerson. She pulled off her headset and smiled. "Hi, how are you doing? How is Matt?"

I wasn't in the mood. "What the hell is this?" I smacked down the file. "You have some explaining to do—not only to me, but to the agent in that field office, Feghali, and the security office."

She picked up the file and slowly turned its pages. "How did you get this? We sent this to the field office in New Jersey almost two weeks ago. Who gave you this?"

"*We?* What do you mean *we?* First of all, you're not a translator. You're a monitor and cannot perform verbatim translations and send them to agents in Counterterrorism without my review. Second, forgery is a crime. How dare you forge my signature and initials on something I haven't even seen? Why did you do this, Jan?"

She coolly stared at me. "*We* means Feghali and me. First: because you're here only on a part-time basis and are not available every day. Second: Feghali has decided that I no longer need your approval and signature. He has given me authority to do all translations. I mean *everything.*"

I sighed. "Stop the BS. Feghali cannot do that. But let's say he did; then why wouldn't you sign *your* name on it? Why would you forge my name, initials and signature?"

She pushed the file back at me. "Here, go and settle it with Feghali. He's the guy in charge, and he decided to do it this way. Plus, what's the big deal? Why would you care about what was translated or mistranslated on some Uzbek and Turkish detainees out in New Jersey? You shouldn't concern yourself with things like that. Just let it go. That's my recommendation."

I went back to my desk and wrote a short memo describing what had occurred and the documentation backing it up. I first e-mailed it to Feghali, and later shoved a folder containing the memo and a copy of the documents with forged signatures under his closed door. He was on vacation.

I stopped by Kevin's desk and told him what had occurred with the documents. Kevin commented in Turkish, "I would watch out for this woman. There is something seriously wrong with her. I was talking about it with Behrooz the other day, since both of us were there when she took the documents out."

"What are you talking about?"

Kevin looked surprised. "Oh, Behrooz didn't tell you? I noticed Dickerson at Omi's desk [the Hebrew translator who had raised hell over his work being sabotaged]; she opened his bottom drawer and pulled out several thick files; then she bent over and put the entire stack inside her duffel bag, the one she always brings in with her. I nudged Behrooz and pointed it out to him. He almost fainted. Haven't you noticed? She always walks in with that shriveled empty duffel bag; but watch her when she gets out: the bag is full and fat!"

I hadn't noticed. I never paid attention to the comings and goings of people in our unit. There are no security checks for the translators entering and leaving the FBI building. Of course, anyone who wanted to could take out a suitcase full of documents and it wouldn't raise an eyebrow. I wondered why she, Dickerson, would steal documents from the Israeli Counterintelligence Desk.

I asked Kevin if he had reported it. "Of course not," he replied. "None of my business. I don't care. I'm just telling you that she is strange. Something is seriously wrong with this woman."

I double-checked with Behrooz; he confirmed the story. I wrote another memo to Feghali reporting the incident, and e-mailed that one too. Things seemed to be piling up with Dickerson. I thought about what Feghali had told me, his attempt to reassure me. Now I wasn't reassured at all.

* * *

On the third day of January I was hard at work when Dickerson stopped by my desk holding a legal-size sheet of paper.

"I've been thinking," she began. "We—the three of us, you and I and Kevin—have been randomly reviewing and translating the incoming intelligence related to these targets." She placed the paper in front of me. "This is not the most efficient way. Instead of doing it this way, we should divide these targets into three groups, and have each group of targets assigned to one of us. This way we will each have a group of targets we regularly monitor and translate."

The crude, hand-drawn chart showed a list of our counterintelligence target ID numbers—more than twenty IDs—divided into three separate groups. The first had an arrow pointing to her name: Melek Can Dickerson; the second had a similar arrow pointing to my name; and the third pointed to Kevin's. I shook my head dismissively. "We don't make the rules on this; Saccher's department is in charge of this. You should be talking to him."

"Why should this be Saccher's business? His objective is to get the translated intelligence; it doesn't make any difference who is doing which target. I believe this will make everything easier and more efficient—"

Reaching for my headset, I repeated, "If he decides to do it, I'll have no problem. Just go and see him to discuss this. He's the agent in charge of this counterintelligence operation."

Dickerson slammed her hand down on my headset. "Why are you being so difficult? I've discussed this with Kevin and he agrees with me; we've already divided the lines between the two of us. Saccher doesn't give a shit about how we do things here; he's not even allowed to come into the unit without us escorting him. He's irrelevant. I don't want you to go over these targets randomly."

Suddenly it hit me. I grabbed the page and looked at it again, this time carefully. Based on Dickerson's division, she would be in charge of a group that included our top two targets—our primary targets, per Saccher. Interestingly enough, both targets were among those the Dickersons had named during their visit to our house, including the colonel, her former boss and the man they visited every week and shopped for at the bakery in Alexandria. She was trying to shield them from us, from the FBI.

I stood and faced her. "I'll go and talk with Kevin myself, alone!"

Dickerson took two steps and blocked me. "I know this is not the career you want to pursue, Sibel. Just do what I asked you to do—a simple request. Why would you want to put yourself in danger by getting in the way?"

"What?" I snapped. "What did you say?"

She stepped aside and let me pass. "I'll take this to Mike Feghali. He's the supervisor; he will decide."

I took long strides to Kevin's station. He looked up and greeted me in Turkish. I waved the paper in front of him. "Do you want to tell me what this is all about? You and Dickerson divide targets and rewrite Saccher's rules and procedures?"

Kevin looked at the paper, then opened his drawer and pulled out a sheet identical to the one I was holding, in Dickerson's handwriting. "Yesterday she came to me and gave me this." He handed me the page. "She said it was your idea, that you'd already agreed this was the best way. So I said OK."

I grabbed a chair and dragged it over. I sat and leaned to face him head on. "Kevin, you were right the other day when you said that she was a dangerous woman. I think she's more dangerous than you think." I told him about the Dickersons' visit to my house and the forged signatures.

Kevin paled. "What are we going to do? What if she gives our names and contact information to the targets? I have family back in Turkey; you do too. What we know can get us killed over there. Why would they let her work here, knowing her history and associates?"

I told him I'd given everything to Feghali, that he'd reported it to the security division and Saccher's unit, and that I hadn't heard anything from either. "Mike instructed me not to mention the report and let him handle it." I paused. Now we had to report this incident, Dickerson's attempt to shield targets. I assured him I would file a report with the unit supervisor; that "someone will get to the bottom of this."

I went back to my desk to write the memo, placed it inside a legal-size envelope with copies of Dickerson's handwritten instructions and sealed it. Then I went to see Feghali in his office. The door was closed. Fifteen minutes later, it was still closed.

I had to leave, so I brought the package to Kevin for him to drop off. I mentioned that Feghali had been in a closed-door meeting for more than an hour.

Kevin pointed to Dickerson's vacant station. "What do you think they're doing in there?"

I didn't know what to say. "Give him the package before he leaves. If you can't, lock it up in your drawer, and I'll take care of it tomorrow." I handed him the envelope and left him looking nervous.

That evening, Kevin called. He had waited until 6:30, he said, but Feghali was still in his office with Dickerson when he left. "I even wiggled the doorknob; he had the door locked. I could hear them whispering inside. . . . What time will you be in tomorrow?" I told him I would be there by ten. The situation was getting out of control; I decided to contact Saccher if this continued.

The next morning I arrived at ten o'clock sharp. I always started off the day by going through my e-mails and phone messages. Almost immediately, Kevin appeared at my desk, with dark circles under his eyes. He looked as though he hadn't slept at all.

As we talked, I glanced at my screen and scanned e-mails. There was one from Feghali, sent the previous evening at 6:41 P.M., addressed to Kevin, Dickerson and me. "After reviewing your workload and projects under Saccher's Counterintelligence division," it began, "I've decided to divide the targets among the three of you, permanently. This will increase the efficiency of processing these lines." Beneath this he listed the target ID numbers and the name of the translators assigned to them. I unlocked my drawer and pulled out Dickerson's handwritten instruction: Feghali's division scheme was identical to it. As a postscript, Feghali added, "Please do NOT discuss this with Special Agent Dennis Saccher. This decision does not concern him and I forbid you to discuss this with anyone but me. Also, from this point on you shall not meet with SA Saccher without notifying me first."

Kevin's face drained of all color. "Shit; I knew she had gotten to him. She's been working on him since she arrived here. . . . Do you know how many behind-closed-door meetings they've had in the past month? Usually after hours? Shit!"

"I'll give Feghali one more chance," I replied. "If that doesn't work, we'll go to Saccher. Based on the bureau's rules, Feghali is not even allowed to know about these targets, their names and their ID numbers . . ."

"Don't underestimate Feghali," Kevin said, deadly serious. "There are other things that you don't know about, Sibel ... let's have coffee outside, I don't want to talk about this here."

I decided to hear Kevin out before giving Feghali the memo. When I got to the coffeehouse, Kevin was already there, looking rattled.

"Do you know how only agents are allowed to know and maintain informants' and assets' identities, contact information?"

I shook my head no. During my work I had not come across anything that involved procedures concerning FBI informants' information, and wondered what this had to do with Feghali or Dickerson.

"Feghali has found a way to access that information," Kevin continued. "I don't know how. Also, according to Sarshar, Feghali has found a way to use and cash in on this information. Again, I don't know how. I'm telling you what I've heard from several sources." He went on to describe illegal transactions involving nepotism and other illicit activities, all of them disturbing. Kevin sounded afraid. He considered Feghali evil. "I won't inform Saccher. I want to stay away from this shit."

I looked him in the eye and told him he didn't have a choice, that if we didn't report this, we would be co-conspirators. "Like it or not, you've been exposed to this; you are a witness." I sighed. "I'll call Saccher tomorrow morning. This information on informants can be huge. Think about it: he could be selling that information to the targets. Do you know how much he can get for that—for ratting out FBI informants? Do you know that this can get some of these informants killed?!"

As I got up to leave, Kevin said he wanted to wait a few minutes; he didn't want us to be seen together by Feghali. *What a paranoid chicken!* I thought. That was then.

When I got to my desk, my phone light was blinking: voice mail. As if connected telepathically, Saccher had left a message, asking me to meet him about something urgent the following morning at nine sharp. Now that was Karma! I thought about Feghali's warning, *You are not allowed to meet with your case agent, Saccher, without notifying me first.* I shrugged and mumbled to myself, "Screw you, Feghali; you and the Dickersons are about to be exposed."

5

Discovery

The following morning, only one day after Feghali's e-mail and before signing in, I stopped by to meet Saccher at his cubicle. He'd left a message that he wanted to see me on some urgent matter. I had no idea what it was about.

When I appeared at his desk, Saccher grabbed a chair from an empty cubicle and rolled it over. After some pleasantries, he began. "Okay . . . I know you're working on many different projects and counterterrorism cases; plus, you're here part-time, so a lot of my CI stuff has been handled by Dickerson for the past month or so. Kevin—well, Kevin is not much of a translator, we both know that. I know how he got in here; I've resigned myself to the bureau's disastrous state in translation and analysis—drowned in corruption, incompetence, nepotism, you name it. I won't even get into that!"

I nodded for him to continue.

"You and I know and have talked about the primary targets—the three most important targets of this operation out of twenty plus—right? Come on, you discovered most of the evidence." He grabbed the file from a stack and handed it to me. "I want you to take a look at this and let me know what jumps out at you, okay?"

I leafed through fifty or so stapled sheets, a collection of Counterintelligence project translations submitted by the Turkish translation unit at the end of each day. I started to hand the file back to Saccher. "So? What is it?"

Saccher pushed it back toward me. "Come on Sibel, just look at it closely. Take a few minutes and go through it. Then tell me what you see."

Now I was curious. I set the file in front of me and paid careful attention to each line, each word. These were not from all three translators in the Turkish unit—they all had been submitted by Melek Can Dickerson. Her name and ID were printed on the top of each sheet. Each page had several target ID numbers followed by either the summary translation of the communication or *Not Pertinent to Be Translated* stamped on them.

On closer inspection, I realized one target in particular had *Not Pertinent* stamped on every single piece of intelligence. That target happened to be the one the Dickersons named during their visit: the colonel they wanted to introduce us to, the man with whom she worked in the past and associated regularly. I started turning pages and scanning for the same target ID number: there it was, on every communication stamped *Not Pertinent to Be Translated*. I could see it all now, plain in full sight: she'd been steadily blocking the translation of her friend and business associate for over a month. *She's shielding the criminals for whom she worked—and who are clearly still her friends*, I thought.

Saccher was watching me intently. I plopped the file back on his desk. "Dennis, it all fits. Now, with everything else you have—the visit and dividing the lines—you can do something about it, right?"

Saccher looked puzzled. "What visit? What dividing?"

"The report," I said. "The report on the Dickersons' visit to my house, the forgery of my initials on CT cases in New Jersey and the latest division instructions!"

"What the hell are you talking about? Are you talking in code? What visit or forgery?"

I felt blood rushing to my face. "I reported several highly suspicious activities involving Dickerson to Feghali, and he said he filed it with personnel security upstairs and sent you a copy on everything. I reported everything in writing, some with backup documentation—her handwritten note on dividing the lines."

Now it was Saccher who flushed. "What report? When? I didn't get a damn thing. Just start from the beginning and tell me everything; from the beginning, Sibel."

It took me nearly thirty minutes to tell him everything: I went down the list, ending with Feghali's recent directive prohibiting Kevin and me from ever meeting with him, Saccher, without first obtaining permission.

With every passing minute Saccher's face grew darker; his pupils dilated and he was breathing hard. When I finished, he jumped to his feet. "Come on; let's go upstairs to the security department. Let's go and check if Feghali ever reported this shit. I also want to check Dickerson's personnel file. Let's go . . ."

We hastened to the eighth floor, which houses the FBI-WFO Personnel Security Division. Saccher had me wait in reception while he went inside.

About ten minutes later he came back extremely agitated, nearly yelling. "There is not a single damn thing in her entire file, Sibel! No report, no memo, no notice—nada! Feghali never reported this. Do you know what this is, Sibel? This is espionage. It smells like it, it sounds like it, and now it sure looks like espionage. This should have been reported to me right away. Oh Sibel, how could you be that stupid? You should have come to me a month ago!"

"I did as I was told," I blurted out. "You should have come to the unit. You should have told me this when you suspected her blocking translations ..."

We were both fuming. He grabbed my elbow and gave it a shake. "Didn't you say she and her husband went to Turkey for a week or so last month?"

Not following completely, I slowly nodded yes.

"Any foreign travel by FBI employees—especially if they're going to the target country—should be filed and reported to the bureau in advance. You're allowed to leave only after it's reported and approved. Dickerson bypassed that. She went to Turkey without reporting it. Nothing is in her file. In fact, I think someone has gone through the file and emptied it. Even her background check and referral sheets are missing. . . . This is a clear case of espionage, Sibel. I have to report this to my boss and unit chief right away. The bureau has been penetrated, and somehow I'm not surprised. The question is how badly . . . how much damage."

He turned around and I followed him back to the elevator. I had never seen Saccher angry, never like this before. *We're all doomed*, I thought; *it's too late, the damage is done.* Knowing these targets, I shivered at all the possibilities—and at the risk Kevin and I now faced.

I followed Saccher to his desk. "What do you want me to do?"

He turned to me and sighed, and apologized for yelling; that this was not my fault. "I have to do something about this now," he explained. "I have to brief my boss and the unit chief. We need to figure out our next step before we hand this over as a counterespionage case. Meanwhile, don't let Feghali know about this meeting. I believe she's hooked him already. . . . Feghali may have given her the Turkish informants list. We have to issue an alert: lives may be at stake." Then he asked, "Are you working next Monday?"

"No, I have school."

"Take a few hours off from your school. This is important. Come to my desk at eight in the morning. Bring Kevin with you. I want the three of us to meet. Not a word to Feghali or Dickerson, understood?"

I nodded.

I took the elevator back down to the fourth floor and noticed I was shaking. I went straight to Kevin's station and told him to meet me in the coatroom in three minutes. When he got there, I quickly explained what happened. He was to meet me in Saccher's office the following Monday at eight without raising any suspicions. Feghali and Dickerson specifically were not to know. Poor Kevin looked devastated.

The following Monday I got to Saccher's unit a few minutes before eight. Kevin arrived moments later and the meeting began. Saccher had met with his boss and the unit chief for counterintelligence. He then explained briefly their decision to collect more evidence before transferring the Dickerson case to the FBI Counterespionage division. He had confirmed, via his sources and informants, that Dickerson indeed had worked for and with certain target entities; and that she and her husband appeared to be part of a larger operation, a global network. The players included U.S. officials—both elected and appointed—and certain Pakistani, Saudi and Israeli elements.

Dickerson's success in penetrating our unit meant that all of the targets already had been tipped off and would no longer be of value. More important, though, was that Saccher's unit had lost any chance of pursuing the U.S. officials under parallel criminal and espionage investigations. Nearly everything Dickerson had blocked dated back to 2000 and early 2001—before she had gotten inside.

The next part of Saccher's plan was to have Kevin and me go through everything—every piece of communication Dickerson had stamped *Not Pertinent* or may well have intentionally mistranslated—translate what was involved, document those considered important, and then translate the select pieces as evidence. Finally, we were to submit them to Saccher's unit.

Dickerson, it was emphasized, must never suspect what we were up to. With our translations of her blocked intelligence in hand, Saccher and his boss planned to interrogate her in a "surprise blast" to try to rattle her into confessing. Saccher's unit then would have enough to transfer the case to Counterespionage under the Justice Department.

When asked how Dickerson could have bypassed the background investigation, Saccher replied that he couldn't be sure, that in addition to her husband's highest level security clearance, they may have other accomplices inside the bureau.

I pointed out the problem with Feghali—how he could and would make life miserable.

Saccher agreed to set up a meeting with the four of us. He dialed Feghali's extension and left a message.

Kevin looked afraid. "She-she knows our last name," he stuttered, "information . . . *contact* information . . . Dennis, you know how dangerous these people are—who's going to watch out for us?"

Saccher smiled. "Don't worry, big man; we'll figure this thing out. As part of our plan, per normal procedures, we'll conduct damage assessment. Just be patient." He told us he would be away for a few days but that in a few weeks' time things would get resolved one way or another.

During my next four working days, I spent time going over Dickerson's blocked communications. Among hundreds of pieces, in every ten or fifteen checked, I would come across a mother lode of hot intel that no translator, no matter how incompetent, would or could ever miss.

We were looking at people involved in sophisticated networks and operations geared to penetrate our nuclear and military technologies and intelligence—that were then sold to the highest bidder in the global black market. This could be a government entity, another network, a front organization, or individuals connected with a known terrorist group. This was not about any one ideology or nationalism; this was about power and money.

We were also dealing with a list of dirty joint CIA and Turkish operatives in Central Asia, Caucasus and the Balkans. As the FBI pursues foreign terrorists who target our nation, other agencies carry out equally bad or worse attacks overseas. Stunningly, some of these black operations employ the same groups accused of carrying out attacks against us.

Within a week I had identified four explosive pieces of communication blocked by Dickerson and was almost finished translating them verbatim. There were hundreds more, but I knew these four were enough for Saccher's planned "blast" interrogation.

Meanwhile, Saccher called to let us know that he had set up the meeting with Feghali for the following Friday, February 1, at 9:30 A.M. I stayed off Feghali's radar until then. I knew how easily he could be provoked; and now Feghali couldn't stand the sight of me.

Kevin too, despite his linguistic shortcomings, discovered three important pieces of intelligence blocked by Dickerson, one of which dealt with the Pentagon's own network of moles. Between the two of us, we were ready for the upcoming meeting.

Prior to the scheduled 9:30 meeting that Friday morning, Kevin and I decided to meet ahead of time and to stop by Saccher's office for any last-minute instructions. By the time I got to the building, Kevin was out front waiting. Without wasting time, we headed inside.

Saccher was in a good mood, a warrior in his element, ready to chase down his prey. He had a list of questions prepared and asked us to let him start the conversation with Feghali. We were to wait to be prompted before saying anything.

We told Saccher what we had unearthed so far. He had the exact same reaction: no one could possibly miss the importance and sensitivity of these four pieces and stamp them as not pertinent to be translated.

Saccher looked at his watch: 9:15. "Okay, the meeting is supposed to start at 9:30. You guys go down and get ready. I'll see you there in fifteen minutes." Kevin and I headed down to the fourth floor.

As soon as we entered, before the glass door even closed behind us, we were face to face with Feghali. He looked and sounded hyper, tapping at his watch. "Come on," he said, "we have the conference room until ten o'clock; we better go in there and start the meeting right now. Let's go."

I looked at him innocently. "Okay, I'll go and grab my notepad; but has Saccher gotten here already?" Feghali had no idea that Kevin and I had just come from Saccher's office.

"Saccher? Oh, Saccher won't be able to make it. He called to cancel earlier today and said he had to go out for some urgent operation."

Without looking, I knew Kevin must have been in shock. I had to speak before he blurted out that we were with Saccher only minutes earlier. "Oh, really?" I jumped in. "Then shouldn't we cancel this meeting anyway? This was a meeting he requested, right? I guess you can postpone it."

Feghali swallowed. "No, we can go ahead and meet; afterwards I'll report back to him and give him the minutes of the meeting. Come on, let's go."

"But this was Saccher's meeting . . . Without Saccher, why would we meet?"

Feghali pointed to the small conference room. "You, Kevin, Dickerson and I will meet in there, right now. Go grab your notepad."

Poor Kevin's apprehension was palpable; I could almost feel him shaking. "Mike," I tried to reason, "when Saccher called to notify us about the meeting, he told Kevin and me not to have anyone but him, you, Kevin and me. He said there were certain specific issues regarding the CI project that he wanted to discuss only with the three of us."

"I decide in here, not Saccher. This is my unit." Feghali narrowed his eyes. "I have a feeling you initiated this meeting in the first place. Want me to tell you what I think? You went behind my back and talked with Saccher, despite my e-mail warning you specifically not to."

"Mike," I protested, defensive now, "I was told by Saccher to follow his instructions. That's what I'm doing."

"Let me tell you something," Feghali screeched. "I've had it with you! Guess who is the person in charge of renewing your contract? Not Saccher! Your contract is up for renewal this month, and HQ will not renew it without my approval. You better understand where your loyalty is supposed to be placed."

Kevin was dead silent. "Mike," I suggested, "since Saccher is not working today and won't make it to this meeting, I think you should either cancel and reschedule it later, or ask another senior supervisor to be present."

Feghali took two steps forward and leaned his face into mine. "I will *not* cancel this meeting," he said acidly. "Saccher wanted a meeting, so I'm having one. Let's go inside the conference room"—he turned to Kevin—"*both* of you."

I'd about had it with his bullying. "I will not go into a meeting with you without another senior supervisor present."

As I turned to go to my desk, Feghali called out, "You 'demand' another supervisor? Fine. I'll go and ask Stephanie Bryan to attend—but you're going to regret everything. Mark my word."

I walked away with Kevin tagging behind. He grabbed my arm. "What are we supposed to do now? Oh shit . . . what kind of game is this, Sibel? What are we going to do, say?"

"Shhh," I tried to calm him. "Go and grab your notepad. We'll go and sit there and see what he has in mind. Afterwards, we'll inform Saccher and see where he goes with this. The reason I asked for another supervisor is so we have another witness present for whatever it is he wants to have this meeting for."

As we entered the conference room, the first thing I saw was Melek Can Dickerson seated at the table. At one end sat Bryan, and at the other end, Feghali. Kevin and I sat together facing Dickerson, with our notepads before us.

Stephanie spoke first. "I understand there are some personal problems between the Turkish translators, Sibel, Kevin, and Jan. This is normal. Whenever you have people, you'll have conflicts, misunderstandings and problems. These issues can be resolved through open communication; through dialogue. That's why we're gathered here today ..."

I could tell she had no idea what this meeting was about. After all, she'd been asked to participate only minutes earlier. I remained silent. With Dickerson present I was not about to say a word.

Feghali interrupted. "First, let me begin by emphasizing the fact that I have been happily married for thirty-four years. Second, I have joined the EEOC board for the FBI-WFO and am fully aware of the implications of sexual impropriety in the workplace. No one—I mean no one—can ever accuse me of sexual misconduct here."

Huh? Feghali must have assumed that this was to be about his behind-the-door liaisons with Dickerson. Were it not for the gravity of the situation, I would have laughed out loud.

Stephanie too seemed taken aback. To me, she added, "So what's the personal conflict and misunderstanding we are dealing with here?"

"I have no idea what this is all about," I told her. "As far as the original intention of the meeting goes, I was instructed by my agent, Dennis Saccher, not to talk about it under these circumstances. I don't know of any personal conflicts."

Kevin spoke next. "I don't know what Feghali meant by 'sexual'; I don't care about people's sexual life. Why is he talking about sex?"

Bryan, confused, closed her notepad. "Mike, I don't even know why we're here. I want to meet with Sibel and Kevin in my office, privately."

During the entire session, Dickerson hadn't said a word. She sat with her eyes narrowed, watching us. We rose and followed Stephanie into her office.

She closed the door. "So, what is this about? Because to be honest with you, I am so sick and tired of Feghali. The man was not qualified for this position, but with threats and blackmail he managed to get it. Since last May I've been going around and picking up all the shit he's been creating. I'm aware of his sexual conduct; in fact, I had to move one of the translators from the unit under his supervision and assign her to me. You know her: the Vietnamese girl, Huan?"

She shook her head. "I've also heard about his escapades with Dickerson after hours. Look, I've been piling up all these incidents in my folder; I'm ready to help you guys bring a formal complaint against him. We can go downstairs to the EEO unit and do it right now. Let's kick the bastard out of this unit!"

"Stephanie," I began, "our case—Dennis Saccher's case—has nothing to do with sex . . ."

Stephanie seemed surprised. "Oh? So then, what's this about?"

Kevin and I exchanged a nervous look. After some hesitation, I decided to give her the general outline, briefly describing our retranslation and review task regarding Dickerson's blocked intelligence documents.

I could see that she was in no way expecting this. As soon as I wrapped up the account, she mumbled half to herself, "My God . . . I can't believe this. I can't believe this has been going on for over a month and Feghali hasn't said a thing..." Kevin told her how afraid he was, not only for us but for our family members in Turkey. "How many of those have you translated already?" she asked me. "I need those translations, right away."

"There are hundreds of them. I went through the first batch, about fifty or so, and have four almost completed, verbatim."

She nodded. "Make sure you bring me those before you leave today. Meanwhile, I want you and Kevin to continue this; review the rest and translate the crucial ones."

I told her that Saccher had asked us to submit the translations directly to his department. "He and his boss are waiting for the first series—"

"I'll take care of them," she cut in. "Submit them to me directly. I'll share those with the appropriate people: Saccher, SAC Thomas Frields and security." She turned to Kevin. "That goes for you too. I want you to translate exactly the same communications; this way, we'll have the two of you verifying the same blocked stuff independently. Do not discuss it with each other—that way, it will be truly independent."

As Kevin and I headed out, Stephanie called me back. "I need to speak with you," she began. "This is what I want to do . . ."

Stephanie outlined her plan. There were "too many holes in the system," she said, fearful of repercussions to the department if word got out. "I want you to put all the memos, letters, e-mails you have sent Feghali on this case, including your verbal reports, in one comprehensive and detailed report. Prepare this memo carefully," she told me, "and make sure you don't leave anything out. Then, submit the memo to me; that way, I can report the case thoroughly to the rest: SAC Frields, Saccher's unit chief . . ."

One more thing: I was not to use my computer at work. Rather, I should do it at home, on my home computer. "Put everything in one comprehensive memo; print the memo and also put it on a disk. Once done, put everything in a large envelope, seal it, and bring it to me."

I told her I'd get the requested material, including the summary of what was in the blocked communications, to her by the following week.

Stephanie smiled, thanked me, and added that she was officially re-moving me from Feghali's supervision. "I'll assign you to me until this is resolved one way or another."

I left her office relieved and very grateful. As soon as I got to my desk, I dialed Saccher's extension. He answered on the second ring.

"What in the world happened to you?" I asked.

"What do you mean? Feghali called me as soon as you and Kevin left and said that he had to cancel the meeting and reschedule it for the fol-lowing week. He had something important on a counterterrorism case involving one of his translators."

This was unbelievable. I told Saccher what Feghali told us: that he, Saccher, had canceled the meeting for a supposedly unexpected field operation.

Before I could even finish recounting, Saccher cut me off. "This is friggin' nuts!" He was yelling. "That bastard . . . that sonuvabitch! I'm going to see him in jail. Meet me at the fire exit—the secondary stairway, on the sixth floor landing."

"What? Why there?"

"We need to talk," he said. "I'll see you there in three minutes sharp." He hung up. *Why there?* I thought, baffled. I started toward the unit exit; then took the stairs two at a time, and when I got there, Saccher was waiting.

He asked me to go over the entire episode, including Dickerson's reactions and body language during the meeting, and tell him word for word what Stephanie had instructed me to do.

"I don't know Stephanie Bryan well," Saccher went on to explain. "I don't know if she's trustworthy or competent. This is not her area. She's only an administrator; she doesn't know a damn thing about this area, about counterespionage investigations. She can ruin the entire case. Don't submit the translations to her," he added. "Drag your feet; bring it to our unit by the end of the day."

I was exhausted, confused, and getting exasperated. "Dennis, I cannot take this anymore. As of today, she is my admin supervisor. She specifically instructed me not to submit the translation to you. She ordered me to prepare a long memo containing everything that occurred and everything I reported to Feghali in writing and verbally."

"Okay, let's go." Saccher, angry now, grabbed my arm and pulled me with him inside. "We're taking this to my boss. I'll ask him to issue a direct order to Stephanie and whoever else in there. I'm going to tell him about this nonsense she's pulling."

Outside the office, Saccher motioned me to wait. "Let me go first. I'll go talk to him; then I'll bring you in, OK?"

I rolled my eyes, but did as I was told. I could hear shouting, a heated exchange; fifteen minutes later, I was face to face with the head of Counterintelligence for the FBI, a man in his early thirties who introduced himself as "John." I had expected someone older, more experienced-looking. He stood up and shook my hand coolly. He didn't ask me to sit.

"Dennis told me what went on there, downstairs. Ms. Edmonds, I have no tolerance for twisted game playing by your administrative supervisors. For years, that department, the translation division, has caused us trouble and headache."

"Sibel is caught in the middle of this shit," Saccher broke in. "Come on, John, it's Feghali and Bryan you should be saying this to—"

His boss didn't let him finish. "It's not only that, Dennis, you know that . . . Ms. Edmonds, the bureau is already under pressure regarding the Turkish operations. The targets, as you are now aware, are connected to people in high places: State Department, Pentagon, White House, Congress ... No one wants any investigation ... The activities have too many beneficiaries in this country—the CIA, weapons companies, military, lobbying firms, Congress, you name it. Now," he continued, "on top of this pressure, we appear to have a 'real spy' problem, the Dickersons. I don't think HQ executives want to know about this; they don't want this to explode. They have made it very clear. Saccher and I tried, but we're being prevented from pursuing this espionage case. They didn't say it in so many words, but I know the lingo. They want this to go away . . ."

I didn't know what to say. I didn't even understand the meaning—the implications—of everything he was telling me.

"This is ridiculous!" Saccher was almost yelling now. "HQ's attitude about this, the bullshit happening downstairs, Bryan asking her to keep translations out of our reach—"

"Drop it, Dennis," John said sharply. "I have a bad feeling on this one, man; my gut feeling says this is going to be bad for all. On top of everything, I don't want you to get dragged in the middle of the war zone in the translation department, you hear me?" He looked straight at me. "Ms. Edmonds, this is going to be a can of worms—a major disaster. I don't want my good men, my agents, my unit caught in the middle of this shit storm."

"Then what do you want me to do?" I meekly mumbled. "I'm being bombarded with instructions; which way do you want me to turn?"

"This is going to be a can of worms," he repeated. "We'll let HQ and the security division handle most of it. I'm willing to bring in Dickerson and put her under a 'blast interrogation.' That's it. OK?"

I nodded, confused. Saccher looked like a bomb about to explode, jaw twitching, his face deep purple red. He shot John an angry look before escorting me out.

"So . . . I guess I'll give the translations to Stephanie, right?"

Saccher shrugged morosely. "We'll see if she keeps her word and sends them to us voluntarily." He added that he hadn't yet given up and that he knew who Dickerson—the spy—was working for. "Our targets are no ordinary criminals," he explained. "These people are involved in nukes, narc, money laundering and espionage ... unfortunately, some of them have their uses for the CIA jackasses . . .You know how they shut down our most important investigation . . ."

I commiserated, allowing that the HQ guys wouldn't let this slip.

"They are not the ultimate decision makers," he assured me. "The pressure to shut this down is coming from others—the hardest from the State Department and Pentagon. I guess I don't have to tell you why, you know what's going on." We had arrived at the elevators.

"Prepare the memo," he told me, "and give Stephanie some of the work. I'll push from this end. By the end of next week we'll be ready to bring Dickerson up here and grill her. . . . We'll have a meeting on this next week."

I returned to the unit deeply frustrated. I was in the middle of a fiasco, a "can of worms," something the bureau didn't even want to acknowledge. My own administrative supervisor was a possible co-conspirator, and I was being asked to prepare a comprehensive memo to be used as evidence.

How had I ended up in this mess?

That weekend was spent at my home computer completing Bryan's memo. I'd asked whether she wanted me to include the 9/11-related cases (she didn't). I was to limit the memo to Dickerson, Feghali, and the blocked intelligence.

More than a month had passed since the Dickersons' visit, and my head was still swirling with too many unanswered questions—almost all of them with frightening implications. Nightmare scenarios had begun to proliferate; there was no end to the awful possibilities.

We now knew, based on Saccher's initial inquiries, that Melek Can Dickerson had indeed worked for some of our operation's primary targets, and that she and her husband associated with them regularly. We also knew that she had deliberately mistranslated and blocked intelligence gathered from these targets for almost two months. We had direct evidence, too, that Dickerson had omitted all information pertaining to her previous employments and her association with foreign entities from her job application with the FBI. Moreover, Bryan and Saccher both suspected Dickerson of having "hooked" Feghali into acting as a co-conspirator, further undermining ongoing FBI investigations and operations.

What remained unanswered, though, was how she had escaped detection during the background investigation for her TS clearance. Not known too was how Major Douglas Dickerson fit into this picture, specifically, how he was able to go undetected by his employers, the Pentagon, considering his level of clearance and his position under Douglas Feith at the Office of Special Plans and the Defense Intelligence Agency. What Saccher meant to determine was how much damage had been inflicted by this penetration, and if the identities of our informants had been compromised. The same sorts of inquiries were being made about the other agencies where Major Dickerson worked. So was Kevin Taskesen right? Were our families and associates in Turkey now in great danger? It would appear more than likely that yes, indeed they were.

All of this left me sickened, and with nothing but mounting questions. Why, for instance, weren't the criminal and terrorism-related aspects of our counterintelligence operation against these specific targets being transferred to the criminal and counterterrorism divisions, as they should be? What was the State Department and Pentagon's role in this, and how could the bureau be so pressured? Why were the (elected or appointed) U.S. persons involved in these criminal networks and operations being so fiercely protected by "people in high places"? I well knew of the involvement and association of certain military-industrial complex moguls, companies and lobbying firms with our target. I knew how much was at stake, particularly for high-level public figures implicated in these investigations. What I didn't appreciate or fully understand was how these same entities could pressure the Pentagon and the U.S. State Department to so directly interfere with the FBI in their behalf.

In time, some of these questions would be answered; some would never be answered concretely; and others would be prevented from being publicly answered—or even addressed—by means of automatic classifications, incessant gag orders, and repeated invocation of executive privileges.

To the unknowing and unaware, the Dickersons' association with powerful organizations such as the American Turkish Council (ATC) and the Assembly of Turkish American Associations (ATAA) may carry little or no significance or cause for alarm. Outwardly, these organizations appear legit; and why not? Their main players happen to be the crème de la crème of the military-industrial center and DC lobbying groups and think tanks. On their boards of directors sit well-known, highly decorated U.S. generals, and their advisors consist of major movers and shakers of beltway politics.

Turkey, one of the closest allies of the United States, is attractive for many reasons: as an artery connecting Europe to Asia, it crosses borders with Iran, Iraq and Syria to the east and south, with the Balkan states to the west and Central Asian nations to the north and northeast. Turkey also is an important member of NATO, a candidate for EU membership, and the only Middle Eastern close ally and partner of Israel—and one of the top U.S. customers for military technology and weapons.

Interestingly too, the same qualities that make Turkey an important ally and strategic partner for the nation states also make it crucial and extremely attractive to global criminal networks. Their activities include the transfer of illegal arms and nuclear technology to rogue states; transporting heroin from Afghanistan through the Central Asian states into Turkey and then through the Balkan states into Western Europe and the United States; and laundering the proceeds of these illegal operations through Turkey's banks and those on neighboring Cyprus and in Dubai. Unfortunately, as well, these same qualities also make Turkey a great operational partner for the unspoken, unsavory actions carried out in Central Asia–Caucasus by the CIA, whose directors and operatives serve the interests of a handful of beneficiaries at the expense of our nation's security and international standing.

Nuclear black market–related activities depend as well on Turkey for manufacturing nuclear components, and on its strategic location as a transit point to move goods and technology to such nations as Iran, Pakistan and others. Turkey's close relationship and partner status with the United States also enables it to obtain—that is, steal—our technology and information. What may not be so well known is that Turkish networks have operatives in several U.S. nuclear labs in addition to others with access on their payroll.

When it comes to criminal and shady global networks, most of us tend to envision either the Mafia, with its own rules and culture of omertà, knife-wielding, semiautomatic-toting Colombian or Mexican drug cartels, or ordinary street-level gangsters with guns. Contrary to these stereotypes, Turkish criminal networks consist mainly of respectable-looking businessmen (some of whom are among the top international CEOs), high-ranking military officers, diplomats, politicians and scholars. Their U.S. counterparts are equally respected and recognized: high-level bureaucrats within the State Department and Pentagon, elected officials, or combination of the two, who now have set up their own companies, NGOs and lobbying groups. When asked, people here in the States generally don't name Turkey as threatening our national security in the fight against terrorism, nuclear proliferation, or international drug trafficking.

Curiously, despite highly publicized reports and acknowledgments of Turkey's role in narcotics, the nuclear black market, terrorism and money laundering, Turkey continues to receive billions in aid and assistance annually from the United States. With its highly placed co-conspirators and connections within the Pentagon, the State Department and NATO, Turkey need never fear sanctions or meaningful scrutiny. The criminal Turkish networks continue their global activities right under the nose of their protector, the United States—and neither the 9/11 catastrophe nor their direct and indirect ties to this attack diminish their participation in the shady worlds of narcotics, money laundering and illegal arms transfers.

The "respectable" Turkish companies have bases in Azerbaijan, Uzbekistan and other former Soviet states. Many of these front compa-nies and nonprofit organizations, disguised as construction and tour-ism entities and Islamic charter schools and mosques, receive millions in grants from the U.S. government to establish and operate criminal networks throughout the region. Among their networking partners are the mujahedeen and the Albanian Mafia. Clearly, having in their pocket high-level congressional representatives on the appropriate commit-tees goes a long way to guarantee the flow of these grants. While the U.S. government painted Islamic charity organizations as the main financial source for Al Qaeda, they were hard at work covering up the terrorists' true financial source: narcotics and illegal arms sales. Why?

Western Europe, followed by the United States, is the principal tar-get of this massive trafficking operation. Yet most of these governments, including that of the United States, prefer to maintain a disturbing and perplexing silence on Turkey's role and dealings in processing and dis-tributing illegal drugs. Why is that the case?

For years on end, information and evidence collected by the coun-terintelligence operations of certain U.S. intelligence and law enforce-ment agencies have been prevented not only from being transferred to criminal and narcotics divisions but also from being shared with the Drug Enforcement Agency and others with prosecutorial power. Those with direct knowledge are prevented from making this information available—and therefore public—under various gag orders and invoca-tion of the State Secrets Privilege. Why?

Might part of the answer be that the existence and survival of many U.S. allies—particularly Turkey, nearly every Central Asian nation, and now Afghanistan—chiefly depend on cultivating, processing, transport-ing and distributing these illegal substances throughout Western Europe and the United States? And might this illegal production and trafficking allow for the procurement of U.S. weapons and technology, our military-industrial complex's bread and butter? Could it be fear of exposure—of our own financial institutions, corrupt officials and lobbying firms—that leads our government's ongoing, ruthless effort to cover up these activities and prevent them from ever being stopped? Or could unceasing gag orders and the relentless invoking of state secrets have more to do with our own unspoken, unofficial black operations and undisclosed agendas set up by unseen, traceless individuals within our shadow government?

As I prepared the comprehensive memo for Bryan, I sensed how I was now being positioned: as the bearer of bad news; the messenger. I knew this shouldn't have been requested of me. The extent of my involvement should have been to give them all the e-mails and written memos I'd sent to Feghali, along with the five completed verbatim translations of Dickerson's evidence. Everything else should have been left to Saccher, his unit, and the security division to handle. Yet here I was, typing away and doing as ordered by my supervisor.

The Dickersons had chosen and approached me; I didn't choose to become their target. As to my signature and initials being forged, not to have reported this to my superiors and notified the recipients could have resulted in serious damage for which I, as the shown signatory, would be liable. With regard to Dickerson's insistence that we divide the targets of our investigations in open defiance of the FBI's own rules—after what had since come to light about the Dickersons and especially after their attempt to recruit me—I could not turn a blind eye and let it go unreported. Having done so, I was then asked to re-review and retranslate Dickerson's previously processed and blocked intelligence. Thus by default I became the first person to process and discover the evidence establishing Dickerson's intentional tampering with and blocking of intelligence.

Somehow I had ended up in the middle of a major espionage scandal within the FBI's Washington field office. Ironic, too, that the agency in charge of investigating all other government agencies' related espionage cases had itself been so easily penetrated. If the FBI could not adequately investigate and protect its own divisions and operations, how could it be capable of protecting and investigating those of others?

I knew that this was one big reason why Saccher's boss was so reluctant to delve any further. FBI management and HQ were not going to take this fiasco lightly, and most likely the messenger—the bearer of ill tidings in the form of evidence and accusations—would take the brunt, in full measure. Moreover, pursuing any case against the Dickersons would inadvertently shine a light on major cover-ups initiated by the State Department and, as a result, expose not only serious criminal activities committed by high-placed U.S. officials but also the subsequent blocking of their investigations.

As the significance and implications of my position and the report I was preparing started to sink in, I felt increasingly uneasy; my intuition was trying to forewarn me. Yet what I could I do? I couldn't turn back the clock, nor could I move forward and pretend that nothing happened. There were no other options. I was already at the point of no return. By default, I was a messenger, like it or not.

III

RETALIATION

6

Memo

The following week, on a bitter cold Thursday, I grabbed a yellow envelope that contained a small disc and two printed copies of the three-page memo and headed out. At work, I stopped by Bryan's office to hand it over. She was on the phone; she nodded, took the package and waved. What a relief. They now had the facts, including incidents of intentional blocking of highly important intelligence and Dickerson's role.

I turned on my computer and got to work. I had a lot to do: in addition to several counterterrorism investigations there was my ongoing Turkish counterintelligence project from Chicago and, of course, my ongoing Turkish Counterintelligence translation tasks involving DC. I put on my headset and began.

My desk phone rang about two hours later. It was Bryan, asking me to come to her office right away.

I turned off my computer, placed my folders inside the drawer and headed to her office. She pointed to a chair. Scattered across her desk was my three-page memo. Next to it was the pile I had turned over to her the previous week, containing selected translations of the top-secret intelligence blocked by Dickerson.

Bryan cleared her throat. "I read the memo. Thorough job, very disturbing; it's worse than I expected. Great job. Thank you."

I got straight to the point. "So, are you taking it to Frields today—right away? Have you sent the copies of the five translated documents to Saccher and his boss? They've been waiting."

She cleared her throat again. "Sibel, you have never worked for the federal government before this job, is that right?"

I was at loss. "No, why?"

"Because things work differently in government. While private companies are concerned with efficiency, security and productivity, the government couldn't care less. Of course, the jobs here come with other pluses: less work, more benefits, retirement . . ." She paused to ensure that I was following this unique revelation. "You need to know a little about some policies that are followed religiously in the FBI. Policy one: one for all, all for one. Policy two: problems and embarrassments are always swept under the rug—*always*. They don't want to know about serious and embarrassing problems, no matter how scandalous. They don't want people reporting these types of issues and cases; especially on the record, in writing."

"And who is this 'they'?"

"You know . . . the management, the headquarters, the director . . ."

I smiled and asked, "Are you included in this 'they' group?"

She returned the smile. "All I want is to run this department and make sure things go smoothly—you know . . . without any scandals. I've been here for a long time; started as a language specialist and worked my way up. . . . I see my younger self in you. You know, I really admire what you're trying to do. You did the right thing: you reported what you should have reported; a serious scandal, this is."

"And . . . what's next?"

Bryan sat up straight, this time without a trace of a smile. "What you reported, what Saccher discovered, this whole thing, especially this memo, are all explosive stuff. I can assure you they don't want to hear about this; they don't want to see anything in writing like this." She pointed to the three-page memo before her. "This will not only affect Dickerson, this will affect everyone: the contract officer at HQ, who may not have done what she should have with Dickerson's application files; the agent who conducted the background check on Dickerson, who may not have done what he had to do to catch this before she penetrated the FBI; the security officers on the eighth floor, who should have seen this coming upon reviewing her file; Feghali . . ."

She took a deep breath. "Especially today, after the horrible Hanssen scandal . . . Needless to say, the involvement of high-profile U.S. persons with the targets of counterintelligence investigations would bring all sorts of political implications—a disaster. This has 'scandal' written all over it."

She finalized this part of her lecture by coming to the point. "Look, you did what you were supposed to do. You reported this to your direct supervisor, to me, and to the agent in charge. You did all you could. No one can ever come and blame you for not doing the right thing. Now, leave this at this point. There is nothing else left for you to follow up on, or pursue."

I could feel every muscle in my body tensing up. I felt sick to my stomach, disgusted to the point of throwing up. I told myself to be calm. "Are you going to send this memo and the package of translated incidents to Frields today?" I repeated. "Saccher and his boss are planning to send this to the counterespionage division. They have Dickerson's application, and the confirmation on her associates and previous employers who happen to be our primary targets. They need the translated incidents before they can move ahead with the next steps."

Bryan responded sternly with a new, sharp edge in her voice. "If you insist, I will; I will send this to Frields. Sibel, I'm trying to warn you here. My advice to you: do not pursue this; do not report this any further than this office. You'll regret notifying higher-ups on this. They will not like it, you'll see. I'm warning you for your own good."

I stood up, leaned over her desk and said, "Stephanie, I really appreciate your considerate warning. The damage has been done: one of the targets is leaving the country after being tipped off by Dickerson; our

state secrets and sensitive intelligence is being sold to the highest bidders; my family's life in Turkey has been directly threatened. There is no
going back on this. Now, please take this to the next step. Saccher and his
boss are waiting for the translated material in order to schedule Dickerson for a surprise interrogation. SAC Thomas Frields is in charge of this
department and needs to be informed. I would appreciate it if you would
set up an appointment for me to meet with Frields to brief him; please
do this as soon as you can."

Bryan pursed her lips and almost in a snarl, said, "Don't tell me I
didn't warn you. You're about to learn a very hard lesson, Sibel. I will
inform Frields today; in fact, this afternoon. I guess this conversation
is over. I did my best to warn you, Sibel; you don't know this agency, but
you're going to learn very quickly."

I stormed out of her office and almost ran to my desk. I sat and tried
to calm myself. Then I picked up the phone and dialed Saccher. I got his
voice mail—again. I had been trying to reach him for the past week and
had left several messages in his voice mail already. I left another, sum-
marizing our status: memo, translation, Bryan, and that the case would
be reported to Frields today. I hung up and tried to do some work, finding it almost impossible to concentrate.

After a long lunch, it was almost three by the time I got back to my
desk. Fifteen minutes later, the phone rang. I picked up, hoping it was
Saccher, but no such luck. It was Bryan. I was to report directly to her
office. Now what?

On the way over I had to pass by Feghali's office. His door was wide
open. I stopped. There were Feghali, Dickerson, and Feghali's daughter—a special agent in the white-collar crime division and an attorney—
seated around the table. On top of it was the yellow manila envelope next
to the stack of translated intelligence intentionally blocked by Dickerson. What the hell was going on? Saccher and his boss were supposed

to set up a surprise interrogation of Dickerson in order to send the case to the counterespionage division. So now the suspect, Dickerson—the person under investigation—is given access to the entire case, the memo and translations?

Feghali saw me and nudged Dickerson. She turned and gave me a lopsided smile. I made tracks to Bryan's office and pointed toward the meeting down the hall. "What the hell is that, Stephanie? What are they doing with my memo and the translated evidence?"

Bryan shrugged. "Oh, that. I took the stuff to Frields per your request. He said that since Feghali and Dickerson are involved and accused, to go ahead and give them the documents and have them review them. They have the right to review any allegations made against them, and respond. He will review the stuff, together with Dickerson's response and also Feghali's, all at one time. So . . . I gave them to Feghali and he's reviewing them with Dickerson. His daughter is here because she's an attorney. She will advise both Dickerson and her dad. I'm sure you understand their need for solid legal advice."

This felt like "The Twilight Zone." "Have you told Saccher? Have you notified him or his boss? This is their area. This is not how the counterespionage investigation is supposed to go. They specifically requested—both from you and me—that this be kept completely away from Dickerson. And what do you mean by his daughter being present as an attorney advising Dickerson and Feghali? This is not a court case, for God's sake!"

Bryan waved her hand dismissively. "Anyway, I asked you to come here for a totally different matter. We have decided that by producing the memo, the one you gave me today, at home, on your home computer, you have violated the security rules of the FBI. The content of your memo involves top secret topics, names and issues. Your conduct needs to be investigated; it may be determined that it is a criminal act. I had to report you and your conduct involving a breach of security to the personnel security investigations office on the eighth floor. The agent investigating you is Melinda Tilton. She wants to interrogate you immediately, today."

She then jotted a few numbers on a yellow Post-It and handed it to me. "Call her immediately—right now. This is a very serious matter and cannot wait. As of this moment you are under investigation, Sibel."

I leaned over her desk. "You've got to be kidding me. Is this real? You specifically instructed me to prepare the memo at home. You said doing it at work would tip off Feghali. You said all this in front of Kevin. You specifically told me what to cover in the memo. Now, suddenly, what I did per your specific instructions is being considered criminal conduct? *I* am the one under investigation? Get real. What kind of silly twisted game are you playing here, Stephanie? Are you running out of your whiskey?" I pointed to where she kept her bottles. I was furious, fuming, shaking with anger.

"Remember that *One for all, all for one* policy I told you about? You just learned how it works. I tried to warn you, but you didn't want to listen. Now, face the consequences, and don't you dare ever blame me. I warned you, damn it."

Back at my desk, I tried Saccher one more time. Voice mail. *Fine*, I decided, *no point in procrastinating. Let the inferno begin*. I dialed Tilton's extension. She picked up on the third ring. When I told her who I was, she asked me to come up to the eighth floor, to her office in the personnel security division, at four o'clock; she would meet me outside the elevators, near reception.

When I got there, the receptionist asked me to wait. A few minutes later, a woman in her early-to-mid thirties with honey blond hair and a few extra pounds came out. "I'm Melinda Tilton, please follow me." We went into her small office, where she pointed to a chair. I sat, and the interrogation began.

She seemed neutral and calm, one of those people who rarely shows emotion; a blank face, expressionless.

First she wanted an account from my perspective, the chronology of events leading to this memo. I started from the beginning: the Dickersons' visit to my home; her list dividing our targets; Saccher's discovery of hundreds of communications that were blocked and mistranslated by her; and his discovery of Dickerson's purged personnel file.

I spoke in detail of what happened after my meeting with Saccher and Kevin: Feghali "investigating" Dickerson; Bryan's request for that memo and her explicit instructions to write it at home on my personal computer; and what had happened that very day—two follow-up conversations with Bryan that could only be described as surreal.

Agent Tilton did not interrupt; she listened carefully and jotted down notes periodically. After I finished, she put down her pen. "I really don't understand," she said. "Why would your division call us up to request an investigation of you? From what I hear and from reviewing the memo you prepared per Ms. Bryan's specific request, I don't see any malice involved and I don't find this to be a case that needs to be investigated. Do you know why they insisted on an investigation of you?"

I first shook my head but then replied, "I can see the administrators, Bryan and Feghali, engaging in this bizarre cover-up attempt due to either incompetence or who knows what else they may be trying to protect. But you said *they*. Are there others outside the Language unit who pressed on this?"

Agent Tilton paused and then answered, "SAC Frields, for one. Also, they notified some people at headquarters and had them call us. I still don't understand."

"What's next? What do you want me to do? Am I still under investigation?"

"Here is what I'm going to do. I'm going to call your unit—Bryan and Feghali—and then I'll also call headquarters and tell them that based on my review of the case and the memo, and based on the interviews I conducted with you and Bryan, I found no malice and no case of a security breach to be investigated." She paused again. "Based on the response I get from them, especially the response from headquarters, we'll either close this investigation or continue. You'll know in a few days, by the end of this week."

I stood up. "Do you have any other questions? Is this over?"

She also stood and replied, "No, that's all for now. Thank you for your cooperation."

I took the elevator back down to the fourth floor. Almost everyone in the unit was gone. Both Bryan and Feghali's doors were half shut and the lights were out. I looked at my watch: almost six. I had spent the entire day dealing with this mess, being accused and threatened, and then interrogated for reporting criminal activities and wrongdoing. I needed to at least do something productive, to get my mind off this situation.

From the corner of my eye I spotted Dickerson, heading in my direction. She came straight up to me and hissed, "You asked for it. What did I tell you about the FBI not giving a damn about it, huh? This is nothing. The worst is yet to come—for your family in Turkey. You can blame yourself for what's to come for them." She then named both my sisters and the neighborhood in Turkey in which the middle one lived.

I was horror stricken, too shocked to respond. She spun around and left. I stood glued to the spot for some time, not moving; then I surveyed my surroundings: there, a translator, four cubicles down. I went over, and she looked up and smiled. "Amerika," I began (that was her real name), "did you happen to hear any of the conversation that took place just now?"

"You mean Dickerson?"

I nodded.

"Not really."

"Did you happen to hear anything?"

She thought a moment. "Something about your family; your sisters. I thought one of their names was very pretty . . ."

This was better than nothing. I thanked her and asked her to remember this, to write it down. She looked puzzled. "Don't worry," I assured her, "just remember, OK? I'll document it." Reluctantly, she nodded again.

Back at my computer, I opened a new file and word document noting the date, time and conversation; I also noted the name of the translator who witnessed the event and what she said she'd heard. I saved it; then I e-mailed both Bryan and Feghali an account of what had occurred with Dickerson. I clicked Send and off it went: I was on record. From that day on, from that moment, I made sure all my communications—everything that occurred at work—were documented and witnessed. This was a battle.

That night, after dinner, I sat down with Matthew and told him everything—omitting only classified details related to names and specific criminal activities. I unloaded nonstop, barely taking time for breath. I'd bottled up so much that now it all came pouring out in a flood. By the time I finished I was exhausted.

Matthew listened intently without interrupting. Although he knew some of the issues, he was stunned by the extent of what had gone on and horrified at the implications. He started to pace. "I think you had better call your sister in Turkey and have her pack her stuff and come here immediately."

"How can she? She has a job, a career! She is engaged to be married next year. What am I going to tell her? Pack and leave everything behind and come over here? What will she do here? How long will she stay? I—"

He cut me off, explaining the stark facts. My sister in Turkey had been named. "At least your other sister is here," he pointed out, "and I'm glad you persuaded your mother not to go back. . . . You know what they can do to you over there; you know there are no laws and no protections over there for either you or your family."

Agreed; but how could I persuade my family? They knew nothing about the situation, nothing about the threats.

"I have a suggestion. Don't make it sound permanent . . . Tell her to take a leave of absence from work for a couple of months—if necessary, without pay. Once she gets here, while she's here, we'll decide what to do. She'll make her decision based on the situation."

"What am I going to tell my mother?"

"For now, I'd say nothing. Let's wait until your sister gets here."

"When should I call?"

"Now. Right now."

I made the call. Even though it was five in the morning there, I wasted no time explaining. I urged her to take a leave of absence, to get here as fast she could. I'd tell her more later, face to face. I mentioned her safety, without going into detail. I knew I didn't make much sense.

My sister responded by telling me about the upcoming busy season in her job, her plans with her fiancé, the wedding, house shopping . . .

"You listen to me," I cut her off. "You know me very well. You've known me your whole life. Have I ever asked something this peculiar from you? Trust me this one time and take my word for it. If I could give you more reasons right now, over the phone, I would. I can't. All I'm asking is for you to trust my judgment and do what I'm asking this one time. Please?"

She sighed. "I'll talk with my boss at work; see how it goes."

I pushed harder. "Talk to them right now. Not tomorrow—today. I'll call you tomorrow. You'll tell me when you're leaving and I'll get your tickets."

My hands were shaking when I hung up the phone.

––––––––––

My next two working days at the FBI were strange. Coworkers openly avoided me. Feghali had spread the word about me being under criminal investigation.

Kevin Taskesen was sent to Guantanamo, Cuba, for an eight-week stint translating interrogation sessions. Kevin—who had failed his proficiency tests for English and even Turkish—was sent to translate for Uzbeks, Turks, Azerbaijanis, Chechens, and all the rest of the other Turkic language-speaking detainees. I remember the day he came to me in tears saying he should not be sent, that he wasn't qualified.

Behrooz Sarshar was sent to "purgatory"—that's what the bureau called it. Those who are subjects of an investigation are placed in low-level positions in a different office during their investigation. This period of purgatory usually, if not always, concludes with that person being fired. Amin and I suspected that in Behrooz's case, he must have decided to notify headquarters about the Iranian informant's warnings prior to 9/11. Now he was paying the price for doing the right thing.

With Behrooz in purgatory, Kevin in Guantanamo, Amin on a TDY (paid travel assignment), and Saccher having disappeared, I had no one left in my corner.

The lull ended the following week, on February 14, Valentine's Day, with a phone call around noon. It was Agent Tilton; she wanted me to go up and see her.

"Sibel," she greeted me cordially. "I did my best to persuade headquarters and Bryan. They still insist on a full-blown investigation of you."

"What's left to investigate? I told you everything. You've seen the memo. I gave you guys the disc. I have nothing more to add."

"Actually you do. They want us to examine your computer—your PC."

"My home computer?" I asked, incredulous.

She nodded. "Of course, you can demand a court-issued subpoena, but I recommend highly against that. We, the security department, know there will be nothing there, but others, as you know, insist."

"That computer is not mine alone, my husband and I share it. He has his and his clients' data on it. After I typed the memo, I put it on a disc and erased the file from the PC, just as Bryan instructed. I gave you guys the disc and the only printed copy."

"I know," she said. "It will take us only a few hours to check the PC and confirm that there is nothing there, then report to headquarters. Let's get this over with ASAP. You don't want this ridiculous investigation hovering over your head. Forcing us to get a subpoena will only aggravate everyone more, and will drag this out longer for you."

I had to think. "When?"

"Today. In a couple of hours."

"I have to call my husband and get his consent," I told her, resigned. "Do I have your word on this entire 'investigation' masquerade being over once you check my computer and find that it's clean?"

"You have my word," she responded quickly.

Once out on the street I pulled out my cell and called Matthew. When I told him about Tilton, he was livid.

"What do you mean by 'making sure it's clean'? What do they think you have in there, secret codes?"

I explained that the longer this dragged out, the more I'd be harassed by Bryan, Feghali and Frields.

"Then tell them to go and get a subpoena. This is a huge privacy issue. All our life is in that computer: our contacts, finances, my client list and their information. I want to see how they are going to come up with a subpoena . . ."

I told him the FBI can get whatever they want from federal judges. I had nothing classified in our computer. "Let's get this over with."

He could hear desperation verging on panic in my voice. "Okay, let them come," he said calmly, "but I'm going to have them sign a sheet agreeing to record the chain of custody of the computer while they have it in their possession. I'll also have them sign an agreement promising to back up everything before they pull out or touch anything in the computer. Understood?"

"Yes, do what you think is right. Let me call Tilton. I'll call you in two minutes."

I called Tilton and gave her the OK. She said they'd be at my house in an hour or so. I called Matthew back and told him they were on their way.

Before he was angry and scared; now he was really pissed off. "The FBI has nothing better to do than send their agents to chase, harass, and investigate law-abiding citizens? These guys are supposed to be out there chasing criminals and terrorists!"

I could almost smile; here was Matthew, ever calm and even-tempered, always the optimist, aflame with this gross injustice. Bravo!

Then they came and took our computer.

It was already dark, and I was one of the few translators who had stayed to work late. I had my headset on, typing, rewinding, and typing again. While focused on the screen, I sensed someone beside me. I turned and there was Saccher, looking at me. I glanced at my watch: it was past six. Saccher usually left no later than three. I hadn't seen him since my home computer was confiscated, and had received no response to the voice mails I'd left. I knew he was under severe pressure from his boss—but I could also tell how angry and frustrated he was.

I removed the headset and put the tape on Pause. "And where have you been? I've left dozens of messages for you! Do you know what I've been going through the past two weeks?"

"Long story; they don't want us to communicate."

"They? Who is *they*?"

"My boss, Frields; you know . . . I stopped by to . . . Sibel, this is bigger than what you think it is . . ."

I threw up my hands. "Bigger than a scandal involving espionage, blocked translations, tipping off FBI targets? Bigger than U.S. officials passing state secrets to criminal thugs? Look, we've got the blocked translations and documented them; we know who she's working for . . . I sent a letter to headquarters—"

Saccher interrupted me. "You don't get it, do you? This goes beyond the Dickersons and the targets. There is no way the bureau will let it go further. Do you realize what they're going to have on their hands if they pursue this? Combine Watergate with Iran-Contra: elected politicians, State guys, Pentagon, MIC, espionage, money laundering, terrorists—"

Now I cut him off. "So? Everything is documented, we have them on tapes . . . once we take it further up, it will be pursued. It's one thing to deal with Frields . . . it's another story when it gets to the guys on top."

By that time we already knew about the previous administration's plan to bring a special prosecutor to look into that part of the scandal involving State Department officials, lobbyists, and some representatives.

He narrowed his eyes. "I was referring to the guys on top," he said in a near whisper. "They want this to go away. No one up there is going to pursue this. Instead, get ready—they'll come after you. Haven't you already realized that much?"

I shrugged and took in a breath. "Fine, then we'll take it to Congress, the Intel Committee, Judiciary—"

He forced a frustrated laugh. "And who are you going to go to in Congress? Let's see, you and I know of a dozen or so dirty ones in Congress—filthy ones involved in this damn thing. How many more are there; those we don't know about? Who in Congress are you going to trust, Sibel?"

Saccher pointed at the area behind me, covered by hundreds of cubicles. "Do you ever wonder how many elected officials are involved in the dirty stuff these people are covering? Chinese, Russians, Saudis, Israelis, Pakistanis . . . I'm asking you again: How will you determine who's clean to go to in Congress? The filth touches both parties, so we don't even have partisanship on our side, my friend. You heard my boss: *This is a can of worms.* Those were his exact words; considering the realities, an understatement. Remember?"

Then it hit me. Saccher now was telling me to let it go. They had gotten to him. "What are you telling me, Dennis? That's it? You're no longer pursuing this? What is it you're asking me to do?"

He pulled a swivel chair from a nearby cubicle and sat to face me. "That's why I came here tonight. I like you, Sibel," he continued, "a lot. You're one of the best language specialists this department has ever had. You're bright, overly qualified, and I hate to see them destroy your life. This place is disgusting. I became an agent believing in it; I was wrong. Know what I'm planning to do? As soon as I get my GS-13 status, I'm out of here, on my way to work for Boeing in California. . . . Now, as a friend, as someone who likes you, respects you, and as someone who knows far more about the shit that goes on here, I have one piece of advice for you: go home tonight, write a one-page resignation letter, submit it tomorrow, and then leave. Run for your life and don't ever look back."

I blinked a few times and said simply, "I'm not going to do that. I just can't. It's already too late." I vowed I would take this as far as I could, adding, "How can you give up?"

His shoulders drooped; the dark circles and heavy rings under his eyes—his whole resigned expression—made him look years older. He stood up slowly. "I have two babies and a wife to take care of, Sibel. I also have more experience with this shit hole than you. I know what they can do to people like you—messengers. They will come after you. They will destroy your marriage, your finances, your future career . . . and there is nowhere to go, nowhere to run to. No one will ever come to rescue you, Sibel, neither the Congress nor the courts. They will make your life miserable. They have already started doing just that. What we know will never see the light of day."

"Dennis, are you telling me that you won't back me up when it gets into the right hands?"

"There's no such a thing, *right people, right hands*. I said what I was going to say. Resign and leave, now. Don't ever say I didn't warn you." Then he walked away.

I watched him until he exited through the double glass doors. That was the last time I saw or spoke to Dennis Saccher. From that point on, the bureau assigned him somewhere else, outside the Washington field office. My operations boss simply disappeared.

Later that evening, when my anger had subsided somewhat, I reflected on our conversation, going over it again and again. What would I have done, if I were he? The bureau operates on the military command model; his boss had ordered him not to pursue this. To continue would mean risking a fifteen-year career and his family's livelihood. Saccher had two young children; his family depended solely on him. I also knew that if Saccher were ever questioned, subpoenaed or placed under oath, he'd tell the truth—he'd tell it all.

I had to get to those who were in a position to bring this corruption into the light. Once this case and the facts were in proper hands, my role would be over. All I needed to do was to find a few good people in our government.

How hard could that be?

More than a week had passed since the infamous memo, yet I had not been given an appointment with the head of our unit, Special Agent in Charge Thomas Frields. There had been no response to my request for a meeting. I did not, however, plan to wait around forever; neither would I bombard Bryan with e-mails for that promised meeting with Frields. Instead, I decided to go to the next level: to report the case to HQ and ask for an investigation.

After some fishing and poking around, I found that the most helpful person to contact would be the executive assistant director for Counter-terrorism and Counterintelligence, Dale Watson.

At home I wrote a brief, one-page letter to Watson and sent it to his office at FBI Headquarters via certified mail. My letter emphasized the urgency of the situation, its impact on the integrity of the translated intelligence and consequences to national security.

About a week after I sent the letter, Bryan called to let me know that Frields wanted to meet with me. The meeting was scheduled for two o'clock at his office. I told her I'd be there. When I entered at two precisely, Bryan was already seated.

SAC Thomas Frields was in his early-to-mid sixties, of average height, with a slight body, heavily wrinkled face, and a set of sharp blue eyes. He spoke with a thick Southern drawl. I had not met him before but had heard him described as a bigot and a sexist who patronized women every chance he got. There were rumors of an ugly past, and of his disdain for and hatred of female agents. How much of this was true I wasn't sure.

Frields shook my hand and guided me to the sofa. I had my pen and notepad with me. He took the chair next to Bryan, so that both sat facing me.

"Ms. Edmonds," Frields began, "I've heard a lot of good stuff about you. I understand you have accumulated quite a file of commendation letters in such a short period of time; agents keep requesting you as their case translator. That's very impressive. I also find your background very impressive. You've lived in Iran, in Turkey; attended school in both countries. I understand you'll graduate this year; criminal justice?"

I was surprised. I didn't see this coming. What was the game? "Yes, criminal justice, and I'm also majoring in psychology."

He nodded. "What are your plans? I understand you've applied for National Security Studies, graduate school. Have you considered becoming an agent? You're a perfect candidate: language skills, international experience, relevant degrees, and obviously meticulous in what you do."

This was getting really strange. "I haven't thought about it."

"Well, I certainly hope that you will at least consider it."

I couldn't prolong this further. We were wasting time with phony niceties. "Agent Frields," I started in, "I understand you were given the memo I wrote two weeks ago and the set of initial audit translations of Ms. Dickerson's work. I'm sure you were also told by SA Saccher about Dickerson's previous employment and associations, all of which were omitted from her application and somehow strangely and unexplainably missed by the background investigator."

Frields raised both hands to stop me. I stopped. "Ms. Edmonds, I got everything. I reviewed everything. In fact, I investigated everything you and SA Saccher had reported. That's why it took a while to grant this meeting. But we are done looking into this stuff. First of all, I want to tell you, thank you for doing the right thing, for bringing this to our attention. You did the right thing. Second, I'm here today, meeting with you, to assure you that everything has been taken care of, everything has been looked at, and that you've got nothing to worry about. You have my word."

I paused and tried to digest what he'd said. I had to think before I replied. Some of it didn't make sense. "As far as I know . . . we haven't even *begun* to go over and audit the blocked translations and those intentionally mistranslated. My family and I have been threatened directly by Ms. Dickerson—twice. We have an unresolved case of my signature being forged on sensitive counterterrorism-related documents by Ms. Dickerson; the case coincidentally involves certain Turkish detainees in New Jersey who happen to be connected to our targets of investigations who, in return, happened to buy their way into the State Department in order to get them released, off the hook—"

Frields cut me off, no longer smiling. "Ms. Edmonds, those things are not for you to worry about. You did your job; you notified us. We did ours, and determined that there is nothing to worry about. Now we all have to move on."

"Agent Frields," I responded quickly, "it *is* my business. When I took this job, I was informed by the briefing security officer that everyone who worked in this unit had to pass thorough background checks. I was assured that neither I nor my family in Turkey would ever be compromised over there, in Turkey, as a result of what I happened to be doing here as my job. If you read those files, you should be very well aware of the fact that the targets of our counterintelligence operations happen to be close associates and former coworkers of Ms. Dickerson. As you know, we are talking about dangerous Mafia-like criminals here who happen to have a free hand in Turkey, with complete immunity. Are you telling me that you are assuring my immediate family's safety in Turkey?"

Frields leaned over and said, "I'm not promising such a thing. I can assure your safety and theirs as long as you are in the United States. That's all. I want to repeat myself one more time: we have decided not to investigate this case because we have found *no need to do so*."

I too leaned over, but for a different reason: I started to write down what Frields had just said. This mightily ticked him off. He instantly changed from Jekyll to Hyde.

"And just what the hell are you doing?"

"I'm taking notes of your assurance on the Dickersons; and I'm taking notes of your statement of deciding not to investigate this case, that's all."

His face turned fiery red and he sharply raised his voice. "I have a question for you. Besides SA Saccher, Ms. Bryan, Agent Tilton and myself, have you taken this issue to anyone else?"

"You mean within the FBI?"

"I mean anywhere."

"I have not taken this issue, reported it, outside the FBI."

"That was not my question. I already named the individuals; I asked you anyone, *anyone*, besides the individuals I named?"

"I understand. I have not reported this issue outside the FBI."

Now he was yelling. "You stop playing games with me, miss! Who else have you told within the bureau? Have you notified anyone at headquarters?"

I answered him calmly. "After waiting for a meeting with you for almost ten days, I did notify an appropriate person at HQ."

Frields stood up and started pacing. He stopped and turned to me. "I want names. Who did you report it to at HQ?"

"I notified an appropriate person, at the executive level."

He pounded his fist into his hand. "I said I wanted *names*. Disclosing this to an unauthorized person will land you in jail. Do you want to be on your way to jail?"

"Are you telling me that the director and assistant directors are not authorized, or not cleared, to know what goes on inside this unit?"

He now towered over me, looking down with an anger I can't even begin to describe. "This is the last time I'm asking you. If you refuse to answer I'll have a security officer put you under arrest for unauthorized disclosure of the highest level state secrets. Do you understand? Now, who did you notify?"

I was dumbfounded. Why would he go into such a panic? If what he said were true—that there was absolutely nothing to investigate or look into—then why would he be so worried about me contacting a senior executive at headquarters? He was threatening me with arrest for writing a letter to the assistant director of Counterintelligence?

"I sent a letter to Dale Watson," I replied, looking Frields in the eye. "I requested a meeting to brief his office on what's been occurring and obviously being covered up here. Now I want to see how you can legally threaten me with investigation and jail time for sending a letter to an assistant director of the Federal Bureau of Investigation."

"When was that letter sent?"

"Three or four days ago."

Frields sprinted toward his desk, grabbed his briefcase and started toward the door. Then he stopped and turned around. "I'm on my way to HQ now," he said to Bryan. "This cannot wait. I'll intercept that letter or make sure it will be intercepted if it hasn't gotten there. I won't have that letter going to Mueller or Watson."

I had forgotten Bryan was there; she hadn't opened her mouth. She stood up and I did the same. As Frields chased into an elevator, Bryan and I went back to the Language unit—separately.

On my way in, I bumped into Amin. He looked at me with concern. "Are you feeling all right? You look so white!" I realized my hands were ice.

"I was in an hour-long meeting with Frields and Bryan. I expect the worst to come."

Amin suggested we go and grab some hot tea. I agreed and we headed to the cafeteria in the basement. The exhaustion hit me as soon as I sat, and the windowless room closed in on me.

"Do you want to talk about it?"

"Have you heard about my situation? Dickerson? Feghali?" I asked him.

Amin mentioned gossip, and that Feghali had been bad-mouthing me. "According to him you are under investigation for a serious security breach and possible espionage; the bureau is about to fire you, and your agent, Saccher, doesn't want to work with you. We all know it's a bunch of boloney."

"*I'm* the one who reported possible espionage! Actually, Saccher is the one who discovered Dickerson's intentional blocking of CI, which in turn led to him checking her employment file and realizing that she worked—and still associates with—our primary two targets." I gave him the thumbnail version of the case.

Amin looked desperately concerned. "You can still back off from the whole thing. Are you sure you want to continue to press on? It seems Saccher is in hiding, shitting in his pants."

I disagreed, explaining about Frields' strenuous objections and Saccher's family situation—but more importantly, that I could not, as a matter of conscience, simply turn around and leave at this point. "We'll see what happens when it gets to HQ," I told him.

"Who did you send it to there?"

"Dale Watson."

Amin dealt with some very high-profile cases and knew just about everyone. "Don't know much about that one; only that he is a pretty boy, risk-averse bureaucrat. I heard he is under tremendous pressure over nine eleven. So it will be tossing the dice for you."

I told him of Frields' plan to intercept and that I would call Watson's office the next day to make sure that he got the letter.

"If I were you, I wouldn't get my hopes up for any action by HQ," Amin continued. "Frields has a lot of friends up there. You think what you see in here is bad! . . . the FBI assigns its worst, most incompetent people to HQ ..."

"Well, that's as high as I can go internally. Where else can I go?" I shook my head in disgust. "What's happening with Behrooz? Did he go to HQ?"

Amin nodded; he looked sad.

"Who in HQ? Amin, I can corroborate his report, at least some of it."

"It went directly to Mueller. They've made his life miserable. I can't tell you everything I know, but I think they will do everything in their power to keep this from coming out." He looked at his watch. "It's time to head up, my friend. Next we'll be accused of conspiring on the job!" He gave a forced laugh. I knew it wasn't meant to be funny. I understood his fear of retaliation from being seen with me. I understood too well.

The following morning I called Dale Watson's office and left a message. His secretary called back and left a voice mail saying the letter had been received a few days earlier. He had gotten it.

I called his office once again for an appointment. The secretary was evasive; she wouldn't give a straight answer. This went on for several days until I received another voice mail from HQ—but not from Watson's office. The woman identified herself as an assistant to Deputy Assistant Director Tim Caruso at FBI HQ. I was asked to call her back to set up an appointment with Mr. Caruso. My letter had gone to Dale Watson, who oversaw the Language unit. Who was this Tim Caruso?

I called her back. She was crisp. "It was decided to transfer your letter to Mr. Caruso and have him handle the meeting you requested."

"Why?" I asked. She didn't know. She scheduled me for March 7 at noon.

The next day at work I stopped by Amin's desk. "Who is Tim Caruso?"

He let out a long low whistle. "Don't tell me *he's* the one who is going to meet with you!"

I was annoyed. "As a matter of fact he is. I got a call from his office. My letter to Dale Watson was transferred to his office and I'm scheduled to meet with him on March seven."

"Now you can say with one hundred percent certainty that your letter was successfully intercepted by Agent Frields!" He laughed unpleasantly.

"What do you mean?"

"Tom Frields and Tim Caruso used to be partners. They both worked for the FBI Washington Field Office Counterterrorism unit dealing with Iran. They're *buddies*. Caruso is Frields' guardian angel at HQ. . . . Caruso has gotten Frields' ass out of trouble more than once . . ."

I tried to digest this new information. Now what was I going to do? After some thought, I decided to go ahead with the meeting. If it ended up disastrous, like my meeting with Frields, I'd insist on seeing Watson, or if necessary, Director Mueller himself.

"I've been thinking," Amin said. ". . . You may want to report the case to OPR."

"What's OPR?"

"FBI's Office of Professional Responsibility; it was established to re-ceive reports of wrongdoing, criminal conduct, harassment, et cetera. Basically it's supposed to be the first stop, the first place to go, for FBI whistleblowers. The next place is DOJ-IG, Department of Justice Office of Inspector General. Of course, they are not independent; how could they be? They get their paychecks from where all of us get ours. Also, they report back to the director and the deputies—the gang itself! I heard this guy, the new OPR director, John Roberts, is supposed to be a decent guy. It seems true, since I also hear that Mueller and the rest of the SES don't like him."

Here, now, was another entity, another person, another possible channel—an internal one. Just in case my meeting with Frields' buddy didn't work out.

I had only a few days to prepare for Caruso. So far I'd heard nothing from the bureau about my computer. Neither was I told anything about the so-called investigation of me instigated by my own unit and unknown individuals at HQ.

When I came to work, I felt like someone with bubonic plague. I was radioactive. Nobody wanted to get on the wrong side of Feghali or Bryan. Behrooz was gone, and I sorely felt his absence, his usual fatherly warmth toward me. Surprisingly, too, I missed Kevin's pathetic neediness. Even Amin, my only genuine friendly coworker, was noticeably cautious.

Another major problem around this time was management tampering with my work projects. Whenever I booted my computer and clicked on a pending task, *access denied* would pop up on my screen. I notified Bryan and Feghali in several formal e-mails but never received a response in writing. Sometimes it took days before problems were corrected; sometimes they weren't corrected at all.

These "denied" tasks included extremely important investigative files: cases involving counterterrorism investigations across the country. Some of them, marked *urgent*, were on short deadlines. The management in the Language unit was not only messing with me, they were messing with agents all over the country who depended on prompt translations; they were messing with detainees whose fate rested on my translation of their files and interrogations. What goes on in the Language unit impacts our national security; these games—at taxpayers' no small expense while I sat there twiddling my thumbs—were unconscionable.

Documents and files also went missing from my "locked" drawer. Again, each incident would be thoroughly reported, in writing, with a full description of the files and contents. I knew Feghali and Bryan possessed master keys to all drawers, yet how could I reasonably accuse supervisors of removing and stealing FBI files? Maybe there was a darker motive. Perhaps they wanted me to report missing top secret files to accuse me of mishandling or even stealing them. Maybe they were setting a trap, which could be used a number of ways against me depending on how I reacted. Perhaps, by tampering with my code, they could more easily establish a poor work record for me? Whatever the reasons, their retaliatory actions created real victims and caused much suffering for others who were not me. Where was the oversight?

That same week, on February 28, I drove to Dulles airport to pick up my sister. Now my entire immediate family that included both my sisters and my mother was in the States, living with me. They were here because I believed this place, the United States, was the safest place for them to be under the circumstances. How long would this situation last? Would they ever feel safe enough to return to their lives back home? Would I ever feel safe enough to go back to visit them and the rest of the family I had there? I had no answers to these questions, questions that didn't leave me day or night.

7

Targeting the Messenger

One evening, a few days after agents had arrived at my house to take away my computer, I was about to leave work when Bryan stopped me. She asked me to follow her into a small printer room to talk. I found that peculiar; her office was only a few feet away. I followed her in.

"Listen," she told me, "the bureau has scheduled you to take a polygraph on Friday, March eighth, at ten in the morning." She handed me a piece of torn paper. "Here is the location of your polygraph session."

I read the address: a building in the middle of Chinatown. That was peculiar too. Headquarters and the Washington field office were within four or five blocks of each other, and both had polygraph units.

Calmly, I asked, "Why am I being forced to take a poly? The bureau gave me a poly before I started working here. I passed it."

"Oh no," she responded. "We're not forcing you to submit to this polygraph. We can't do that. We're giving you three options: one, you can refuse to take it. You have the right to refuse, but then we'll fire you for refusing. Two, you can take it, and if you fail the test, we'll fire you based on that. And finally, you can take it, and if you pass it . . . hmm . . . well, we'll see about that."

I was impressed. No, they weren't forcing me; rather, they were presenting me with this Kafkaesque menu of options so that I was doomed no matter what. "Okay, here's the deal," I said. "You give me this request in writing. In your letter, your request for this poly, you will provide me with the reasons I'm being asked to submit to this polygraph. OK?"

"Oh no," she quickly replied, shaking her head. "We never do anything like that. These types of requests are never given in writing. All you have to do is say no. Of course, we'll be forced to fire you, but you still have the right to refuse to take this polygraph."

The level of retaliation was being kicked up a notch. I offered her the fakest smile I could muster and in a calm voice replied, "Okay Stephanie, here is what we are going to do. I'm going to put this request and notes of this conversation in writing. Then, I'm going to send you and the rest of the FBI-WFO management a formal letter stating that I'm being asked to take a polygraph, and that once you guys provide me with reasons for this request—in writing, of course—I'll be willing to take it. You'll get my letter in two or three days."

Bryan curled her lips then shrieked, "You will never get any response from us in writing! Go ahead and send your letter to anyone you wish—but don't expect anything in writing . . . I told you to expect this, didn't I? It was your decision, now face the consequences." She spun on her heels and marched out.

That night I barely touched my dinner, a fact that did not go unnoticed by Matthew. He had a right to know. After all, he'd been dragged into this. I asked him to follow me to a place where we could have some privacy. I closed the door and told him about the polygraph request.

"You realize this is pure retaliation, right? It looks like they've decided to shoot the messenger. Do you still want to press on?"

I thought for a moment. "What? What am I going to do? Turn around and run as if nothing happened? Do you think that's what I should do?"

He shook his head. "It's your decision, Sibel. I want to make sure you understand that this is retaliation, and that from this point on, things will get worse, that's all."

I started to think about how much worse things could get.

"I think your idea to write them a letter, to go on record and ask for reasons . . . excellent thinking. Let's do that. You should sit and write this thing tonight. After all, you have less than three weeks until this scheduled polygraph. Meanwhile," he continued, "I'll do some research on employment laws and laws associated with whistleblowers—"

"Whistleblowers?" I interrupted. "I'm not a whistleblower. I'm not blowing any whistle. I reported these issues internally. Saccher already decided that this is an espionage case and reported it himself. I brought this to FBI management's attention. That's not whistleblowing."

"Nonetheless . . . I'll see what I can dig up."

The final letter—citing whistleblower laws to remind them that their actions could only be interpreted as retaliation for my having reported agency-related wrongdoing—was sent two days later. I went on record stating that I would only be willing to take the polygraph *after* I was provided with reasons in writing. Copies went to Bryan, Frields, Stuckenbroker (in personnel security) and Tilton via certified mail and fax.

I waited for several days, but received no response from FBI management. Did I need an attorney? Could now be the time to take this to Congress and DOJ-IG? I hadn't planned on it, although I had already begun to research whistleblowers and disclosure laws.

My frustration grew as the date for the scheduled polygraph drew closer. One morning, I decided to have a chat with my neighbor, who worked for Senator Daschle at the time. Although we had been neighbors for almost two years, we hadn't had much contact and she didn't know that I worked for the FBI as a language specialist. When I knocked, it was very early. Surprised to see me and still in her robes, she nevertheless graciously asked me in.

I didn't want to take up her time and came straight to the point, outlining my predicament. She listened attentively, and when I finished, appeared to be thinking. "Have you taken it to upper management?" she asked. I told her I'd begun to do just that when things turned quickly against me: a retaliation full force, mounting in intensity.

She sounded concerned. "The appropriate committees in the Senate are the Judiciary and the Intelligence Committees. I'll talk with a few people in the next few days and let you know what I come up with. I'll try to find the best person for you to talk to on the Judiciary Committee."

I thanked her several times, and as I was leaving, she brought up my family. It must have appeared strange, seeing them all move in with us at once. I told her they were safe, as long as they stayed here in United States. I said good-bye and left.

About two days later, she called in the evening and gave me the name of the legal counsel for Senator Leahy, Beryl Howell, who would be available to talk with me whenever I was ready. She also said that Leahy had a good reputation as ranking minority member of the Senate Judiciary Committee. I thanked her again. Here, at least, was one potential contact outside the bureau. Already I began to feel better.

We decided to contact attorneys experienced in the area of federal government employment laws. We'd been given two referrals and made appointments with each in one day, and Matthew accompanied me to both meetings.

The first didn't last more than fifteen minutes. As soon as he heard the summary, the middle-aged, distinguished-looking attorney stood up. "I'm sorry," he said. "We cannot help you with this case. We don't want to get involved with the FBI. . . . They have a way of making people's lives miserable, and this includes their attorneys. These agencies—CIA, FBI, et cetera—can be very scary; especially now, after nine eleven."

I was dumbfounded. Was he saying that the FBI is above the law? What did he mean by "scary"? This sounded eerily like what I grew up with in Third World countries, where the police and intelligence agencies rule with one hundred percent impunity; where the people have no due process and the government or monarchy have unchecked powers. This "reputable" and experienced attorney, who happens to be an American, is telling me that it is hopeless to pursue justice when it comes to our law enforcement and intelligence agencies? This goes against everything I believed to be true about this country, everything I thought I'd learned in the fourteen years I'd lived here.

The second attorney's office was more modest. This one was a bit younger and didn't seem as flashy. He had the mien of someone who dealt with labor unions and underdogs. He was sympathetic and gave me his full attention while I talked about my situation and the upcoming polygraph session. Based partly on what happened with the other lawyer, I emphasized I was *not* planning to bring a claim against the government, that I was there solely to get advice on this recent order (to submit to a polygraph test, etc.) and what my rights were under the circumstances.

"May I ask you why you haven't resigned under these excruciating circumstances?" His voice was gentle.

"My reports are all documented," I told him. "I did what any conscientious bureau employee should do. I did what I was supposed to do. I'm not the one engaged in any wrongdoing. . . . Now, with all the harassments and threats I've been dealing with in the past two months, why the hell would *I* resign?"

He smiled a little sadly. "Because this is not a fair and rational world you are dealing with. Because those who choose to fight government wrongdoings, especially those in the law enforcement and intelligence-related agencies, swim against the current. Because no matter how right you are or how wrong they are, no matter how the nation may suffer the consequences of these issues, they—the bureau—will wear you down if you choose to fight them. They have all the power and all the money. You have no power and no money to stand up to these giants, no matter how right you are."

"Are you saying I should just turn around and walk away?"

"I'm giving you my expert advice. . . . The decision is yours. I know what the agency is capable of doing to you, to your loved ones; to your life. . . . The best thing you can do, the wisest decision you can make, is to send them your resignation letter and continue with your life."

"That sounds familiar, but I'm not at that point yet. I haven't taken this up far enough. As far as the polygraph goes, what rights do I have?"

He paused to consider. "They cannot force you to take it, but they can fire you if you don't take it—which is, in a way, forcing you to take it. Also, the bureau has a bad reputation as far as their polygraph ethics are concerned . . . don't risk a pseudo investigation by taking a tampered polygraph. If you pass, they will never mention it. If you fail, they'll use it to investigate you, fire you."

"I think I'll take my chances. I have zero to hide."

"Ms. Edmonds, the bureau seems to have skeletons to hide. The further you push with your attempts to expose these skeletons, the harder they will fight against you and your reports. . . . I know you'll find it a hard pill to swallow—to run away from a fight against what you believe to be serious issues with national security implications. However, for your own good, for your husband's and family's good, the best option is to resign and put this behind you; to go on with your life."

Our one-hour appointment had come to an end. I looked at Matthew and tried to read what he was thinking. I knew the decision was all mine.

"I know this is not what you wanted to hear," he said, shaking my hand.

"I understand and appreciate your candor," I said. "I'm doing only what I know I'm supposed to be doing; doing the right thing. I may lose in the short run, but as my father always said, in the long run the truth will prevail. I have one last question: Can I call you with questions if anything happens before or during the polygraph?"

"Of course." He jotted down his number on the back of his business card. Then he wished us luck.

My meeting with Deputy Executive Administrative Director (DEAD) Tim Caruso was for noon on Thursday, March 7, in his office at FBI Headquarters. When I arrived fifteen minutes early, I looked for something—anything—to help me pass the anxious waiting time. There wasn't a single thing to read, so I tried a meditative breathing exercise for the thousandth time and failed, again.

DEAD Caruso entered the waiting area a few minutes before the hour. Tall, erect, slim, and with a pair of razor-sharp blue eyes so bright it hurt to look into them. His suit was impeccable: not a single crease. When he moved in to shake my hand, his spicy aftershave tingled in my nose. I followed him into his office.

He hadn't a notepad, paper or pen. I looked around: nothing on the coffee table either. "Ms. Edmonds," he stated curtly, "thank you for coming to see me. We received your letter. You asked to meet with us to report serious issues. This is the meeting you requested. Please begin."

I was startled but gathered myself quickly and started right in, from the beginning: order to slow down translations to increase the backlog; intentional blocking of some counterterrorism investigations of 9/11; blueprints case; Saccher's discovery; Dickerson; the memo . . . Caruso listened with a blank face. He took no notes. This was even more disturbing than the attacks I had come to expect. I was unnerved. I paused. "Are you going to take any notes?"

He shook his head and waved me off. "Please go on."

Without knowing what else to do, I continued.

Forty-five minutes later, Caruso still hadn't moved so much as a finger or toe, not even an eyelash. I don't think he blinked once.

He asked, "Are you done?"

"Yes . . . do you have any questions?"

"No, none at all."

"Are you planning to look into these issues? Investigate this?"

"No."

"I don't understand," I said, exasperated. "You took no notes. You asked no questions. You're saying you won't look into this. What's this about?"

He responded slowly and precisely, articulating every word. "Ms.

Edmonds, your letter asked for a meeting. We provided you with one. In your letter you asked to brief us. I just did that: let you brief us. In your letter you did not ask us to take any notes or ask questions. Also in your letter you did not ask us to take any action on your briefing. We did exactly what you asked for; nothing more, nothing less. This meeting is over."

He stood and politely walked me out. I was shocked. This was worse than I expected—it was passively vicious. I turned to leave when he called my name. I turned back. "You are a very brave lady," he said, "very brave indeed to pursue this. Have a good day and good luck; you will need plenty of that." Then he went back into his office.

I was dumbstruck. What was that supposed to mean? Was it a coded message? What the hell did he mean?

In time, I would find out.

When I phoned Matthew and he asked how it went, I mumbled something about Kafka. Though I wasn't in the least bit hungry, he thought a nice lunch at the Capitol Grill might cheer me up. He dropped me off in front of the restaurant and went to look for a parking spot. I went in to find a table.

It was past one and the lunch crowd was thinning. The bar area was almost empty. I chose a table tucked in the corner for privacy and waited for Matthew. A few minutes later he joined me, and while the two of us were looking over the menu, a heavyset man in his fifties walked in and surveyed the bar. He wore light gray slacks, a navy blazer and a blue-striped white shirt. By now most of the tables were cleared and set up. He asked the waiter over and requested that the table next to ours be cleared. He stood in the corner and waited while the table was bused, then he took a chair, positioned it to face us and sat. This was certainly odd, but we continued our conversation.

Within a few minutes, another man, who looked familiar, joined the older one. He too was clad in a blue blazer and gray slacks. He pulled up a chair as the other had done, took out his cell phone, flipped the cover open and placed it on the table.

The two men sat and stared. I well knew that FBI cell phones were often used as transmitters; voice recorders. Matthew was getting annoyed. He turned his chair and glared at them. They didn't care; the older one even smiled, half crookedly.

I gave his arm a nudge. "Just ignore them. This is not surveillance. This is just an intimidation tactic by the bureau—they want us to know they are 'watching' us. Let them watch and listen . . . Hey, stop looking at them!"

Matthew turned back. By now our food had arrived. The men ordered coffee only. The situation kept up until we left, whereupon we were followed.

So this was the bureau's new tactic: 24/7 surveillance! What would be next?

I dialed the FBI Office of Professional Responsibility (OPR) as soon as I got home and asked for John Roberts, the agent in charge recommended by Amin. After I gave him a summary of my case, he said he'd have one of his investigators call to set up an interview. I told him about the polygraph session scheduled the following day.

He laughed sadly. "Welcome to the club. That's one of the first things they do to any whistleblower in this agency. It's part of their game. They'll try everything to trip you up. Don't give them the opportunity."

"You mean I shouldn't take it?"

"No, go ahead and take it if you want, but don't let them get under your skin—either before or during the polygraph session. They'll try their best."

He asked me to fax a summary and chronology of my report (unclassified, of course) and the name of the investigator who was to set up an interview time; then he hung up.

That night, unable to fall asleep, I went over all that had come to pass since Saccher's discovery of Dickerson. For the past eight weeks my life had been a roller-coaster ride of threats, retaliation and intimidation by the best known, most powerful law enforcement agency in the world.

If I were to tell the story of what this agency is doing, I wondered, would anyone even believe me? What if I went to Congress, to the appropriate committee? Would they believe me? I didn't think so; I knew then I had to have documents, as many as possible. So far, I'd kept my promise to myself to put everything in writing: I had e-mails, memos and letters—but were they enough? From now on, I had to think and act strategically. It could not simply be my word against theirs—the all-powerful FBI—whose ruthless management was resolved to make me disappear.

8

Shooting the Messenger

That morning, Friday, March 8, the day of my scheduled polygraph, Matthew prepared a big breakfast. I was having none of it. "The worst thing you can do is to load yourself up with coffee and take the test on an empty stomach," he gently scolded. "Lack of sleep, no food, and caffeine! I thought you were determined to fight this with all you've got?"

I was in no mood. I drained my coffee cup and headed for the shower. After going through the mechanics of dressing, I looked at myself in the mirror: haggard, gaunt, with sallow skin. I didn't look or feel like a fighter. Maybe I could fake it—start by putting on some makeup. Next, straighten my shoulders and raise my chin. Already I felt better, stronger. By the time I finished and came downstairs, I was ready to fight. I even took a croissant.

On the way, neither of us spoke. Traffic downtown was congested, and the building was difficult to find. I looked again at the address: there we were, but no signs indicating FBI anywhere in sight.

"Let's see if there's a sign inside." We went into the building. Next to an art gallery on the entrance floor was a spiral staircase on the right. I started up, with Matthew a few steps behind. On the second floor, through tinted double glass, was a reception area, scarcely visible. I could just make out a small FBI sign posted at the unmanned desk. I pushed on the door: locked. Then I noticed the buzzer, pushed it twice and waited.

Moments later, a stocky man in his early forties with a thin mustache opened the door and asked us in.

"I am the FBI agent in charge. You must be Sibel Edmonds," he said, pronouncing my name *Cybil*.

Let it go.

The man didn't look happy that I was accompanied. He asked us to have a seat, explaining quickly that he needed to go set up the room.

"I have a question: to this date I have not been given a request for this polygraph in writing, and despite my repeated requests, verbally and in writing, I have not been provided with any reasons for it."

The agent in charge frowned. "No one can force you to take this polygraph. You still have the right to refuse."

I told him I didn't have a choice if I wanted to keep my job.

The agent replied that it wasn't his problem, that if I didn't want the test I should tell him now. "I have an examiner here from the FBI-Baltimore field office; he has come all the way to DC to administer this polygraph."

Why would the FBI bring an examiner from Baltimore when they have so many of them here in DC?

"I can do one thing, though," he continued. "After you take the polygraph, we'll provide you with the results; so you'll know before you leave this building. Now, are you going to take this or not?"

I looked to Matthew; he nodded. He too had heard the agent's promise. I agreed.

Five minutes later, the agent returned and led me through a maze of corridors to the polygraph room, a small office with a desk, a test giver, some machines, and a large two-way mirror. Let the circus begin!

The young, clean-faced agent stood and introduced himself. We shook hands and he asked me to take a seat next to his desk. The agent in charge left us.

"First you need to fill out and sign a few forms," the agent began, "then I have some test questions to go over, and afterwards you'll take the polygraph test itself."

He handed me a stack of papers and pen; then he too left the room. I started to review and fill out the standard forms, one of which listed my legal rights with regard to the polygraph test. The final paragraph stated, *I have been provided with and fully briefed on the reasons for this polygraph* . . . I stopped and read it again. I was not about to sign any such statement without indicating someplace on the form that this was certainly *not* the case—that I had *not* been given any reasons for this polygraph. I drew a circle around that paragraph with an arrow pointing to the margin, where I noted, in pen, *Despite my verbal and written requests, the agency has not provided me with reasons for this polygraph, and I have been told that I would be fired if I were to refuse to take this polygraph.*

The young agent returned and started going through the forms when he stopped at once and shrieked, "You cannot make any notes or changes on these forms! What is this?"

Calmly, I explained.

"But you cannot do that! You either sign it or don't sign it!" Then he stormed out with the forms.

This went back and forth until I finally called my attorney, to see where we stood with regard to the law.

"You did the right thing," he assured me. "They cannot object to the note. What did I tell you about these bastards, huh?" I thanked him and hung up. Matthew too agreed.

I walked back in. "Are you going to administer this polygraph or not?" I asked them. "The forms will stay the way they are; you can call my attorney regarding my rights if you wish." The agent in charge left in a fury. The other began his pretest questions.

The polygraph session took approximately an hour and a half. I was asked the same questions over and over. Despite all the stress and chaos, I felt calm and unusually confident.

The young agent walked me back to reception, where Matthew was waiting. He looked up. "So?" I shrugged. Soon we would find out.

The agent in charge reappeared and motioned us to the exit. "The session is over, have a good day."

"And the results?"

"The results are complicated and inconclusive," he said. "You won't be getting any results."

Now it was Matthew's turn to get mad. "This is not what you told us. You were very specific—you would give us the results of the polygraph before we left."

"I know what I told you," the agent responded. "I changed my mind; I don't have to give you any information."

Matthew's color deepened to purple red. "Shame on you people ... I'm ashamed of this government," was all he could utter.

I grabbed his arm and steered toward the exit.

That day, I came to the conclusion that pursuing this case internally within the FBI was futile. The polygraph clinched it. I decided it was time to take this to the appropriate committees in Congress. That day too, I prepared my request to submit to the Department of Justice Office of the Inspector General (DOJ-IG) for an independent investigation.

The FBI knew beyond a reasonable doubt and with documented evidence that it had been penetrated by criminal foreign elements.

Armed with this knowledge, they had decided on a single course of action: shoot the messenger and cover it all up.

I couldn't waste time. That evening I called Beryl Howell, the lead person in Senator Leahy's office on the Judiciary Committee, and got contact information for both the DOJ-IG and the Senate Intelligence Committee. She advised me to start with the DOJ-IG's office, to request an investigation, the sooner the better. She also planned to set up appointments for me to brief the appropriate staff in the Judiciary Committee: primarily Senator Grassley's staff, accustomed to dealing with FBI whistleblowers. That was the first I'd heard of others like me. I was glad.

By ten o'clock the following morning I had faxed letters and reports to DOJ-IG and the Senate Intelligence and Judiciary Committees. I had officially stepped outside the FBI.

My first appointment for an interview by the FBI's Office of Professional Responsibility was set for Friday, March 15, one week after the polygraph session. I met the investigators, two female agents in their mid-thirties, in a conference room in the OPR unit in FBI Headquarters.

Both women sat across from me around the conference table. First they asked me to go through the entire case history. I retold the story, everything in chronological order. I stayed away from issues involving the targets of FBI investigations and actual cases under both Counterintelligence and Counterterrorism. The focus was mainly on Dickerson, Feghali, and the sorry state of the FBI-WFO Language unit. Both agents took notes.

The entire session lasted nearly three hours. I was told to expect either follow-up phone calls or another, similar session. They requested that I document everything and notify them of any new developments, threats or further retaliation. Once they finished transcribing, they would have me back to review the transcript and vouch for its accuracy under oath. This would take approximately two weeks.

Five days later they called. I went there to review the transcript of our interview, my reports. They appeared accurate, to which I testified under oath.

I was unsure whether news of my reports to OPR and IG had gotten to management in the Washington field office, though the unit felt unusually calm. Both Feghali and Bryan stayed clear of me; yet, I still could not access many pending investigative files. I continued to be blocked. Instinct told me this was the quiet before the storm—but what kind, and how was I going to deal with it?

On Friday, March 22, I started my work at ten in the morning. I spent the day working mainly on Chicago files. Of the counterintelligence cases I'd worked on, this was by far the most intriguing and contained the most explosive elements: well-known Chicago political figures—including certain Illinois representatives in Congress—who were directly involved with targeted Turkish operatives, some of whom were among Interpol's most wanted fugitives. I had placed most of my focus on files dating from mid-1996 to January 2002, as well as ongoing DC counter-intelligence—part of which I was still going through, auditing those that had been reviewed by Dickerson. Since no one specifically asked me to stop going over those documents, I chose to press on—assuming I was still under the same order.

I went through and documented each thoroughly. On this day too I spent a couple of hours going over Dickerson's cover-up, in the middle of which I hit a new mother lode. Five or six pieces of additional audio communications—all stamped as not pertinent by Dickerson—contained information so volatile that I had to bite the bullet and report it to Saccher's unit. The information included specific U.S. persons, facilities and payments, all involving U.S. nuclear secrets being passed to foreign entities who then offered them to the highest bidder. In one case, the highest bidder who purchased one of these illegally obtained, highly classified information sets happened to be a non-state group with highly likely ties to a Middle Eastern terrorist organization. The players involved high-profile Pentagon and State Department figures, congressional staff, academic and think-tank-based individuals. The penetration went as deep as top nuclear labs, U.S. Air Force nuclear weapons labs and research facilities, and the RAND Corporation.

I translated those specific five communications verbatim and made four sets of copies, placing each in a large yellow envelope. I took one to Saccher's unit. He was still away, so I placed it on his desk and marked it EXTREMELY URGENT in big black letters. I took the second set upstairs, to security officer SA Tilton's office and dropped it into her slot. I came back to the Language unit and filed the third set in the unit's shared file cabinet. I didn't want to take any chances: I didn't want these documents to disappear, be destroyed or who knows what else, under the circumstances.

Even today, all these years later, I still don't know what made me do what I did so urgently on that day; it was as though a voice inside were telling me, *this is your last chance.*

At four o'clock that same Friday, March 22, 2002, I turned off my computer, locked my file drawers and went to grab my coat. As I was putting it on, I heard Stephanie right behind me.

"Sibel, Tom Frields wants to see you before you leave. It's urgent."

I turned around. "Now what? What's this about?"

"You'll find out soon. Please come and sit in my office. I'll go to Frields' office and let him know that you're ready."

I followed her to her office and took a seat. She left, leaving the door half open.

I looked at my watch: it was already 4:05. I knew Matthew's car was out in front. Well aware of security rules with respect to parked vehicles near FBI buildings, I decided to call Matthew and let him know of the delay. I reached over to the desk phone and dialed Matthew's cell. I told him I had been summoned and it would be another five or ten minutes before I could leave.

As soon as I hung up, I noticed Feghali standing outside Stephanie's office, staring at me. He tapped on his watch with great show. "In less than ten minutes," he crowed, "you are going to be fired, you *whore*. You are finished here." Then he turned and walked away.

I sat stunned, digesting the insult. Then I redialed Matthew. "This is going to take more than five minutes. I believe I'm about to be fired." Then I quickly hung up.

Stephanie returned and asked me to follow her to Frields' office. Waiting there were Frields and a stubby, shabby-looking agent named George Stuckenbroker, from personnel security.

Stuckenbroker pointed to a seat on the leather sofa, where I had been threatened with arrest only a month earlier.

"Sibel," he began, "I would like you to hand over your ID badge, entrance key and any other FBI properties you have."

I swallowed hard. So Feghali was right. I told myself to stay calm, though my heart was racing. I reached for my bag, hoping they wouldn't see me trembling. I pulled out my ID badge, keys, and a pen and notepad, placing the latter two before me. Then I handed him my keys and ID.

"I assume I'm fired. May I ask why and based on what?"

Frields broke in. "No, you may not ask why. You don't have the right to know why. We are under no obligation to provide you with any reasons. We are the FBI."

His face was ruby red; he sounded angry and out of breath. Now I felt cool in comparison.

Stuckenbroker put his hand up. "Come on Frields, you can do better than that . . . Give her some reasons; any reason."

Frields nodded. "Okay, do you want to know why we're firing you? Here is why: because of the way you walk—like a snob; because of the way you dress—like a stuffy snob; because of the way you talk and because of the way . . . just the way you *are*," he chuffed. "That's why."

"Okay," I responded, doing my best imitation of calm. "If I'm hearing you right, you're firing me because . . ." I then listed such despicable attributes as respectful work attire, proper etiquette, professionalism, good posture ... "Correct? In fact, I would like to note this, write this down now, since to date I have not been provided with anything in writing from you."

I took up the pen and started writing. Frields screamed to the other man, "You see what I'm talking about?" He yelled back at me, "No! You have no right to take notes! You have no right to ask questions! In fact, you have zero rights; this is the FBI, who the f— do you think you are here?"

"No sir," I responded, "you are wrong. I do have rights. I have my rights under the Constitution as a citizen of this country. I have my rights under this country's labor laws. I have my rights under the FBI's own rules and regulations, at least the written ones—"

Stuckenbroker stood up, interrupting me. "This conversation is over. We'll escort you out, Sibel. By the way, the FBI is not firing you; *we* are firing you. You are not fired from the FBI, you are fired by the FBI Washington Field Office."

Waiting outside the door was a uniformed security guard. Here I was, a petite five-foot-three female being escorted out by three burly FBI guys, one of them security, as though I were a criminal. I prayed my knees wouldn't buckle. I did my best to walk out of there straight, to keep my chin up high.

Once in the elevator, Frields laid it out straight. "I want to make sure you understand," he snarled, "that everything about today, your case, your employment with the bureau—I mean *everything*—is considered highly classified; top secret. You are not allowed to talk to anyone about any of these. Do you understand? You may think you have a right to an attorney. I have to tell you that you *don't*. You cannot even speak to an attorney, unless that attorney is cleared and approved by *us*. Do you understand?" By this point we had reached the exit.

Frields pulled open the heavy double door. "I'm warning you, Sibel. We'll be watching you. We'll be listening to your calls. If you even attempt to discuss this case, these issues, with anyone—this includes attorneys and Congress—the next time I'll see you will be in jail."

I couldn't take it anymore. "Frields," I told him, inches from his face, "it may be in jail, but I won't be the one behind the bars. Now do *you* understand this?"

I turned and walked out, taking quick long strides. The cold and bitter wind hit me like a knife. I was shaking. I couldn't see Matthew's car anywhere so I kept on down the block, my face half frozen, numb—and damp. It was wet. I was crying.

"So it's over," Matthew told me in the car. "You did all the right things and took all the appropriate steps to resolve this internally. . . . It's time to take this elsewhere: Inspector General's Office, Ashcroft and the Congress. By the way, while I was waiting for you I called Don Stone from the Senate Intelligence Committee. I told him about you getting fired. They're going to set up a time and place to interview y—"

"Drive to headquarters," I cut him off. "I'm going to OPR, to see John Roberts, right now."

There was no reasoning with me. He shook his head, made a U-turn and headed toward HQ. We got there exactly at five. I ran out of the car and went straight to the security desk.

I no longer had my ID badge so I couldn't just sign in. I would need an appointment and an escort. I don't know how, but I managed to smile at the guard, whom I'd seen on previous visits. "Oh God," I told him, "SA Roberts has been waiting for me since four thirty. I'm late and I'm sure he's utterly pissed since it's Friday, past five. I have to run up and see him for an urgent case."

The guard smiled. "You bet; almost everybody is gone already."

I handed him my driver's license. "I'll run up quickly, I don't want to hold him up any longer." He buzzed me in.

When I reached the OPR unit's office, the door was locked. They'd all gone home. I pressed the buzzer twice. Nothing. I felt defeated; I slid to the floor outside the door. What would I do now? I couldn't wait until Monday.

I spotted two men walking toward me. I scrambled to my feet; the last thing I needed was to be reported to security. One of them looked to be in his late forties, almost albino, with eyelashes the color of snow. The other was a little younger, with a salt-and- pepper mustache. They stopped and looked at me curiously.

The one with the mustache spoke first. "Miss, can I help you?"

"Oh . . . I'm late for an appointment with OPR. I came to see Special Agent Roberts. They seem to be gone for the day."

The albino-looking agent smiled and extended his hand. "You must be Ms. Edmonds. I'm John Roberts. Please, come with me." He took his key out and unlocked the unit door.

I was momentarily taken aback; I felt stupid, but lucky stupid. I followed him through another door into a smaller office, where I collapsed in a chair in front of his desk. I didn't know how to begin or what to say.

He spoke first. "I assume they fired you today. From your look, I can tell they did it in their usual vicious way. Why don't you tell me? I'm very familiar with your file; your case."

I tried to respond, but instead of words an uncontrollable sob came out. I hardly ever cried. What was happening to me?

"Here . . ." he handed me a box of tissues. "Take a few minutes and breathe deeply. They know how to make people miserable. They know how to rattle them. Welcome to the world of FBI whistleblowers, Ms. Edmonds."

I did as he suggested, then began. He listened patiently, without interruption, taking occasional notes.

"Just the usual," he said once I'd finished. "I know it's no consolation, but you are not alone. This fits the pattern of how the bureau reacts to messengers bearing bad or embarrassing news . . . *truth*."

I asked him what being fired "only from the FBI Washington Field Office" meant.

"That's pure bullshit. You are not officially fired by the FBI until they send you a formal termination letter. Usually it takes a couple of weeks; but you can be certain that you are fired. I understand you've also contacted Congress," he continued, "a very good move." He then explained that the DOJ Inspector General's Office was reviewing the case. If they decide to take it on, he said, OPR then turns everything over to the IG office. "We'll know in a few weeks."

"What do I do now? What should I do?"

"My recommendation: go and hire a good attorney; follow up with the Congress, especially the Judiciary Committee. You are up against an ugly beast who's decided to come after you, Ms. Edmonds."

I told him what Frields had said about my not having any rights to an attorney.

"That's a belligerent lie." Roberts shook his head in disgust. "You are an American citizen; no one can take your rights away, including the right to an attorney."

I liked this man. I knew he was trustworthy and had integrity. In less than a year, he too would be harassed, threatened and fired; SA Roberts would join the infamous FBI whistleblower club.

"By the way," he said, walking me out, "you may consider this good news. This morning I took it upon myself to go directly to the polygraph office and ask for your polygraph file and results: you passed with zero glitches. It was as conclusive and clean as polygraph test results ever get. I'm sure they were very pissed; they wanted to use the polygraph result to fire you. You took that reason away. With your computer one hundred percent clean, with all the commendation letters and positive job evaluations you had gathered, with all your allegations and reports documented and witnessed, and with passing the polygraph test with no glitches, they ran out of legitimate reasons to fire you. Your future lawyer will have a great case, a slam dunk case."

Walking out of there, I started thinking: How *are* they going to justify firing me? Roberts was right; I had done nothing wrong. What could they use as a legitimate reason?

Two weeks later, my questions were answered. According to the termination letter, the FBI had decided to terminate my contract "solely for the convenience of the government." So that was it. The government didn't need any reasons. I was an inconvenience.

IV

PURSUING ALL FOUR BRANCHES

9

Warrant

The day after I was fired, I began looking for an attorney, which proved difficult. Good, affordable attorneys willing to take on the FBI and Justice Department are a rarity in Washington, DC. As far as government watchdog and whistleblower organizations go, none of them call back unless you happen to be famous. (It took me years to understand the game: high-profile cases are cash cows for many of these groups, who use the funds they raise to pay the salaries of their staffs, none of whom are whistleblowers.)

After a long, frustrating search, Beryl Howell (Senator Leahy's chief counsel) helped me get in touch with Kohn, Kohn & Colapinto, a DC law firm with expertise in whistleblower and employment laws. The firm's chief investigator, Kris Kolesnik, had worked for Senator Grassley and was a seasoned investigator in whistleblower cases, especially those involving the FBI. It seemed a perfect fit.

Matthew thought that lunch—just the two of us—might be a good idea. In a house full of in-laws and relatives, we tried not to talk about the case, but so much was happening so fast. The date sounded perfect. The day too was perfect, sunny and unusually warm so early in May.

We met at a quaint family-owned café in Old Town Alexandria. During our lunch we discussed my upcoming IG interview; I would be accompanied by my attorneys. It was a relief to have someone who worked for my interests and stood by my side for a change. While we waited for our coffees, my cell phone rang. It was my middle sister, Lena. She sounded shaken up and asked when I would be coming home. We were only five minutes away. "What's wrong?" I asked. "Something happened?"

"That's okay ... I'll wait until you get home. We just got some news from Turkey. It doesn't sound good. I'll see you in a few minutes."

My stomach clenched. "I think it's my grandmother," I told Matthew. "I think she's dead. I'll have to go to Turkey if that's the case. I won't let threats or the bureau stop me from being there for my grandmother."

He reached out and held my hand. "You don't know that it's about your grandmother. Don't jump to conclusions, Sibel. And no matter what, you cannot go back to Turkey—ever. You know very well what they'd do to you over there."

When we walked in the door, my mother and sisters were seated around the family room in a state of abject gloom. My mother gave me the look: she was *furious*. I stepped into the middle of the circle. "Well? What happened?"

"I got a call from our neighbor in Istanbul," Lena calmly explained. "They said three Turkish police officers came to our house and knocked on our door several times. Not finding anyone, they went over and knocked on our neighbors' door and asked them about my whereabouts. They told our neighbors that this was their second visit; they had an interrogation warrant to serve me with, and that if I didn't respond to it in seven days, they'd come back with an arrest warrant."

I froze. The day I had dreaded for the past two months had arrived. My nightmares had come true. I avoided my mother's eyes. "Okay," I said to Lena, "I want all the details. Did they leave the warrant with your neighbor?"

"Yes," she said. "In fact, the father—my neighbor's father—is very well connected with the main police HQ in Istanbul. He made a trip there and spoke with his contact. His contact, a high-level officer there, said that the source of this particular warrant was MIT [the main intelligence agency in Turkey], and that he couldn't find out any more details since it was considered a sensitive intelligence matter."

I looked at Matthew then turned to her again. "Lena, I want you to think, and think very hard. Can you think of any unresolved matter, any financial dispute, any parking tickets . . . *anything* from the past? Think hard and respond honestly and truthfully."

She shook her head no and I believed her. Lena lived the life of a young, outgoing woman who never bothered with politics. Why would anyone from Intelligence want to interrogate her? There could be only one answer, and the thought sent cold shivers through me: Melek Can Dickerson, who was specific in her threat; she had named Lena and repeated her address.

I got the neighbor's number and arranged for her to fax us the warrant right away. Then I baby-sat the fax machine and counted the seconds. Fifteen minutes later, the one-page warrant slowly emerged, with the logo and stamp of the Turkish police. I read the four short sentences over and over: this was a warrant for interrogation; it cited certain laws and stated that arrest was the penalty for not showing up in seven days. I had to think fast.

I called my new attorney, Dave Colapinto, and bombarded him with questions. Sensing panic, he patiently went over what we might do. Together we decided that notifying Congress and the Office of Inspector General (IG) were the best options under the circumstances. I was to translate the warrant into English, then draft a short letter with an account of the events leading to the warrant; then fax everything to him. He would send the entire package, along with his letter requesting help, to the offices of Senators Grassley and Leahy.

It took me an hour to prepare the letter, translate the warrant, and send them to Colapinto. This helped me focus my anger and frustration on something other than simply being a victim—it made me feel of some use, rather than helpless in the face of something unbearable happening to my faraway sister. Now I had to go downstairs, talk to Lena and try to calm her down; and then, inevitably, face my mother.

When I went downstairs, my sister had already gone to bed. My mother was at the kitchen table drinking herbal tea. I pulled up a chair.

She quietly sipped her tea for another few minutes, which felt like hours to me. I knew what was coming and dreaded it. She was waiting for an opening. I began.

"I'm so sorry for this situation. I didn't go looking for it, and I didn't choose to get involved in this mess. I chose to do the job for my country after the terrorist attacks, and as I was doing just that, I stumbled upon this, I tripped all over it. I hope you understand that, Mom. I had two options: to lay down and sink quietly, keep my mouth shut and deny its implication for the country and our national security; or to take a stand and fight it—fight all the way to get the truth out and to have the issues addressed—for everyone's sake: yours, mine and the people of this country. Obviously, I chose the second option; the fight has just begun." I'd said the entire thing without a pause, and by the time I finished I realized I was out of breath. Now it was her turn.

She shook her head, narrowed her eyes and began in a low voice. "Remember what your grandfather always said about working for or getting involved with the government? He said, *Stay away from the government—it involves nothing but mud, dirt, corruption.* There are so many ways to make a living; there are so many jobs to be had, and there are so many businesses and people to associate with. Why would you choose to get involved with the government here, and of all its agencies, why in the world would you pick the worst part of it—intelligence and law enforcement, where all the fascists, crooks and despots get together? Why?"

Now *I* shook my head. "Mom, this is not Turkey. You don't know the government here. Things are different here. The laws and the way the government is set up is totally different from what you know—Turkey, Iran, Azerbaijan. In Turkey, there is no constitution guaranteeing freedom: freedom of the press and speech; there are no rights of due process . . . Here things are different. FBI doesn't equal MIT . . ."

"No, that's your mistake," she replied. "You are the one who doesn't understand. You are the one who is naïve; like your father, you are the one who lives in an idealistic world. That world does not exist, Sibel. Governments, be it Turkey, Germany, Egypt or the United States, are all the same. They want one thing: power; power to rule. They cannot tolerate truth or dissent. You either play the game with them by their rules, be a good team player, or they chew you alive and spit you out before you know what hit you." She took a big, deep breath and went on. "In fact, I'd say it is worse here. Do you know why? Because at least over there the government doesn't pretend to be such a goody-goody; they don't pretend to be a great democracy; so people know what to expect from them and they watch out. Here, they pretend to be the land of the free and the government of the people. When in reality, as you are learning and paying the price for it, they are equally despotic and power-driven. And when that power turns against you, its force is far more destructive."

I was doing my best not to explode. This exchange brought out all the bottled-up feelings I'd accumulated since I was a child. My mother had always made her resentment and disapproval of my father's quest for freedom and justice loud and clear.

"No wonder things are the way they are over there in Turkey," I lashed out. "When people assume an attitude and thinking process like yours, when they timidly look down and refuse to acknowledge their rights, when they accept despotism and censorship as a fact of life . . . they deserve what they get. I believe in what my dad taught me by example; I refuse to be victimized and live in fear. As he said, life is too short; you get to live this life once. You can either choose to live it in fear and intimidation, or to live it based on your principles and beliefs."

She stood up and made her position clear. "You can choose to do whatever you want or believe, as long as you are the only person responsible for it—as long as only *you* pay the price for it. With what you decided to do, you have dragged all of us into it. You expect us to pay the price for what you have chosen. Is that fair, Sibel? Your course of action has put me, your sisters, and the rest of our family in Turkey in danger. Your selfish idealism is going to cost us all. It already has. I know what I think and believe is not going to change you or your decision. In fact, it never did. You are your father's daughter; he spent his entire life in a never-ending search for nonexistent justice and ideals. Go ahead and do the same, I cannot stop you. But I am responsible for protecting my two daughters, my family. I have to do whatever I must to shield them from the consequences of your 'quest.' Just remember, you are not swimming against the current; this is more than a current—it is Niagara Falls!"

So there it was. She wanted me to quit, turn around and run, keep my head down and pretend that I see no evil, hear no evil. I tried my best to hold back the tears welling up. "I'm not the person causing this ... this fell upon me. I'm sorry for you being affected and dragged into this. I understand your anger and your decision. I'm fighting this not only for myself, but also for you, for the country. I'm not going to quit, Mom. Obviously, you won't stand by my side—"

She cut me off. "You won't have anyone on your side. Just watch and see how every friend you have, everyone you've come to know and associate with, will desert you. I've been there and seen it happen. They will disappear from your life one by one."

"Then so be it. At least I have my partner, Matthew, who stands by my side. My father didn't even have that much. While you're at it, why don't you go ahead and disown me?"

I stormed out of the kitchen and ran up the stairs to the office, shutting the door behind me. I sank down next to the fireplace and closed my eyes. Hearing my own mother repeating Saccher, Bryan and those so-called legal advisors had begun to plant horrific doubts. What if she were right? Just three months in, I felt I was already drowning. If this were only the beginning, what would it be like to continue forward?

I looked up and the first thing that caught my eye was a photograph of my dad on the mantel. Young, handsome, with dark hair and olive green eyes, he looked at me right back. I could hear his words.

"Sibel . . . no matter how hard and excruciating, always stick with truth and justice; in the long term you'll always prevail. Telling the truth and standing by it may come with its own punishment. Go ahead and take it, because the alternative will be much uglier and harsher. . . . We are given this opportunity, this life, only once: you can choose to live it with integrity, principle and honesty; or you can give in to fear, duck your head, timidly follow the unjust rules imposed upon you and live a life—but not *yours*."

A soft knock on the door brought me back. It was my "baby sister" (we called her that owing to the difference in our ages). I felt protective of her, almost as a mother would her nineteen year old. I had to remind myself to treat her not as a child but as a young woman. Not easy.

"I heard your conversation with Mom, Sibel. I don't know the details of those things that led you to this situation, but I want you to know I support you and what you are doing. I know our dad would have stood by your side and fought this together with you. I miss him so much. I'm not our dad, and I know there's not much I can do to help, but I will stand by your side. You can count on me."

My baby sister had grown up. Yet I knew that she faced real danger. "All I want you to do," I implored, "is to focus on your studies, and *do not mention this to anyone*—not a single person. You have friends, some of whom you trust very much, but please let this issue, let these problems, stay right here. Do not say a word about this to anyone; *anyone*."

She promised. As soon as she left, I began to think of everything I had to do to shield my family. Considering all the secrecy, classification and cover-ups involved, I was confident that this matter would be limited to a precious few, only those with Top Secret Clearance in the FBI, DOJ or in Congress. At the time, that gave me cause to feel somewhat relieved. I knew that the Dickersons, for example, had already reported us to the FBI targets, but I believed that threat was limited to what they could do to my family in Turkey, not anything here in the States.

So much for what I believed!

My first formal interview session with the Department of Justice Office of the Inspector General was scheduled for mid-April. Kohn, Kohn &

Colapinto would accompany me. I didn't know what to expect: Would it be similar to what I went through with the FBI-OPR, or would it be antagonistic and accusatory, like the meetings I had with FBI management at the Washington field office? Either way, I felt more secure and empowered to have a savvy attorney present as a witness and supporter who knew the government's limitations.

The day of the interview arrived. I met Colapinto in front of the Justice Department fifteen minutes early. After passing through security, we were escorted upstairs, where we were met by Kris Kolesnik, the law firm's senior investigator. From the DOJ-IG were the lead investigator, in her mid-to-late thirties, and her assistant investigator, a former Secret Service man in his early fifties.

The meeting started with a cursory interview covering the general issues in my case. The lead investigator asked open-ended questions and allowed me time to answer them; in this way, we established a chronology of events. My attorney refereed the questions and took very detailed notes.

I was asked about Feghali and the work slowdowns. How had he handled my first reports and memo on Dickerson? and so on. Then they asked how translators were hired, about nepotism and cronyism, and about incompetence.

Next they asked about my background, education and previous employment. What was I planning to do now that I had lost my contract with the bureau?

Once we'd gotten over preliminaries, the lead investigator said she needed details. "We need to know about the targets of investigations, the specific Turkish operations, the methods . . . the Dickersons and who they were connected to . . . basically, all classified information pertinent to this investigation. I understand you [indicating my attorney and Kolesnik] don't have Top Secret Clearance, thus you cannot be present for this segment of our interview with Sibel. We need to take her inside a SCIF—that is, a Sensitive Compartmented Information Facility—where she can freely disclose sensitive and top- secret information."

My attorney asked if they would be recording the session.

"No, we do not record our interviews," she answered. ". . . After all, this is only our initial interview. We will have follow-up interviews, some of which may require additional SCIF sessions."

I left my attorneys and was escorted by a guard into a windowless vault-like room with a heavy metal door that looked like a safe. Furnishings consisted of a medium-sized conference table and six chairs.

The session lasted about forty-five minutes, during which I answered questions regarding the nature of some of the counterintelligence operations I had translated, the file names and numbers, locations, the priority targets—particularly those related to or associated with the Dickersons; and the Chicago files dating back to 1996. I told them about the five main criminal activities the primary targets were involved in: narcotics, money laundering, illegal arms sales, the nuclear black market, and obtaining U.S. intelligence and military secrets and selling them to the highest bidders. I gave them specifics on extortion and bribery cases involving representatives in the U.S. Congress as well as general information about U.S. persons and officials involved—both elected and within the Pentagon and State Department. I was asked to provide further information on the forged signature incidents related to counterterrorism investigations on 9/11.

I easily could have spent dozens of hours providing every last detail. Yet, considering their position, that wouldn't be necessary: all they had to do was ask the FBI to turn over those case files; they could also subpoena them.

"Listen," I told them, "you don't really need my words, my account and allegations. All you have to do is get those files. We—that includes the FBI—already know the two foreign organizations Dickerson worked for prior to joining the bureau. It's already been established that she and her husband continued to closely associate with two primary target individuals within these organizations, and that they were active members and employees of others. The recorded communication of these individuals and entities will tell you all about the criminal activities they were engaged in here in the States and, more importantly, the high-level U.S. persons involved ..."

"Right. We will do that. That's a good idea. We'll have you come back and check those records, audios and documents, to make sure we have all the right ones. Afterwards, if it's necessary, we'll have follow-up sessions in a SCIF. Of course," she continued, "we will have to find competent and independent translators of our own and get them the necessary clearance in order to retranslate the audio and documents relevant to your case."

"The interesting thing," I told her, "is that some don't even need to be translated, since some of these conversations, those involving U.S. persons on their payroll, are mainly in English."

She paused. "Have you provided the same information to Congress—to the Senate Judiciary Committee?"

I had been advised by my attorneys not to respond to any question they might ask on either the scope of my activities or the information requested by and provided to the Senate investigators.

"I cannot discuss with you what I've discussed with the appropriate Senate staff. You can contact my attorneys if you have any problem with this."

"No," she replied, "not at all."

I followed them back to where my attorney and Kolesnik were waiting. The lead investigator told my attorney, "Well, I think we have enough, more than enough, for our initial meeting. As I told your client, Ms. Edmonds, we'll get all the case files she dealt with at the bureau. Then, we'll have you come back, and have Ms. Edmonds verify every single file, audio and document just to make sure that the bureau turns over everything pertinent to this case. Considering their reputation, we won't take a chance. Afterwards, we may have independent translators go over those considered pertinent by Ms. Edmonds and retranslate them. I believe your client believes this to be the best course of action too."

I agreed. "Everything you need is documented, recorded. With the information you have already, all you need is to have these audiotapes and documents. You won't need my words."

All agreed.

We left that long, exhausting meeting with the understanding that the IG would request and receive all the relevant case files then have us come back to verify. This was expected to take no more than a few weeks.

One sunny, cool morning in mid-May, I was in-between exams on campus when my cell phone rang. I nearly choked when I heard the voice: SAC George Stuckenbroker. I never thought I would hear that voice again.

"Hello, Sibel. Sorry to bother you, but we needed to reach you urgently."

"What do you want?"

"Well . . . I guess you've gotten what you pushed for . . . an investigation. We need to schedule you to come over here to WFO, ASAP. We need to question—uh, *interview* you regarding the issues, the case. We need that for our investigations, including the investigations under our counterespionage unit."

"Investigations? Who or what is it that you are now investigating?"

He paused. "I cannot discuss the details of this over the phone. Let's confirm the day and the time for now. Once you get here, you'll understand."

Here we go again. In a cool voice, I said, "George, as you know, I no longer work for your bureau; I received your formal letter of termination. You want something, then go ahead and contact my attorney." I gave him the number and hung up.

My palms were sweaty. I was breathing as though I had run a mile. Hearing his voice triggered all the rage and anxiety I'd felt the day I was fired. I dialed my attorney, told him about Stuckenbroker's request and asked what he thought of it. Colapinto was pleased with the way I'd handled the call, said he'd take care of it, and that in no way was I to go back there without his being present. First, they had to provide him with more information regarding the so-called investigation and its targets; second, WFO would only see or question me with my lawyers by my side.

I was relieved. I now had an attorney and advisor, someone they couldn't walk over—and more important, someone who wouldn't allow them to walk over *me*.

The following day I met Colapinto at his office and we strategized about upcoming meetings with Congress and the IG.

Colapinto planned to file a formal request under the Freedom of Information Act (FOIA) to obtain from the FBI what legally belonged to me. Materials and documents requested, to which I had a right, included all my personal belongings (including photographs); copies of my commendation letters and performance evaluation; all my memos and letters; all letters and memos related to me; my original application and subsequent information provided by me to the bureau; the polygraph result; and the formal order for confiscation of my home computer and the result of their examination of it.

Some of these documents were needed as well for our future lawsuit dealing with my wrongful termination. The FBI clearly had violated my First Amendment rights and the right to due process. In my attorney's view, based on positive performance evaluations and numerous commendation letters, a no-glitch polygraph result, and their inability to establish any security violation, the bureau had zero grounds for firing me. My bosses at the FBI had me fired for one reason: retaliation, against a whistleblower.

I understood all that, yet what bothered me most was still left unaddressed: the *cause* of this whole mess. Yes, I had wrongfully been fired and suffered humiliation and threats; but I knew that our lawsuit was not going to the heart of the issue: espionage, political corruption and cover-ups that included spectacular intelligence failures both before and after 9/11, and more. My family too was paying a terrible price, a direct result of the bureau's incompetence, inaction, and fearsome retaliation. What could fix the damage done to *their* lives?

I did my best to articulate these profound concerns without revealing to my lawyer details that were classified. Colapinto assured me that I would be given the opportunity to bring these issues to light during the discovery and depositions, and that the court process alone would expose the truth. I had to concede his point and stay positive. I was placing my faith and trust in the American justice system.

We discussed the progress of my case. Colapinto had received a copy of the IG letter to the bureau regarding my personal property—yet *nothing* on the IG's request for the FBI investigation files dealing with my translations. He'd also faxed them the interrogation warrant issued to my sister by Turkish Intelligence but hadn't received any acknowledgment or response.

I asked Colapinto about Stuckenbroker. He told me they had a short but strange conversation. My attorney had pressed for more information, specifically on whether or not I was a target for their alleged investigation. Stuckenbroker evidently refused to provide a clear answer to any question touching the subject of an investigation, yet after persistent grilling, admitted I was not their "target." He was to call back with possible dates for the interview, and that's where the conversation ended. He never called back.

Next we discussed the status of congressional activities with respect to my case. I had met with the staffs of Senators Grassley (R-IO) and Leahy (D-VT) several times and provided them with general information. I was told by my attorney to expect another SCIF session, this time with congressional staff. Investigators from both Senate offices apparently planned to have a session dealing with more detailed and sensitive information. Colapinto assured me both offices were working diligently on the case and that their initial investigation was moving forward: they'd contacted the IG's office and were expecting a thorough and expedited report.

Colapinto then handed me a sheet of paper with a big smile. It was a letter from Senator Grassley to the Immigration Department requesting that they process my sister's application for political asylum. This was a very kind gesture but I felt no joy; rather, the feeling was bittersweet. Here was yet more evidence of the price being paid by my family. My mother's words echoed in my heart. This was the best I could do to protect my sister. I knew she wouldn't have perceived it as such.

10

Leaks

A t seven in the evening of June 7, I got a call from Colapinto. The first words out of the box were, "Are you sitting? Because if you're not, you better do so before I tell you what I called to tell you ..." What was *this* about? As far as I knew, things were going well; we had filed our FOIA request, Congress was pursuing the case diligently, and an IG investigation was under way.

Dave cleared his throat. "Sibel, we got a call from John Solomon, a reporter with AP. He called to ask for our comment regarding your case. Obviously, certain people within the bureau and the Justice Department decided to leak your case to the press. He put the story on the wire; it's already picked up. It will be all over the place by tomorrow morning. They have fed him a bunch of lies, saying that you were the one under investigation. I am so sorry, Sibel. I guess they, the bureau, have decided to get nasty. Usually they follow these types of leaks with a name-smearing campaign. Get ready, the attacks have begun."

Now I had to sit. My blood pressure dropped and my fingers, gripping the phone, turned ice cold. This would be a disaster—for me, for my family—damaging everything I could think of, starting with the ongoing IG and Senate investigations. Weren't they the ones who told me that my case and everything touching it was Top Secret Classified and ultrasensitive? How could they leak the case and jeopardize my family's safety? Was there anything we could do?

Dave tried hard to calm and reassure me. He didn't succeed. "At least we gave Solomon the true version," he said, "of course, in a very general and cryptic way, but still. They will regret this, Sibel. Now, in addition to violating your First Amendment rights and wrongfully terminating you, they've violated your right to privacy. This will come back to haunt them, Sibel. I promise we won't let them get away with this; neither will the courts."

"Dave . . . what are we going to do meanwhile? I don't even know if I can keep my mother here any longer; she's getting so restless, she wants to go back to her life, career and family. Do you know what the Turkish government—or worse, the criminal thugs and operatives—can do to them over there? Even here!"

After an agony of silence, Dave finally spoke. "I am so sorry, Sibel. What they did here is not unusual. In almost every whistleblower case they do similar things . . . it is part of their intimidation tactics. It's to send a strong message to any potential whistleblower. This is what they call 'shooting the messenger.' However . . . with your case, the implications apply to your family; there are international concerns involved. . . . We'll contact the Senate offices . . . I know they're going to be pissed, very angry. Hang in there, okay?"

I hung up and sank deeper in the chair. I wanted to curl up in a ball and cry. I couldn't do that. I had to stay strong, force myself to think clearly and fast. I had to do some damage control; but how? This was so beyond me. This was already a congressional case, Inspector General's case, and now, of course, a public and media case. With each day that passed, I further lost my grip. It had a momentum all its own, dragging me and my family through the mud and sludge in its horrific wake.

I went to find Matthew, closed the door, and quietly told him about the latest development, afraid of being overheard. "Are you going to tell them?" he asked. I knew he meant my family.

"No, let's wait and see how wide it spreads. I don't want any newspapers here at home. Grab them and toss them out first thing . . . I'll also monitor Turkish news on the Web. This may die down ..." I knew it was wishful thinking.

The AP story was picked up by a few news outlets but not by TV news. It merely mentioned the case as possibly involving espionage, claiming I was fired as a result of a security breach. I checked all the Turkish papers online and didn't find anything. The story hadn't hit—but it did manage to snag the attention of a few major newspaper reporters, who called my attorneys to request interviews, to go on record. We had gotten onto their radar. It was only a matter of time before the inevitable storm.

From the moment I was fired, with few exceptions I had not been in touch with my FBI co-workers. Most had begun to keep a cool distance during my last two months at the bureau. They were afraid. Associating with me had become dangerous.

Those with whom I kept in touch, mainly through e-mail, were Shahla, a female Farsi translator, and Zuzanna, a female Russian linguist. Behrooz Sarshar thus far had not returned my calls. I knew Taskesen was still in Guantanamo and would be very unlikely to contact me.

Toward the end of May, Shahla asked me to lunch near the FBI-WFO. At first, I cringed at the idea of being anywhere near that place, but on second thought decided to go ahead and meet. I missed the friendly office interaction and was curious what might be happening there. We chose Andale, a chic contemporary restaurant only four or five blocks from the FBI-WFO. I cautioned her not to mention our lunch date to anyone and was given careful reassurance before we hung up.

Shahla arrived on time. After ordering, we began to chat. I casually asked about the climate in the Language unit. She spoke of being warned in subtle ways about the danger of associating with me; she said she didn't care, didn't take the warnings seriously. She knew next to nothing about what took place during my last two months there, having been gone during most of that period on various travel assignments. She did tell me, however, that "one late afternoon, after you were fired, before I was getting ready to leave, Stephanie and Feghali came to my desk and asked me if I had anything that belonged to you. I pointed at your drawer and told them everything you had was right there." According to Shahla, Stephanie and Feghali then went to the drawer, emptied all its contents—including my photographs, other personal items and leather organizer—into a large cardboard box and went back into Stephanie's office. I asked her the date; she paused and gave it to me. I took out my notepad and wrote it down, also recording the time and place of our lunch and Shahla's full name. I told her that even though more than two months had passed, I had yet to recover my things. I specifically asked whether she was sure she saw the photographs. Yes, she was sure.

At that precise moment, three young men in nondescript suits approached our table. One stood right behind me, at the entrance to the restroom, while the other two stood next to Shahla's chair less than ten feet away. Then one of them flipped his cell phone open. Shahla's face went white. She asked with trembling lips, "What the hell?! My God, are they going to arrest us? I know one of them, I've seen him before—he's with the CI unit at HQ."

I leaned over and said in a low voice, "Shahla, did you tell anyone about this lunch? Think hard."

She shook her head several times; then paused. "Well . . . only Stephanie."

"What?" I shrieked. "Why?"

"It was strange," she said, "because right after we spoke on the phone, she called me to her office and asked me whether or not I was still in touch with you. I told her *but of course, yes; why?* Stephanie said, *oh, nothing, just was wondering how she was doing, that's all.* Then, today, as I was getting ready to leave, she stopped me right in the hall and asked me where I was going. I told her to lunch. Then she asked me, *who with?* I didn't see any harm in telling her, so I told her with you."

"Did you tell her where?"

Shahla didn't remember. I'd suspected my phones were tapped. I don't believe in coincidences.

The three men remained where they were—at their posts. I knew they were there not to conduct surveillance but to intimidate Shahla. They didn't want anyone from the bureau to associate with me. Were they afraid that we would subpoena them as witnesses? Were they nervous about me collecting information from my former colleagues and collating further data? I bet they were.

I tried to calm Shahla down; I didn't succeed. She quickly asked for the check and looked like she was ready to take off—to sprint right out of the restaurant. As soon as we paid, she got up nervously. "I'm *so sorry* for this situation you're in, Sibel. I have to go—I've got a lot of work waiting for me. Best of luck, and please watch out for yourself." Then she hurried off without so much as a good-bye air kiss.

That was the last time I ever heard from Shahla.

The day after the AP article came out I received a call from Zuzanna, a veteran translator at the FBI's Russian CI division. I was surprised to hear from her. After what happened with Shahla, I figured that was that.

Zuzanna first said hi and immediately began, "Sibel, today Feghali asked every translator in the unit to gather around him for an important announcement. We all gathered around him in a circle. He actually climbed and stood up on one of the translators' desk, and while waving a sheet of paper in his hand said, 'Dear translators, today this article came out in all the major papers; it is from the Associated Press. This article makes it clear that your former colleague, Sibel Edmonds, is under FBI investigation and surveillance due to possible espionage activities and security breaches. I understand she is under twenty-four seven surveillance by the bureau. This is a huge scandal and embarrassment for the bureau; for all of us. She has betrayed our trust and good will. Why am I telling you this? Because I want to warn you: this is exactly what happens to those who choose to betray the bureau. We are a family in here. Sibel chose to go against this family; against all of us. Now, I want to warn you,

you'll be jeopardizing yourself and your career if you choose to associate with her or simply talk to her. My job is to protect this unit, to protect you. As I said, we are a family here. Of course the decision is all yours; we cannot force you to do anything, but you don't want to be found guilty simply for associating with or talking with that woman.'"

I knew Zuzanna was straightforward, not the type to embellish or exaggerate. It sounded exactly like something Feghali would do: outrageous lies, deception and a vicious smear campaign. I felt sorry too for Zuzanna and other former colleagues who had to put up with that—to feel intimidated by the bureau. I thanked her and took careful notes while she talked.

Zuzanna, though, wasn't yet finished. "Sibel," she explained, "I like you very much. I don't think you made the right choice here . . . the bureau is like a beast and too big to challenge. What the hell did you think you were going to get when you reported those cases? How could you even think for a second that you had any chance against these people? Man, was that naïve or *what*?" She paused to catch her breath. "I'm sorry, I didn't mean to say that. I'm just so angry and disgusted with this entire situation; with what they are doing to you. I called you, this one last time, to tell you that I won't be in touch with you any longer, at least for a while. Don't expect any e-mail or phone calls from me. I'm only three years from my retirement; at least until then. OK? I'm so sorry, but I cannot risk it. Do you understand?"

"Of course I do, Zuzanna." I smiled, even though she couldn't see. "You guys are one big family; remember what Feghali said? You have given this agency twenty plus years, and I do not expect to hear from you again. I understand, Zuzanna."

"Thank you; thank you for understanding my position. One last thing: your phone is 'dirty.' Watch out, Sibel, watch out for the monsters. Bye."

After I hung up I felt numb. No feelings anymore. Was this to last forever?

I went up to my office and made an entry into my log of events, dates, names. Stripped of nearly everything else, I was damned if I would let them strip me of my integrity and determination. I knew the price I had paid, was paying, and would pay; but what choice did I have?

A few days after the leak, I received a call from Kris Kolesnik, who wanted to get together to go over a few issues that dealt with Congress. During our conversation, he mentioned a tentative meeting set up by Senator Grassley's office for the following day to discuss some questions. Though short notice, I told him I would make myself available.

I now had three channels to pursue and Congress was one of them. During my congressional interview, I'd told them essentially what I'd told the IG: subpoena the relevant documents and audios from the FBI and let that material tell the whole story. Why waste valuable time questioning me when you can get everything you need straight from the source? I didn't know if they ever made the request.

That evening I met Kolesnik at a pub only a few blocks from where I lived. According to Kris, the Senate staff had already met with and questioned several FBI officials regarding my case. They wanted to meet with me again and have me provide answers to their follow-up questions right away, the next day. He didn't have any further details, and nothing about what questions were asked during that meeting or the bureau officials' responses. I asked him about the request for documents by Senate investigators: Had they obtained those files and materials? Kolesnik didn't know but expected that if they hadn't already, they surely would after having met with the FBI officials.

We also discussed my FOIA case. The bureau had three weeks to respond and release to us the requested documents under FOIA regulations, and they had already gone beyond that time. KKC sent a follow-up letter. If their stonewalling continued, we would file a court case against them—my first court claim against the FBI.

This was more than darkly troubling, it was Theater of the Absurd. If government agencies can so easily refuse to abide by it, what is the point of having such a law? Refusal to comply—in fact, a violation—means it is now *our* burden to pay legal fees and spend time and energy fighting in court. What kind of justice system is this? Then again, what are my choices? In the time that followed, this simple FOIA request would take years and tens of thousands of dollars battling in court.

On the afternoon of the day I met with Senate investigators to answer their follow-up questions, my home phone rang while I was cooking. I answered it, cradling the receiver in the crook of my neck while I rinsed my garlicky hands in the sink. It was the lead investigator from the Inspector General's office.

"Today we received a report from the FBI regarding your visit to certain Senate offices," she informed me.

"Since when do they report to you regarding my whereabouts?"

"According to the FBI," she went on, ignoring me, "two agents were in that same Senate building when they noticed you in the hall walking toward one of the offices. According to their report, you had with you a folder filled with top-secret classified and extremely sensitive FBI-related documents."

That did it. Time to set aside cordiality. "You listen to me," I lit into her, "how stupid can you be to even question me about something so ridiculous and outrageous! One, I did go to the Senate; I have the right and freedom to do so. Two, two FBI agents just happened to be there in the same building, on the same floor, and in the same hallway by this cosmic coincidence, huh? Three, they happen to know what I look like and recognized me—wow! Four, and here I was, stupid and mentally challenged, to carry with me a folder filled with top secret and sensitive documents. Five, I was either psychotic or crazy enough to label my file 'Top Secret and Sensitive FBI Documents,' which supposedly I carried openly, or these bastards have X-ray vision like the Six Million Dollar Man and can see inside my file and what it contains! Are you guys playing mind games here? You go ahead and call my attorney; I have nothing further to say."

I hung up on her, sank to the kitchen floor, bent over and laughed—an angry, hysterical laugh.

Later I called my attorney and reported the conversation. Now it was his turn to laugh. He was disgusted, and by then both of us knew that this most likely would be a kangaroo investigation. He said he would call the Senate offices then call me back. (He did.) We were to meet in the Senate the following day, and from there, accompanied by Senator Grassley's staff, would march to the IG office to straighten out this pathetic new twist.

I showed up at the Senate Dirksen Building on time. My attorney and Kolesnik were already there, in a small conference room in the Judiciary Committee's office. It took me several minutes to go over the phone conversation I'd had earlier with the IG lead investigator. The Senate investigators shook their heads in disgust. One phone call from my attorney later, we all headed out. I asked what they were planning.

"We'll go there," Kolesnik replied, "and the Senate staff will meet with the IG investigators and demand an explanation for this ludicrous intimidation tactic—geared to making whistleblowers wary of contacting or visiting the Congress. They may have questions for you, so you're going with us."

After going through the usual excruciating security procedures to enter the Department of Justice building, we were escorted to the IG unit. The Senate investigators went in first and met with two IG investigators behind closed doors while Kolesnik, Colapinto and I stood outside and waited. They were in there for a good thirty minutes. Theirs must have been a heated exchange; at certain points we could hear yelling. Then they came out. The Senate staff told Kolesnik and my attorney that the IG investigators had further questions for me. They had to leave, they said, and asked Kolesnik to keep them informed of how things went.

The lead female IG investigator stepped forward. "We need to ask Sibel a few questions. However, we have to do this inside the SCIF. You guys can either wait outside or leave."

Here we were again: another claustrophobic SCIF session. The windowless, heavy atmosphere had begun to cause shortness of breath, agitation and anxiety in me. I dreaded another session. I hoped my attorneys would refuse. No such luck! Kolesnik and Colapinto opted to leave. They asked me to come to their office afterwards for a short meeting. Then they left.

I followed the investigator into the almost airless, dimly lit chamber and sat in the exact same chair. She opened her book and noted the date and time. "We talked with the FBI again regarding their report on your divulging classified data to the Senate staff. They said they were wrong and the incident was different than what they had claimed previously. They now say you have divulged classified and sensitive FBI information to your family members."

I gave her the look and then shook my head. "And how is that?"

"According to them, you, your mother and one of your sisters went to a restaurant for lunch. Two FBI agents were having lunch there, and happened to sit right next to your table. During lunch they overheard you telling your mother and sister about ongoing FBI investigations, targets, and highly sensitive and classified intelligence regarding Turkey. So, they came back to FBI HQ and reported it."

I let out a scornful laugh. "Okay, so two FBI agents just happened to be there, and happened to be seated right next to us, just like that. Now, considering the fact that my mother doesn't speak English, that I only speak Turkish with my immediate family, did these assholes happen to be fluent in Turkish to understand all the top secret stories I was divulging in Turkish? Huh?"

She hadn't expected this. She leaned over to her colleague and whispered something; then they excused themselves and exited. A few minutes later they returned. "We called the FBI and asked for clarification," the lead investigator began. "No, they didn't speak any Turkish and could not understand what you were talking about. So, they taped the conversation you were having with your family and took it back to the bureau for translation."

"Yeah right!" I shot back. "Two agents happened to be there, coincidentally; they happened to be seated right next to us, what Karma; then, they happened to recognize me and guessed what I was talking about in Turkish without understanding Turkish; oh—and they happened to have a tape recorder with them! Just listen to yourself. Are you telling me you bought into this outrageous and ludicrous story fed to you by the bureau?"

"Ms. Edmonds," she responded, "I am only telling you what's reported to us. You only need to confirm or deny, okay? Did this incident take place a week ago?"

"No."

"Okay then," she continued, "let's move to our next topic. You and Dennis Saccher worked closely, right?"

"I only worked twenty to twenty-five hours a week. Sometimes I didn't even see Saccher, since I was busy working on other priority counterterrorism cases; sometimes I did. Of course, I told you about them removing him from FBI-WFO during my last month with the bureau."

"I understand, but generally speaking, you regularly met and discussed the ongoing counterintelligence operations assigned to you. He consulted with you frequently regarding certain targets; you served as an analyst for the primary Turkish CI case . . . so on and so forth. Right?"

"Yes."

"You also went out for coffee breaks. Is that correct?"

"Yes; we grabbed coffee from a coffee shop located two blocks from FBI-WFO."

"We were told you had lunch dates frequently?"

I could see where they were going: an improper relationship, maybe an affair between Saccher and me. I remembered what my attorney had warned me about. "No, we only had two lunch sessions. Kevin Taskesen, the other Turkish translator, was present during one of them."

"But they were not all during your work, during weekdays," she continued to suggest. "You also met with him on weekends; to dine and spend personal time."

I was near the end of my patience. "Only once, with my husband, Saccher's mother, his wife and two baby daughters present—and no, we did not engage in group sex!"

She ignored my gibe. "Some people describe your relationship with Saccher as intimate. They believe it went beyond a simple working relationship. He has been known to be fond of you. Do you deny that?"

I stood up, ready to leave. "Why don't you ask Saccher? He'll sue your ass for even implying such nonsense. He loves and adores his family; that's what he lives for. I have a successful marriage. I am not going to sit here and take shit from either of you. I am done here." I paused and added, "By the way, why did you make this ridiculous session a *SCIF* session? Does the government consider questions regarding my relationship with Saccher classified? You told my attorneys that your questions could not be asked in their presence . . . obviously, another dirty trick!"

They walked me into the hall. Familiar with the building by now, I left them behind as fast as I could.

Outside, I started smoking. *When is the next attack coming?* I asked myself. *Are they going to accuse me of having an affair, and leak it to the press? Oh my God—how will Matthew deal with this? Our neighbors, my family, Matthew's clients—how are we going to explain this to them? How can anyone deal with this kind of situation?* I spent nearly thirty minutes there, smoking and worrying.

Later, meeting with my attorneys, I told them what went on inside the SCIF, making it clear that I would never again talk to any of those investigators without my attorneys present, and that never again would I step inside that secret airless room. Fair enough, they nodded. They would go on record about this incident with a letter to the IG, with copies to Congress. Now I had to go home and prepare my family for what promised to be a disaster.

The only good news I received that day was that the Senate Judiciary Committee had made a formal request to IG to expedite its investigation and report on my case. I was told to expect this report no later than October 2002. If the IG did what it was supposed to do—an independent and thorough investigation—my case and I would be fully vindicated. Yet after what happened with their lead investigator inside the SCIF, what were the chances of that? I began to count the days to October.

As promised, my attorneys reported the AP leak to the Senate Judiciary Committee, already deep into its investigation of my case. What may be inferred from such a leak and all that it implies is serious, and, as had been expected by Colapinto, the investigative staff was duly outraged by this callous move by the bureau. This breach to the media was added to the list of claims we planned to file with the court. What the government had done was a clear violation of the Privacy Act.

During June and early July, the Senate Judiciary staff summoned those FBI officials in charge of the FBI-WFO Language unit and personnel security to several meetings. The meetings were not classified. (The Senate staff was not cleared for top secret briefings, nor did FBI officials ask that all staff members present be cleared.) All we were told by the Senate investigative staff was that during these meetings they thoroughly questioned the FBI officials and had gotten all they needed to establish my full credibility and the validity of my allegations and reports. I still didn't know precisely who these FBI officials were; neither did I know what specific questions were asked or answers provided.

The dreaded media storm hit one week later on Wednesday, June 19, 2002, beginning with a national story in the *Washington Post*. The fairly long and detailed article gave a brief summary of the Dickerson case and characterized it as a "possible case of espionage." It also stated that "Under pressure, FBI officials have investigated and verified the veracity of parts of Edmonds' story, according to documents and people familiar with an FBI briefing of congressional staff. Leahy and Grassley summoned the FBI to Capitol Hill on Monday for a private explanation, people familiar with the briefing said."

Amazingly enough, based on the congressional letters obtained by the *Washington Post*, "The FBI confirmed that Edmonds' co-worker had been part of an organization that was a target of top-secret surveillance and that the same co-worker had 'unreported contacts' with a foreign government official subject to the surveillance, according to a letter from the two senators to the Justice Department's Office of the Inspector General. In addition, the linguist failed to translate two communications from the targeted foreign government official, the letter said."

Senator Charles Grassley was quoted as saying, "This whistleblower raised serious questions about potential security problems and the integrity of important translations made by the FBI. She made these allegations in good faith and even though the deck was stacked against her. The FBI even admits to a number of her allegations, and on other allegations, the bureau's explanation leaves me skeptical."

Considering the fact that this story broke in the wake of the highly publicized whistleblower case of FBI Agent Coleen Rowley, who complained about systemic problems before the September 11 attacks, the *Post* coverage was fairly comprehensive and damning of the FBI.

At once, I was struck by the implications of what was about to happen. First, I was relieved to be vindicated in the mainstream press after the false and derogatory leak: this article had established my legitimacy. Yet I knew that this story could no longer be contained. Very soon my name, my case, and the classified nature of the sensitive issues involved were going to reach other places, including the Turkish press. No longer could I tell my family that this dangerous situation was only temporary and that I would have it resolved; now there was no turning back.

That night at dinner, Matthew and I delivered the news to my family and showed them a copy of the *Post* article. No response from my younger sister; my middle sister started to cry, unable to speak. As to my mother and our fraught relationship, it now had reached the point of no return. Their lives had changed *forever*; I would never be forgiven. With my sisters, only time would tell.

Within days we started to receive calls from Turkey. My uncles, aunt, cousins, friends and neighbors all called to let us know that every newspaper, TV and radio channel had given extensive coverage to my case—and every one pejorative. According to their reports, I was now considered an enemy of the state, a traitor, a U.S. spy undercover against Turkey and its reputation, and on and on. Some accounts even named me as a CIA operative who worked against Turkish interests. All depicted the case as something that would expose the Turkish government and its activities. How could they not? The major facts and exonerating details were still unknown and classified; they had no idea which players or what targets were working against the national security and interests of Turkey. Turkish media and journalists remained very much in the dark about who was using their power and influence to obtain and sell sensitive U.S. intelligence and nuclear and military technology.

My sister's fiancé (soon to be ex) called to report on a segment aired on a popular radio show. They attacked me as an agent for Armenians, that I was spying on Turks, divulging their national secrets and intelligence in order to damage Turkey's reputation for her enemies. Apparently there were calls for my hanging, that I should be burned to death, that the Turkish government needed to "take me out."

Then a unanimous decision was made by my extended family members in Turkey never to contact me by phone or e-mail. Each had to protect her- or himself from being blacklisted by the Turkish government and quite possibly becoming a target. All had come to pass, as promised: I was now endangering and threatening their safety and well-being. The result, as far as I could tell, was to be cut off from my extended family—permanently. With my mother, it was only a matter of time.

11

On the Lam

n July 2002, I focused on the two lawsuits we were about to file. The FBI had thus far refused to turn over a single page of the documents we had requested under FOIA and also had refused to return my personal belongings.

We also planned to file our primary claim under the Privacy Act for violations as a result of the leak to the press: the false and wrongful disclosure of confidential information about me; under the First Amendment for FBI retaliation against me as a result of my disclosure of serious wrongdoings (whistleblowing); and under the Fifth Amendment, since the bureau violated my right to procedural due process. Defendants in my primary court case were the FBI, DOJ, Director Mueller, Thomas Frields, George Stuckenbroker and John Ashcroft.

Each claim was relevant to the others. To establish my case under the Privacy Act and First Amendment, I needed to have the requested documents released by the FBI. These documents belonged to me; they concerned my performance and included commendation letters and job evaluation. These documents showed how I went about reporting the issues and wrongdoing, the result of my polygraph test, and the status of the FBI's so-called investigation of me.

I hoped that as my primary case proceeded in court, the serious issues—with even more serious consequences that could devastatingly compromise our national security—would surface in the glare of media scrutiny. This was the only way I could see how to draw attention to these problems. Investigating these matters internally had come to naught; the public needed to know what was being done with their money and trust. Here was an opportunity.

As we prepared for court, my attorneys and I spent considerable time going over facts and chronology. My course work was completed: I graduated with degrees in criminal justice and psychology. Prior to working with the bureau, I had planned to go to graduate school and major in national security studies. Yet, after what I had been through in the last six months, I would in no way consider anything having to do with intelligence or law enforcement. Instead, I applied for an advanced degree in public policy. My focus was so intent on Congress and its oversight function that everything I read, listened to, studied or watched had to do with Congress and the judiciary branch. If I was to be in it for the long haul, I might as well get myself the knowledge to understand and deal with it.

In early July we filed our case under the Freedom of Information Act with the U.S. District Court, District of Columbia. The case was assigned to Judge Ellen Segal Huvelle. Colapinto didn't know much about Judge Huvelle, other than that she was appointed to the bench in 1999 and had a mixed record ruling on cases brought against the federal government.

Then, on July 22, we filed our primary case: our First Amendment–Privacy Act claim, with the same court in the District of Columbia. Our case was assigned to Judge James Robertson. Judge Robertson had been appointed U.S. District Judge in 1994 during the Clinton administration and had served as chief counsel with the Lawyers' Committee for Civil Rights Under Law in the State of Mississippi. My attorneys were happy with this. They knew Robertson as a fair and straightforward judge with great respect for civil liberties, and we considered ourselves lucky to have him presiding on our primary case. Four years later, Judge Robertson would be the first and only judge to resign from the highly secretive

FISA court in protest of the NSA Illegal Domestic Eavesdropping scandal, subsequently confirming our high opinion of him.

During one intense session, my attorney brought to my attention an angle I had previously overlooked. "Oh, before I forget," he said over sandwiches, "I was thinking about Major Douglas Dickerson the other day and it hit me: this guy has Top Secret Clearance and is still employed by the Department of Defense with access to sensitive and national security documents—information."

I nodded. "Yes. And?"

"Look, the Senate is investigating this as an espionage case. The IG at the Justice Department is investigating this and the Dickersons as an espionage case. We've had these newspaper articles confirming that Dickerson actually worked for and associated with those thugs who were under the bureau's counterintelligence investigations, both before her employment with the bureau and during, right?"

"Exactly. What's your point?"

He motioned me to wait; then he turned back to his computer and typed as he talked. "So, the point is, I got curious and checked the Defense Department's own security rules and regulations, those that deal with Top Secret Clearance holders . . . aaannnd . . . *Bingo*."

He clicked on Print and waited for the paper to emerge. I could hardly wait.

He gathered the documents and handed them to me. "This is DOD Inspector General regulation fifty-two hundred. According to their own regulations at DOD, Major Dickerson and his wife, Melek Can Dickerson, have committed numerous violations of the U.S. Department of Defense Personnel Security Program. I believe there is credible evidence to indicate that both Major Dickerson and his wife have been subjected to improper 'foreign influence'; indicated a 'foreign preference'; involved themselves with 'outside activities' and 'membership in organizations that could create an increased risk of unauthorized disclosure of classified information, had improper and unreported contacts with foreign officials and/or other entities under the control of foreign influence'; and both of them have engaged in other conduct that would make them untrustworthy and unreliable for the purpose of maintaining a security clearance with the United States government." He stopped, leaned back and smiled.

I grabbed the document and began to read. The regulation essentially states that if a person's spouse, partner, or living companion is under the influence of any foreign government or entity, or has loyalty to foreign individuals, government or organizations, then that person must undergo investigation by the DOD Inspector General's Office and his or her clearance must be removed and put on hold until he or she is cleared.

Major Douglas Dickerson's wife did in fact work for foreign organizations that were under FBI surveillance. She had ongoing relationships with at least two of the FBI targets, both socially and financially. Douglas Dickerson was the person who tried to recruit my husband and me into one of those foreign organizations, offering to help get Matthew in by telling that organization what I did at the FBI. Colapinto was right. Now, officially, the Dickersons were under investigation by the Senate Judiciary Committee and the Inspector General of the Justice Department. Their names had become public. How could Douglas Dickerson retain his clearance under these circumstances? How could he continue to have access to our sensitive defense intelligence and technology and be entrusted with them?

"Here is what I'm going to do," said Colapinto. "I'm going to draft a letter to DOD-IG and the air force to ask them to open an investigation on Douglas Dickerson, and I'll point out why. I'll also attach the newspaper articles and the letters by Senators Grassley and Leahy to Mueller, IG, and Ashcroft. I'll start on it right away, and should have it ready in a week or two."

OK again. This was good strategic thinking. I started to feel a bit more optimistic about our upcoming court battles. I had confirmation by the

Senate offices. And pretty soon I would have the final IG report that we so desperately needed to further vindicate me and thus proceed to court. I actually looked forward to October.

One evening toward the end of July, Matthew and I were on our way out for fresh air during a concert intermission when I felt a tap on my shoulder. It was my coworker from the bureau, Amerika. What a lovely surprise too that she didn't pretend not to see me. After greeting each other warmly, we stepped aside and chatted briefly; small talk. As usual, I tried in my not so subtle way to acquire information. "What's up with Dickerson?" I asked. "When did she leave?"

"Oh," she said, "you haven't heard? She took off for her maternity leave last week, but she and her husband are leaving permanently at the end of August or first week of September."

I felt as though I'd been kicked but feigned casual. "Leaving? . . . Where are they going?"

"As far as I know, first they are going to Belgium, where her husband will have an assignment for a while, but then they will go to Turkey and will permanently settle there."

So they're running away; escaping! . . . We chatted a few more minutes and then it was time to go in. *Running away* . . . It figured. She was under two active investigations. Along with the Dickersons, my concentration had taken flight. I didn't register a single note of the entire second half.

By the time we got home it was too late to call Colapinto. I tossed and turned, unable to sleep. Insomnia had become the norm. I thought, planned, strategized, grieved, cried and agonized in the dead of night, when everyone else was asleep. Bedtime now was a never-ending episode of "This Is Your Life," where the past was always revisited, events deconstructed, the latest gone over to the nth degree while I lay there listening to my father's voice, imagining him comforting me.

The following morning I called Colapinto and told him about the Dickersons' plans. He said he'd sent the letter to the Department of Defense and U.S. Air Force Office of Inspector General. Not only were there now active investigations of Dickerson by the Senate Judiciary Committee and the Justice Department's IG, there was also a possibility of DOD starting its own separate investigation of Douglas Dickerson. Colapinto himself would check the extradition treaties between the United States and Turkey, as well as those Central Asian countries in which the Dickersons were involved. Depending on his findings, he said, he might need to petition Judge Robertson to issue an emergency subpoena for both Dickersons' depositions before they left the country.

My attorney called later that evening; as expected, the United States did not have a sound extradition treaty with Turkey or other Central Asian countries. He would notify Judge Robertson's court and request an emergency and expedited subpoena for the Dickersons' depositions. We only had a month. He suggested I put together a set of relevant questions to be asked of them.

I spent several days carefully drafting questions for the Dickersons' depositions. Matthew and I were scheduled to leave for a weeklong vacation and I wanted to get this out of the way before we took off. When finished, I had filled several pages with precise and detailed questions that I hand-delivered to my attorney's office.

The day after our return, I received an official letter, dated August 22, 2002, from the Department of Defense Office of Inspector General: DOD had officially begun its investigation of Major Douglas Dickerson. This was a positive development. Since, according to the letter, the formal investigation was expected to take at least six months, the Dickersons were bound to stay in the country.

Colapinto shared my optimism. He told me to expect another set of interviews, this time by DOD. (Since Matthew too had been present during the home visit, he would be considered another key witness who had to be interviewed.) Colapinto assured us he would be present during all interview sessions.

The very next day, my doorbell rang. When I asked who it was, the man identified himself as an officer with the DOD Inspector General's Office; he and his assistant needed to speak with me for a few minutes. I immediately dialed Colapinto, who was out, so I asked for his partner, Steve Kohn. When Steve's voice came on and I told him about my visitors, he advised me not to answer any questions and instead forward them to Colapinto.

I went downstairs to let them in, asking first for identification and DOD credentials. I told them what my attorneys had instructed me to say, that they had to contact them and schedule a meeting to interview me in their presence.

"We understand, Ms. Edmonds, and we are going to contact them and schedule our formal interview. This is not an interview; we only have a few general questions in order to prepare for the intensive investigation ahead when we will interview you and all other relevant witnesses."

He seemed very polite and respectful. I stepped aside and pointed to the family room. They walked in and took their seats on the sofa. The younger one pulled out a small notepad while the other one asked, "Is this the place where the Dickersons visited you?"

"Yes."

"Do you remember the date?"

"First Sunday in December."

"May I ask who else was present besides you and Major Dickerson?"

"His wife, Melek Can Dickerson, and my husband, Matthew Edmonds."

"Is it true that Douglas Dickerson mentioned certain foreign organizations and individuals?"

I stood up. "I will not talk about this without my attorneys present. I believe this visit has ended."

"Fair enough. We'll contact your attorneys right away and will be seeing you soon."

They respectfully shook my hand and walked to the door. I handed them two of Colapinto's business cards, just in case. They said good-bye and left. I went upstairs and called Steve Kohn to give him a detailed account of what had occurred and exactly what was said.

On Friday, August 30, 2002, Judge James Robertson granted our request and issued an expedited subpoena to depose the Dickersons. Next, we had Kris Kolesnik (who happened to live nearby), serve both Dickersons with the subpoena.

In the meantime, Colapinto had been trying to coordinate our schedules for the requested interviews with the men from DOD's IG office. Contrary to what those two officers assured me, no one from DOD contacted my attorney's office and they hadn't returned his calls. We found that peculiar. First they rush to show up at my door claiming urgency, and now they don't even return our calls. What happened to their investigations?

On Wednesday, September 4, 2002—one day prior to the scheduled deposition for the Dickersons—Colapinto called me at home. He sounded furious. He had shocking news, he said.

"There will be no deposition tomorrow; it got canceled."

"*What?*"

"Several attorneys from the Justice Department and Department of Defense appeared before the judge and successfully blocked the deposition. They persuaded the judge to have the Dickersons deposed later. They provided him with affidavits from both Dickersons stating that they promise to make themselves available for any deposition in the future. Also, the heads of both agencies, DOD and DOJ, issued affidavits stating that they would make the Dickersons available if needed in the future, that they would even pay for the Dickersons' airplane tickets and personally escort them if necessary."

A thousand questions entered my mind; I didn't know where to start. "What do they mean, *if necessary*? The court had already agreed that it was necessary. What's the difference between having them provide statements— depositions—right now and bringing them in later? Why would DOD postpone this and accept paying for travel expenses when they are here and available right now? Why—"

"I know, I know," Colapinto cut in. "It is mind-boggling, doesn't make any sense at all. Also, now we have DOD getting itself into this battle. I don't know what else they may have in their hats but this stinks, big time."

"When are they leaving the country, the Dickersons?"

"On September ninth, five days from today."

There was a long silence. "Just like that, huh? Espionage charges, active DOJ-IG investigation, DOD-IG investigation, Senate investigation, yet they are on their way to escaping it all. . . . Call the press and let them know. I bet they'll find it just as strange and peculiar!"

"I've already let one of our reporter contacts know. He needed more information, like airline, flight time, et cetera. We'll see. Here is what I suggest we do: come over next week; we'll sit and discuss strategies, okay?"

"Yeah right, strategy! The targets—the key witnesses, the *real* criminals—are flying into the sunset with DOJ and DOD's unconditional cooperation and support. We, on the other hand, are sitting and talking about strategies."

He sighed. "I know how this must feel for you. I've never seen anything like this myself. The resources they're putting into this, bringing in all these high-powered attorneys, so many of them, from both agencies, tells me that they have something to hide, something very big."

We set the meeting time for Wednesday the following week.

When I showed up at my attorney's office for our lunch meeting, Colapinto was talking on the phone; he waved and smiled a bitter smile. I knew his body language by now and this didn't bode well.

I paced his office and looked at all the files and boxes with my name on them. They were piled everywhere. I spied the list with my questions for the Dickersons' subpoena. *So much for the depositions.* Deep in my gut, I knew they would never return to this country.

Colapinto hung up and grabbed his sport jacket. "Let's go. I'll give you more bad news once I let you eat."

That was it. More bad news. As I followed him out, my mind started to race with unanswered questions.

After we were finally seated and had ordered our food, Colapinto started with small talk. He was preparing me, massaging, working up to something, which only increased my agitation. When he saw I could wait no longer, he spilled it.

"Okay ... we got an official letter, faxed to us, on Douglas Dickerson's investigation. It says they have done a thorough job investigating Dickerson and have decided that he has not engaged in any wrongdoing. Therefore, they closed the case as of yesterday."

I almost choked on my chicken. I started to cough violently and grabbed the water glass, taking big swallows.

"What the hell is *that* supposed to mean, Dave? What investigation? They started the so-called investigation less than three weeks ago! They haven't interviewed me, they haven't interviewed Matthew, they haven't asked for any documentation—they haven't even started!"

"I know ... I'm going to write a long letter and say just that. I'll include the letters and statements by Senators Grassley and Leahy, and the major articles on the case."

I pointed out the absurdity—these investigations were supposed to take 180 days minimum, by their own rules—and the conspicuous disappearance of the targets, how conveniently well-timed. All of which was met with promises by my attorney that something would be done.

"I know exactly why the Pentagon would want to cover this up," I told him. "I know it too well. This will expose some of the traitors in there, those engaged in selling military intelligence and secrets—"

Colapinto cut me off. "Sibel, let's not discuss this in here, please! We'll talk about it in my office. Also, on the positive side, I want to talk to you about something else, a solid strategy you should consider ..."

As I walked back to his office, I began to think. And the more I thought, the more overwhelmed I became. How many more blows could I take? How could I fight all these actions? Things were only getting worse. How could I even dream of taking on this leviathan, set to fight me all the way?

Back at Colapinto's office, I was handed the one-page letter from DOD stating they'd terminated their investigation of Dickerson. I read it over three times. It was one paragraph long, less than two hundred words. Then something caught my eye: "The Air Force Office of Special Investigations (AFOSI) conducted a complete and thorough review of Major Dickerson's relationship with *the American Turkish Council* (ATC)" (emphasis mine).

I pointed out the section to Colapinto. "I never named any targets—organizations or individuals—when their investigators came to my house. Look, they're naming one organization that I can't! This should make our case even stronger. They're saying Douglas Dickerson had and has a relationship with ATC. Based on what Dennis Saccher found out, Dickerson did not mention her previous employment with these foreign organizations; neither did she disclose the fact that they had continued the relationship with these organizations and certain target individuals within. The Defense Department has gone on record naming one of the organizations in question, Dave! This letter is not classified; they cannot put the cat back in the bag. ATC's name is fair game, as far as we're concerned!"

This caught his attention. "Wow. That's a very interesting point. We'll make sure we put that in the letter to DOD. You are sure you didn't mention ATC, right?"

"Of course I'm sure! I transcribed the entire conversation that same day and sent it to Steve. Haven't you seen it? I could not disclose FBI targets during an unclassified meeting with these people. Even with DOJ-IG and the Congress, I only named them inside the SCIF ... Have a little faith in me!"

"Okay. . . . Now, that brings us to what I wanted to discuss with you. Are you ready?"

I looked, waiting.

"Remember the request we got from "60 Minutes" after the *Post* article came out? Remember what you said about never being willing to go on camera or have your picture taken by the press?"

Certainly I did. Right after the series of articles on Dickerson and my case appeared in July, we had received interview requests from several TV news programs and monthly magazines. I didn't want my face out there, so I refused every one of them—including "60 Minutes."

"Look, you've done all the right things," he continued, "have taken all the right steps. The FBI is the one who leaked the story to the media, not you. Also, now you have two senior senators who have come out publicly and confirmed your case and vouched for your credibility. They need your help in garnering public support to push this further. . . . Neither Ashcroft nor Mueller has even bothered responding to the numerous letters sent to them by Senators Grassley and Leahy. They will do everything they can for this case, for you, to go away. You shouldn't let them succeed. ... What I'm advising you to do is to reconsider your position on not going to the public with your case."

"But the story is already out there. *The Washington Post, Chicago Tribune* . . ."

He shook his head. "That's not the same as coming out directly from you. The public hasn't heard from you. They want to put a face with the story. They need to hear you telling them what they've been putting you through, and how they—the FBI and the Justice Department—are endangering national security. The senators, the Congress, will have a greater chance of success if they're able to have the public pushing for this. You believe in the public's right to know, don't you?"

Of course I did; but I had already caused so much pain for my family. This would destroy them and with it, my relationship with them. I also had to consider the danger, including the physical one, that I would be placing myself in once my face could be recognized by certain criminal targets of the FBI investigations. What would I do then, go into witness protection?

Yet, the latest developments, particularly the cover-up by DOD in their non-investigation of Douglas Dickerson, all indicated how tough this fight would be, whether in court or Congress.

"What exactly do they want, the "60 Minutes" people?"

"You won't even come near anything classified," he began. "We will not allow that, as you know; basically, the Dickersons—both of them; the espionage case and blocking intelligence; the disastrous translation department in the FBI and the consequences on our war against terrorism. That's it."

Many consider the media the fourth branch of government. When I had made the decision to proceed with my case and do whatever it takes to shine a big light on what I knew at firsthand to be genuine threats to our security and interests, I resolved to pursue all available channels. I had pursued the obvious three: the Congress, the courts, and, of course, the investigative bodies within the executive branch. The media—the fourth pillar—plays a vital role both as an independent channel and as a mechanism to bring needed pressure on elected officials, particularly those in Congress.

Before a case is pursued by the Congress, it first must become a public issue. Of the one hundred members of the Senate, I had garnered support from only two; as for the House, I had none. My last direct communication and past experience with the DOJ's Office of Inspector General indicated enormous pressure on the investigators and dirty maneuvers by the bureau and Justice Department to steer them as far away as possible from the real issues and threats: those that affect every one of us and have the greatest potential to do us harm. Our latest legal round only reaffirmed our fear that the Justice Department would do everything in its considerable power to prevent us from utilizing the courts to bring about justice and accountability. In my case, I couldn't shake the feeling that the rule of law had been put on hold indefinitely.

"Okay," I said. "Let's do it. When can they come and conduct the on-camera interview?"

Colapinto looked pleased and a bit relieved. "ASAP. I'll call them today and let them know. They'll be here in a few days. I'll be right next to you during the entire interview."

"Okay. Now I'll have to go and drop the bombshell at home. My mother will write me off. Permanently."

He looked genuinely sad. "Tell her it's already out. The warrant for your sister's interrogation by Turkish Intelligence has already proved the fact that their safety was jeopardized when the bureau hired and took in Melek Can Dickerson. In time she'll understand, Sibel." He continued, ". . . Which brings me to my latest news."

I was already rattled. I told him I couldn't take any more news.

He mentioned John Roberts, director of FBI-OPR, to whom I reported my case. "Roberts has officially become our client, as of last month. We now represent his case: a new FBI whistleblower!"

"He blew the whistle? On what? Have they already retaliated against him?"

"Yes and yes. He's been reporting wrongdoing and cover-up of OPR investigations by FBI management for a while. He's been under retaliation for a while, long before you met him."

Apparently, Roberts too couldn't take any more. He'd gone to the same Inspector General and the Senate Judiciary Committee, but the case was not yet public.

"He may appear on the same "60 Minutes" show—with you."

I didn't know what to say. A man in his position, in charge of OPR, was being retaliated against. I thought what happened to me was largely attributable to my low position in the bureau. I was wrong. They didn't at all mind going after bigger fish; they were determined to shoot any messenger, regardless.

By the time I got home, my head was spinning with overload and turmoil from news and developments and decision making. I couldn't go through another trauma, not yet. I decided to wait a few days before breaking the news to my family.

I was going public.

The producers for "60 Minutes" responded as Colapinto had expected. They scheduled our filming for the following week. I had several short pre-shoot interviews with them and a dinner; they wanted me to be comfortable with them. I liked their professional yet sympathetic demeanor.

On the day of filming I took a taxi to a boutique hotel on the edge of Georgetown. CBS had reserved and set up their equipment in one of the hotel's presidential suites. I was nervous and already sweating. By the time I arrived my attorneys were there, waiting. Ed Bradley was in the next room having his makeup applied. I'd done the best I could with my own makeup, focused mainly on hiding the dark circles under my eyes. Thank God they found it sufficient; except for a light dusting of powder, they left me and my face alone.

Ed Bradley entered the main room, where they were all set up and ready. In addition, there were the crew (at least four people), my two attorneys and Matthew. Bradley talked with me for a few minutes, light chat, what they call "icebreakers." My anxiety was building with every passing second. The soundman threaded the cord under my jacket and secured it under my lapel. He asked me to count from one to ten so they could check the sound levels. I did as requested.

They dimmed the room and adjusted the lights to focus on me and on Bradley, sitting only a few feet away. The cameras started rolling and the interview began. Bradley led off with general questions: the importance of translations, and so on. I began to feel more comfortable a few minutes in, but my body was a few steps behind; it was still shaking inside and pouring sweat.

Toward the middle of the session, Bradley asked me about the threats from Dickerson and what it meant to my immediate family in Turkey. I froze; then, as I started to answer, I broke into a violent coughing fit—one of those dry hacking coughs that nests in your windpipe and spews every time you try to speak. They stopped the cameras and handed me water. One crew member brought a few throat lozenges. I chewed the first tablet and sucked on the second. What was happening to me? I am not by nature a shy, timid or nervous person. This was a completely new experience.

They rolled the camera and Bradley continued with other questions. I seemed to be doing just fine, at least until Bradley revisited that question. I had the same violent reaction, a coughing spasm that couldn't be suppressed. That was it. On the deepest level, my body was responding to a suggested threat—in this case, the real one my family faced that moment in Turkey. It was not only embarrassing but also extremely upsetting, for a host of reasons. I turned around and looked at my attorneys, who seemed puzzled and concerned; then I scanned the room and found Matthew. He was standing in the corner, so saddened; he knew exactly what was wrong.

The retakes continued; we tried it several times. At last, with tablets under my tongue during the final minutes, we managed to complete the shoot. I felt so relieved when it was over; my body ceased its frenzied sweat production. I was sure I looked awful and awkward. I didn't care anymore. Most likely, I'd blown it. Maybe they'd decide not to run it.

They asked to let them film me walking with Bradley in the hotel's manicured garden, which we did without sound. Then, thankfully, it was over. I asked the producer when the segment was scheduled to air. He guessed either the third or fourth week in October. That was only slightly more than a month away.

Colapinto approached as I was getting ready to leave. "Now we're going to the next recording," he said. "John Roberts is here and is going on camera in a few minutes."

I asked if I could stop by and see him, to talk with him for a few seconds. Colapinto thought a moment. "I don't think it's a good idea. He may end up becoming one of our witnesses in your case. He may be subpoenaed by Congress on your case or interviewed by DOJ-IG. We don't want anyone to claim that you had talked to each other or synchronized your statements."

I understood; his points made sense. I was exhausted anyway. The anxiety and level of focus it took to answer each question accurately without unintentionally divulging classified information—on top of that neurotic cough, like a panic attack—had utterly worn me out. I wanted to sleep forever, or at least until this nightmare was over. And I still had my family to face. They did not yet know about "60 Minutes" and the path I had just set us on.

The reaction from my mother and sisters on telling them the news was milder than expected, or so I first thought. Instead of the usual hurt and anger, my mother merely nodded, exchanging a look with my middle sister. She talked in a reasonable tone. "In fact, we wanted to talk with you, too. Your sister and I have been discussing this for a while. I guess this is the right time to share our plans with you."

Alarmed, I looked to my sisters and then to my mom. "What plans?"

"Look," she said, "you're thirty-two years old and in charge of your own life. You have all the right to make your own decisions, based on what you believe. We need to think about our life and make decisions for ourselves. We believe now that Lena and your younger sister are working part-time, we can manage to live in our own place. This way we won't burden you with our constant presence; you guys need your privacy too. We've checked out a few places," she continued, "and found a small flat with reasonable rent. Last week we paid the required deposit. We'll move by the end of this month."

I couldn't believe, despite all of us living under the same roof, they had chosen not to tell me until now. "Wow," I said, "you should get a job with the Secret Service. You sure kept this classified."

"Considering all the hardship you've been going through and your hectic schedule, we didn't want to bother you with this. Don't try to make it anything more than that." Then she added, "Do you want us to be exposed to some camera crew that may camp out in front of your house? Do you want our pictures to appear in Turkish papers, TV? You may not care for your face, your picture, being pasted all over the world; we do! For the time being, the further we stay from you the less in danger we'll be. Look, your 'baby sister' is in college, where many other Turkish students happen to attend. She is a much easier target than you, don't you agree?"

"All I want is honesty from you," I replied. "Just be straightforward with me. I understand completely your decision to have a place where you'll have more privacy. I also get your point that the further you are from me the safer you'll be. Then why not let me in on your 'plan'? What kind of a family have we become?" I faced my sisters. "I've been doing my utter best to protect you; maybe unsuccessfully, but I have done my best. What I'm doing today is *not* for some personal selfish reasons, for me. Neither have I chosen this path. I ended up on it before I knew what was happening. Do you understand?"

My younger sister nodded. Lena showed no reaction. I sighed. "I'll help you out with the move and furnishings. You can take anything you want; furniture, kitchenware, et cetera."

I did just that. By October 2, they had moved out.

Gone.

V

STATE SECRETS

12

Invoking the Privilege

In early October 2002, Matthew surprised me with an unexpected tenth year wedding anniversary gift: three full days in London. We were scheduled to leave on Wednesday, October 16, and return on Sunday the 20th. At Matthew's insistence we made a pact: I was not to check my e-mails more than once a day during our trip, and we were not to talk about the case. I accepted his proposal and agreed to live up to my end of it.

Our flight arrived in London at seven in the morning. Despite our inability to sleep during the flight, we decided to start our exploration of London anyway: Covent Garden, a leisurely late breakfast, and afterwards, the entire day on foot, where we checked out exhibits at the National Gallery and Tate Museum, sat by the fireplace in a historic pub and dined at a fantastic Indian restaurant on Oxford Street. That night I slept—more like collapsed—uninterrupted by the usual anxieties. We made it through our first twenty-four hours without a single mention of my case, a major success.

The following day, our anniversary, we explored sites and returned to our hotel late in the afternoon to change for dinner and the theater. We loved the play (Shaw, whom I adore). The evening so far was magical; I couldn't imagine anything more wonderful. We had made it to a decade.

Upon our return to the hotel, as agreed, I went to their 24-hour business center to check e-mails. I logged on and immediately spotted one from my attorney, with a subject line reading *Very Urgent, call me*. I dread-

ed the news. The anxiety and tightness in my chest returned. I turned to
check on Matthew; he was outside, waiting in the lobby. I turned back to
the monitor again, grabbed the mouse tightly and clicked:

Sibel, today Attorney General Ashcroft publicly announced that he was
invoking State Secrets Privilege in your case. It will be all over the news
by tomorrow a.m. This is unbelievable. We are still shocked. This is a
very rare and unknown privilege, worse than the President's Executive
Privilege. I'll go to the library and do research on it; mind-boggling.
Here is the release from his office:

STATEMENT OF BARBARA COMSTOCK, DIRECTOR OF PUB-
LIC AFFAIRS, REGARDING TODAY'S FILING IN SIBEL ED-
MONDS V. DEPARTMENT OF JUSTICE:

"To prevent disclosure of certain classified and sensitive national
security information, Attorney General Ashcroft today asserted the state
secrets privilege in *Sibel Edmonds v. Department of Justice*. This assertion
was made at the request of FBI Director Robert Mueller in papers filed
today in the U.S. District Court for the District of Columbia. The Department of Justice also filed a motion to dismiss the case, because the
litigation creates substantial risks of disclosing classified and sensitive
national security information that could cause serious damage to our
country's security.

"The state secrets privilege is well-established in federal law. It has
been recognized by U.S. courts as far back as the 19th century, and al-
lows the Executive Branch to safeguard vital information regarding the
nation's security or diplomatic relations. In the past, this privilege has
been applied many times to protect our nation's secrets from disclosure,
and to require dismissal of cases when other litigation mechanisms
would be inadequate. It is an absolute privilege that renders the information unavailable in litigation."

I sat and stared at what was before me. I kept reading and reread-
ing the e-mail. What in the name of God was *State Secrets Privilege*? What

did they mean by "to protect national security"? From what I knew, what these agencies were covering up was *endangering* national security. Why had the Justice Department, the attorney general, decided to go this far to cover up my case, my report? I could see the State Department or Pentagon attempting such an outrageous move, but DOJ? How would this affect my IG investigation and their report, expected this month? The IG investigators' boss was Ashcroft—who kept them employed and paid their salaries. How could they issue a real report? My mind was racing, my heart was pounding, and my body had started sweating again.

There were so many questions, and so many possible answers. I knew a lot. What caused this move by Ashcroft? Was it congressional corruption that involved one of the most powerful men in Congress and a few others there? Was it government officials within the State Department and Pentagon, on the payroll of foreign entities who sold our secrets, intelligence and technology? Did this have anything to do with narcotics trafficking, with some of those involved connected to the higher-ups at the State Department, Pentagon, NATO, as well as certain lobbyists? Was it the cover-up related to 9/11—those issues we'd all been warned to keep quiet about?

The more I thought, the more questions arose, and with them, possible answers. Matthew's voice startled me.

"What's wrong? What is it?"

I asked him to come and read it for himself.

Matthew shook his head. "Sibel, what is it that you know that they're after so badly? It must be more than just some FBI incompetence or the Dickersons. It must be something highly explosive. Otherwise, they wouldn't go this far, and we don't know what they may do next. I worry about your safety."

"Not yours?"

"No; I really fear for your safety. We may want to consider moving out of the country for a while. This keeps escalating. Who knows what they may do next?"

"If someone really wanted to do something like that, they could do it easily," I replied. "There really would be no safe place to hide. No bodyguard would be able to protect us."

As soon as we returned home, I Googled *State Secrets Privilege*. The search produced only seven hits. The little I was able to obtain indicated that the privilege was invoked only rarely; it could not be found in the U.S. Code (the code of federal regulations) or the Constitution; it allowed the government to tell a judge that a civil case may expose information detrimental to national security and to ask that testimony or documents be hidden or a lawsuit dismissed.

The privilege, when used, was to prevent plaintiffs from getting hold of very specific, sensitive evidence in an ongoing lawsuit; it was seldom invoked to dismiss entire cases. Yet this is precisely what the attorney general was asking the courts to do. I hoped that my attorneys would be able to shed more light on the privilege and our position to counter it.

When I arrived at Colapinto's office, Kolesnik and Steve Kohn were already waiting. Kolesnik tried to break the ice by joking, "I surely don't want to know what you know; oh man, it must be something!"

It didn't help to break the solemn mood. The question was, now what? What could we do?

On the positive side, Kohn said, the government might be shooting itself in the foot by using this "nuclear option" of all legal maneuvers—that it might end up backfiring. It might get Congress outraged and add media frenzy. On the negative side, if they can use 9/11 to justify this unprecedented level of secrecy to persuade the courts, then we'll have little chance to succeed.

"Sibel," he continued, "when we took your case we thought it was going to be a straightforward whistleblower case. . . . But here we are, facing a completely different case, one characterized by an unseen level of secrecy, espionage, and high-level corruption and criminal acts."

"You're telling me! I didn't even decide to become a whistleblower. I tried to tell you the magnitude of wrongdoing involved . . . The Dickersons are only a fraction of what lies beneath. When the facts come to light, there will be high-level elected and appointed officials standing trial and criminal prosecution. Of course, there are also certain aspects that directly relate to nine eleven."

Kolesnik whistled. "Oh man!"

Kohn shook his head and mumbled, "We didn't sign up for this. Let's see what we can do . . . I'm not optimistic."

I asked about the stalled IG investigation and their report.

Alluding to the requested FBI documents and audio files, Colapinto responded, "We don't know the facts. Maybe they decided not to have you verify them. Either way, that will give us ammunition to hold them liable and responsible if the final report ends up being a half-ass job and a whitewash. Since everything is on record, we'll hold their feet to the fire. I'll call the IG and Senator Grassley's office to check the status of the report." He then continued, "As far as our primary court case goes, the government has asked for an extension due to the latest developments. As soon as they file their response, we'll find out what their argument and strategy is. Then, it will take a tremendous amount of time to research and file our response."

"Guys," Kolesnik reminded them, "don't forget "60 Minutes." It'll be aired in less than a week, and we have to let them know about the privilege. They should mention it in the segment. If it's all right with you, I'll call them and let them know." Everyone agreed. Now, we would buckle up and wait for the segment to air.

Only three days before "60 Minutes" was to air, while we were seated around the dinner table, the phone rang. To my surprise it was Behrooz Sarshar.

He sounded unusually unsure of himself and hesitant to speak. He talked of his battle with FBI management; they had placed him on administrative leave and were ready to fire him soon. He couldn't discuss details and would rather discuss it in person. He mentioned the *Post* article and upcoming CBS program; he said there were other issues he wanted to tell me about related to certain aspects of my case, and wanted to know whether I could meet with him as soon as possible.

I paused. Was he now a plant, sent to milk me for information and trip me up? I didn't want to think that way, so negatively; after all, he had always been kind to me. Yet, I found his timing curious, only days before the piece would air. I could tell from his voice he was distressed and nervous.

"Fine," I said, trusting this wouldn't be a mistake. "Let's meet tomorrow, early afternoon, lunch. Suggest a place." We decided to meet at an Italian café in the mall in Tysons Corner.

After I told Matthew about the meeting and my suspicions, he offered to observe us and our surroundings from a distant table. I thought it was a good idea.

The next day, when I saw Sarshar, he looked sickly and worn out; the spark in his eye was gone. He insisted on treating me to lunch. I accepted and went to grab a table while he waited for our order. I looked around for Matthew. I couldn't find him. Then I looked to see if I could spot the FBI; before I was able to complete my scan, Sarshar showed up with our food.

He began to tell his story. After he had reported to FBI HQ the 9/11-related case involving the Iranian informant and two other cases I hadn't previously known about, management's attitude toward him drastically changed. First, they pulled him off his two most important assignments. Then they called him into a meeting where he was confronted with vague allegations of misconduct. Later, in February (while I was still working there), the bureau interrogated him, charging that he had disclosed classified information about an ongoing FBI investigation under court review. They followed that up with a coerced polygraph test and withheld the results. This was beginning to sound familiar! He was open and sincere. If he were lying, then he sure had me fooled.

Sarshar expected he would be fired in a matter of days. He said he needed legal advice, attorneys.

I told him about my attorney and his law firm. Then he said, "When I reported my case to Mueller and HQ, I also told them about issues that involved your case: about the blueprints case; that on two occasions I had seen Dickerson filling up her large duffel bag with FBI classified documents; that I had seen her removing documents from others' desks, including the Hebrew guy; and that I was aware of indecent relationships between her and Feghali in his office after hours."

I was surprised. I had not expected that much courage from him. Before I was able to ask him anything further, I saw his face turn white, eyes fixed on a spot behind me. He leaned forward and whispered, "I can't believe this. They're here, following us. I recognize one of the guys from HQ, a young agent named Steve. There are two of them standing right behind you, the other one holding a recording device."

I turned around. They were there, all right—they hadn't even taken off their sunglasses, here indoors. "Don't worry," I said. "I'm used to this. They only want to intimidate you. Just ignore them."

At that moment my cell phone rang; it was Matthew. "Hey, I'm sitting on the left side furthest from your table. First I noticed a group of four very FBI-looking guys walk in from outside. Two split off, came to stand right behind you less than ten feet away with something that looks like a recorder. As to the other two, one is standing right outside the entrance door to the mall, and I lost the fourth one."

"Okay, I am aware of the two behind me. We'll leave in a few minutes. Meet us at the exit door on the second floor of Neiman Marcus. Bye."

I told Sarshar about Matthew conducting surveillance. Having four of them tagging us was unusual.

"I also wanted to let you know that the bureau has tapped your phone," Sarshar told me in low tones. "They've been listening to your calls since May; when you speak in Turkish or Farsi, they record it and then have translators go to the second floor and translate it there."

I knew of that possibility, but to have it confirmed was something else. I was outraged.

"Listen," I told him. "I have an idea. I'm going to call my attorneys right now and have them meet with you right away; an hour from now, max. I want you to tell them everything—everything unclassified. I want you to tell them about Dickerson, blueprints, Feghali and, of course, the phone tap and how you got that information. In return, I'm going to ask them—beg them, if necessary—to take your case. What do you say?"

He nodded yes. I called and got Steve Kohn. I brought him up to speed and urged him to meet with Sarshar. Kohn asked us to be there ASAP.

We headed toward Neiman Marcus with two FBI agents shadowing us.

When we met Matthew outside the parking lot, I quickly filled him in. Since he had to work and the attorneys' office was on the way, we decided to have him follow us to Georgetown, with me riding shotgun with Sarshar. Once we were on the highway, my cell phone rang. It was Matthew, calling to let us know that we were being tailed by a white van.

We arrived at the law office and parked a block away. Kolesnik and Kohn were waiting. I told them about the tail and the team in the mall. Kolesnik went outside to look, then came back in. "Guys, come out and look." He motioned to us. "The white van is right in front of our building, illegally parked in the space reserved for loading."

We all stepped outside and looked. The van's passenger door swung open and a clean-shaven white guy in his early thirties, dressed in a crisp white shirt, tie and khakis stepped out. He shut the door, leaned with his back against the vehicle and stared at us. Then he pulled out sunglasses, put them on and smirked.

Kohn asked us back in. They were clearly rattled. They told me that as a caution against tainting a possible future witness I couldn't be present during their meeting with Sarshar.

Sarshar's session with my attorneys lasted more than an hour. He would report his case to the IG and FBI-OPR. Until he was fired, Sarshar couldn't bring any case in court. I asked Kohn whether they'd gotten his statements regarding my case and Dickerson. He smiled. "But of course, with Kolesnik present as a witness." I was relieved; we had our first official witness.

When we left, the white van was still there.

My segment on "60 Minutes" was due to air on October 27, 2002, a Sunday. That morning I went out to buy a blank tape, and by the time I returned there was a message from Colapinto asking me to call him at home. *Hmm*, I wondered. *Have they canceled the segment?*

He answered the phone with, "You won't believe these FBI clowns, they are f—ing out of their mind!"

"Now what?" I asked wearily.

"Last night, knowing that it was Saturday, knowing that it was evening, they faxed us this ridiculous letter saying that they had found out about "60 Minutes" and that you had no right to appear on that show and make comments not approved or reviewed by them! Can you believe these jerks? Basically, at the eleventh hour they are asking you to back out; they're threatening you with criminal prosecution—as if your attorneys were born yesterday!"

"Well, can they come and arrest me? Can they prosecute me criminally? I didn't divulge anything classified!"

"They're stupid enough to try. They won't get anywhere with it. This is another intimidation tactic by them; just the usual."

"What will I do if they show up to arrest me?"

". . . Write down Steve's home number and you have mine. Anything happens you call us; do not answer any questions without us present. Understood?" He gave me Steve's home number and we hung up.

That night, as Matthew and I watched the segment, I was holding a page with the list of numbers to call and persons to contact in case they came knocking on our door. I had also instructed Matthew to call my attorneys, Kolesnik, "60 Minutes" investigators and all the major newspapers in the country. I thought, *This must be how people under Fascist regimes feel, not only for one night, but for years, for their entire lifetime.*

The knock didn't come that night. Nor did it come the following morning. Yet all my tension, fear and violent emotions would stay with me—not as intimidation, a deterrent, but rather as a catalyst to fight back, to resist, and to pursue what our country had cherished for centuries: the freedom to speak out.

My father, F. R. Deniz, during college-1964

My father (on the far right) in medical school during his residency exam-1966

My mother, S. Deniz, in Istanbul-1968

My parents during their
engagement party

Wedding picture of my parents

I am three months old and enjoying the warm afternoon sun
during the winter with my parents

Riding my first pretend horse at 9 months of age

Riding the waves with my parents in the Caspian Sea - Azerbaijan

Victory was one of the first sign languages my father taught me. Here I am practicing it with my father on the hospital grounds where my father worked.

My Pre-school Entry Photo in Istanbul

My father as the director of the hospital during the Shah's visit in Tehran-1978

Enjoying the weekend at the park with my sister a few months before the regime change in Iran-1978

My sister and I clad in mandatory scarf and covering for primary
school post revolution in 1981

With my two sisters during one of our transition periods

College years in Washington DC   Skiing in Colorado

Our wedding in 1992
in the mountains of
Virginia

Wedding photograph
with my parents

Blown by the wind in St. Petersburg, Russia during our work project-1993

With the director of the children's hospital in St. Petersburg, Russia during our work project

Enjoying a long weekend with my dad in Charlottesville, Virginia-1994

Summer in the middle of snow in Switzerland-1995

"60 Minutes" and my first media exposure and interview-2002

produced by
MICHAEL RADUTZKY
TANYA SIMON

LOST in Translation

Does this woman know too much?

Edmonds took her charges to the U.S. Senate.

Sibel Edmonds says she has damning evidence of security breaches at the FBI. Her supporters call her a brave whistle-blower; her critics have taken steps to silence her. Here's why she won't back down——and what it's cost her. By Sheila Weller

A shot taken by Glamour Magazine during one of my congressional visits to deliver petitions

Vanity Fair Article right before my Supreme Court Case decision in September 2005

With Dr. Jeff Fudin during one of our many meetings on government whistleblowers legislation

With whistleblower Russ Tice, John Cole and Lt. Col. Anthony Shaffer during the first ever national security whistleblowers conference and retreat in Chincoteague, Virginia

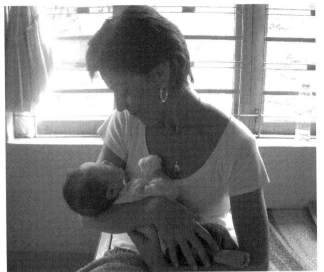

One of my most favorite photos with my daughter, Ela, at Phu Hai orphanage in Vietnam

At Phu Hai Orphanage, spending every day with Ela

Ela's first dress-up session on her first day in our hotel room in Mui Ne, Vietnam

On the beach with Ela in front of our hotel suite on Mui Ne Beach

Enjoying full-time motherhood upon our return from Vietnam

Our long weekend hiking trip in July 2009 to celebrate Ela's first birthday

NOVEMBER 2009

The American Conservative

Who's Afraid of Sibel Edmonds?
The gagged FBI whistleblower
on espionage, al-Qaeda,
and secrets for sale

The Five Faces of Jerry Brown
Jesse Walker

We Are Not All Keynesians Yet
William A. Niskanen

The Wrong Way to Reform the Right
W. James Antle III

American Conservative
Magazine Cover for
October 2009

Launching Boiling Frogs
Post news and editorial site
to counter the mainstream
media

13

The Judge Game

For the first four months after Attorney General Ashcroft invoked the (then) ultra-rare State Secrets Privilege to block my case from moving forward in the courts—in effect, gagging me and my reports—activity in my court case consisted of the government requesting delays in filing its response and the IG postponing release of its report.

During the first week in November 2002 I called my attorney to inquire about the status of the IG report. After contacting the Senate offices that same day, Colapinto called to let me know that the IG had extended the release date to early January. According to the Senate staff, the IG had been unsuccessful in obtaining the relevant files from the bureau and had come up with additional witnesses who had to be interviewed—in other words, more foot-dragging. Was this a coordinated attempt by the DOJ and the IG office? How would this affect everything else we were doing: our FOIA claim, our primary case, and the ongoing congressional investigation that was largely dependent on completion of this report?

Colapinto shared my concerns, yet our hands were tied, he said. We had to sit and wait. One positive note, he assured me: our case was in the hands of a reputable judge, Judge James Robertson. Once the case got to the discovery stage and hearings, he promised, we would be vindicated.

That only cause for optimism, our one good fortune in having a just judge, would be taken away in less than three months. The government that had gone to such lengths had more in store for me; and as my attorneys and I waited for justice to take its course, unseen actors were plotting their next move to shoot the downed messenger again.

On February 6, 2003, about six months after we had filed our primary case with the district court and less than four months after the attorney general had invoked the State Secrets Privilege, the court notified us that my case had been removed from Judge Robertson and was now assigned to Judge Reggie Walton—a recent appointee of President George W. Bush. No reason was cited by the court for this unforeseen and highly suspicious move.

Very briefly, from what Colapinto had been able to find out, Judge Walton had assumed his position as a U.S. District Judge for the District of Columbia in October 2001 after being nominated to the position by Bush and confirmed by the Senate. Between 1989 and 1991, he had served as Poppy Bush's associate director of the Office of National Drug Control Policy in the White House. Walton had been a Bush-team insider for years. He had risen quickly in the Washington legal establishment, earning an appointment from former president Reagan to a District of Columbia superior court judgeship. He was later taken under the wing of the self-styled man of virtue William Bennett, serving as a top gun in the White House Office of National Drug Control Policy during Bennett's tenure there.

Based on this scrap, I could smell conspiracy and predict with near certainty an upcoming disaster for us in this man's court. The bureau's retaliation against my report and the arcane state secrets ploy had occurred on this administration's watch, more likely than not with their knowledge and approval. Walton was their pick; he was their man.

I was concerned about Walton's previous position in the office of the drug czar. I knew of illegal narcotics activities that involved obtaining, moving and distributing opium-derived products from the East—mainly Afghanistan—to Western Europe and the United States by Joint Turkish and Albanian organized crime, with full cooperation of certain arms of NATO and with the full knowledge of the State Department and certain individuals in the Pentagon. I was also aware of the intentional cover-up by the U.S. government, or at least certain components, that included not only protecting the players from becoming targets of real investigations by U.S. law enforcement agencies (including the DEA) but in some cases supplementing their operations. After all, the proceeds from these illegal activities went a long way toward enabling Turkey and some Central Asian countries to procure U.S.–made weapons and materiel, some of which ended up in countries under international sanctions via false end user certificates and other illegal arms sales channels.

In 2003, we were not aware of *half* of the red flags alerting us to Reggie Walton. In the years ahead, other deeply troubling facts about him would come to light.

All federal judges are required under ethics rules to file what are known as *financial disclosure reports*. The disclosure statement filed by Walton, obtained in 2005 by a conservative watchdog group, Judicial Watch, was completely redacted, every line of it. The entire document was blacked out.

Judge Walton was one of a very few—in fact, less than a handful—of federal judges who had redacted every single word from his financial disclosure statement. What was hiding in his fiscal closet? He refused to disclose his participation or interest in any businesses outside his job with the court. Did he have financial shares in any of the more than one hundred foreign front companies engaged in narcotics, money laundering and illegal arms sales (and, thus, the necessary bribing and blackmailing of elected and appointed U.S. government officials)? Did Walton serve on the boards of any of the many nonprofit and lobbying front organizations that were movers and shakers within these shadowy, illegal networks?

Also, notably, that same year Judge Walton just happened to be "randomly" assigned to another high-profile whistleblower's case, in which a top White House aide, Scooter Libby, was indicted: the so-called Valerie Plame affair. Joseph Wilson, Plame's husband and a former ambassador, alleged (along with others) that the disclosure of Plame's identity as a former CIA agent was done purposely, in retaliation for Wilson's criticism and whistleblowing, and that such illegal disclosure, or "outing," did in fact endanger both Plame and national security. Per the CIA's request, a special counsel was appointed to lead the investigation, and when the case targeting primarily White House officials was filed, low and behold, Walton appeared as the judge. Quite randomly, I'm sure.

I wanted a straightforward counterattack. My attorneys tried to persuade me otherwise, yet I asked them nonetheless to file a motion with the courts requesting that they investigate this suspicious transfer—to at least give us one good reason why it was done. I was told of the unwritten pact among judges to protect one another and watch each other's backs. According to my attorneys, if we were to do what I suggested, we'd "piss off" Walton and get on the wrong side of the court and other judges.

"Are you suggesting that we do nothing and let them get away with this?"

They had a plan, Colapinto explained. "You have another case: your FOIA claim before Judge Huvelle. That case was filed before your primary case . . . There is a law . . . that says if two separate claims are relevant, deal with the same plaintiff and defendant, then if one case, for whatever reason, has to be transferred from one judge to another, the presiding judge on the other relevant claim should be given the case." He continued, "Basically, according to this law, we can file a claim with the court saying that your cases are considered relevant 'sister' cases. Thus this case should be removed from Walton and assigned to Huvelle, who has presided on your FOIA case since July."

That made perfect sense. They would file the request within the next four weeks.

I asked them about the IG report. Here it was already February, and I had not heard anything. None of my calls to the Senate had been returned. I had asked my attorney and Kolesnik, who had high-level contacts at Senator Grassley's office, to look into it.

They exchanged peculiar glances. Finally, Colapinto cleared his throat. "Sibel, we finally got a response from the senator's office. The IG notified them of another short delay, extension. They promised the Senate the report will be released by the end of April, only two months from now . . . this time they actually promised. According to what we heard from the Senate, the IG is done with the investigation and is busy typing and reviewing the final report before releasing it."

I exploded. "What do they mean by that? They haven't responded to Sarshar's request to be interviewed; he is one of my witnesses. According to Sarshar, the IG has not contacted the two counterterrorism agents or Amin for an interview. Matthew has not been interviewed. Now they say they're finished? Typing my ass! What's the Senate going to do? Just sit there and take this bullshit indefinitely? . . . What's the point in asking for an expedited and thorough report, when these guys lie through their teeth and make a mockery of this entire process?"

I paused to catch my breath. "I'm tired of this. I've had it. I cannot take this anymore . . ."

"Okay, you know what, I had forgotten about these witnesses not being interviewed," Colapinto admitted, partly, I'm sure, to try to calm me. "I'll draft a letter this evening and send it to the IG. I promise." I silently nodded. Everybody sat there in silence. The meeting was obviously over.

On March 13, 2003, one month after the case was mysteriously transferred to Judge Walton, we filed our motion to retransfer the case to Judge Ellen Huvelle, the presiding judge over my FOIA case, based on the fact that the two cases were related.

To our joy and relief, on May 7, the court granted our motion. They removed my case from Walton and transferred it to Huvelle.

The sense of vindication and relief lasted only two short days. On May 9, two days after we were notified of our victory, we received a court notification letter informing us that they had retransferred the case from Huvelle back to Walton. No reason provided.

The Department of Justice and FBI had not given up their game of shopping for judges. I was now up against the director of the FBI, Mueller; the attorney general of the United States, Ashcroft; the Justice Department's IG, Glenn Fine; and the federal court in DC.

There was nothing else we could do. We had to bite the bullet and fight a losing battle. Not only that, come April, the IG once again failed to issue any report. This time, the IG didn't even bother to provide an expected release date.

In early April, after letters from Colapinto, the IG finally interviewed Matthew in the presence of my attorneys. They had yet to interview Sarshar, though, and I had not been asked to go and verify the FBI files that would vindicate me. I knew that report would never come out. Sure, they'd release something once the 2004 presidential election was over, after all the key suspects and witnesses were long gone, including Ashcroft. Whatever ended up being released, I was quite certain that the substance of their internal investigation would be classified, falsified, or diluted completely.

Then, too, the Senate became puzzlingly quiet. They were no longer communicating with my attorneys or with me. Had the government gotten to our supporters and allies in Congress? Was it as Agent Saccher had warned me about—that these senators had been blackmailed into silence? I was told the administration played rough.

Strangest of all was the resignation and coolness I'd detected in my attorneys that month. I knew they had not expected this. I had seen their shock and fear; I saw their justifiable reluctance to take on Walton.

My attorneys had recently experienced another rare and unexpected development: on our FOIA case, Judge Huvelle had ordered the FBI to present the court with a Vaughn Index (an index–list) of every document they were withholding. The government had produced the list but requested that it be released only to the judge, ex parte and in camera.

They asked the judge to withhold it from us, citing sensitivity, secrecy and national security. Even more unsettling, Huvelle had granted their request. So here we were, ready to file, but how could we argue against something we didn't know? The reasons and list were secret. We couldn't have access to either. Yet we were expected to argue against them.

Our earlier court date of March 6, 2003, had been postponed at the eleventh hour by Walton until July 25—over four months. While disappointed, my attorneys were not too upset, since they believed we would have at that time the much-anticipated IG report, which was expected to play a major role in the hearing and bolster the strength of their argument.

Of course, the IG report was *not* released by July, and our FOIA case hit an appalling snag. In a rare move, the government decided to classify the entire list of items they were withholding—the entire Vaughn Index. Still, we looked forward to the status hearing and our chance to actually argue the case and respond to the government's assertions.

Less than twenty-four hours before the scheduled date on July 25, Judge Walton's clerk issued another notification letter. The hearing, scheduled for the following day, was now canceled and postponed until mid-October. Again, no reasons were given.

Walton lived up to our predictions. He would drag this out and prevent a public hearing for as long as he could—and that proved a long time. The scheduled October hearing would be canceled almost without notice. No other hearing date was set. He would sit on this case for almost two years before deciding to inflict one last orchestrated blow.

By the end of July, my relationship with my attorneys—the only people I had truly relied on and worked with since the day I was fired—had come to its end.

I knew they were competent. I trusted their judgment and sound strategic planning. But now, at this stage, I could see that they had lost their focus and, in a way, their faith in pursuing the case. They had not signed up for the State Secrets Privilege, the spy game, and a mammoth government scandal.

At the end of July, we finally had the inevitable meeting: the point at which we parted ways. After a year and a half of nonstop roller coaster, I had reached the end of one stage and begun the next without even realizing it. My case was most likely a losing proposition, but I was resolved in my demand for unconditional faith and the quest for truth in my attorneys, whoever they might be. I wanted someone who would fight based on principles, not a settlement. For me, winning is and always will be about accountability, bringing about needed changes and reform: true vindication. As to compensation, think about it: if it were that easy to turn a blind eye to secrecy, lawbreaking and systemic corruption, I could have kept my mouth shut and spared everyone such agony.

I know those who call themselves realists, those who practice in private law, the politicians, would consider my quest and objectives futile, unrealistic, naïve; maybe even downright stupid. Maybe they had given up on those principles—if they ever had them in the first place. Regardless of their warnings and advice, I would remain true to my beliefs. I would be true to myself. I would be my father's daughter, for as long as I could, for as long as I lived.

14

9/11 Commission

In May 2003, during the height of the publicity and intense media coverage on the formation of the 9/11 Commission to investigate all the facts and issues related to the terrorists' attack, I decided to contact the commission and offer my report. I prepared a short letter to introduce myself with my request that I be interviewed. I sent the letter to the commission's two offices in DC, and after many follow-ups, I was finally able to speak with the person in charge of scheduling witnesses to be interviewed.

After confirming that they had received my fax and letter, the woman told me that due to limited time, they would not be able to schedule an interview session for me.

I asked whether she wanted the names of special agents and language specialists who could provide them with extremely important information. She declined my offer and hung up without waiting for my response. I shrugged and gave up trying. I had become numb to our government's indifference. I was already drowning in my own battle, and considering the colossal failure of the Congressional Joint Intelligence Inquiry to investigate, address and get to the bottom of 9/11, I decided to not bother pursuing the so-called commission.

The summer of 2003 went by fast. I had already given up on the Justice Department's Inspector General's report; they had gone a year beyond the promised delivery date and didn't seem likely to release anything anytime soon. I had lost my FOIA case due to the government's secrecy tactics, which included classifying even the *list* of items in their possession. Of more than 1,500 pages of documents on my case, the judge ordered the government to release about 200 pages, which consisted of several copies of my own attorneys' letters to them and their written responses, several copies of each article printed in the media dealing with my case, and numerous copies of public letters sent by congressional members to the FBI and Justice Department.

As far as my primary court case went, with Walton as the presiding judge, I couldn't see a single reason for optimism. In addition, I no longer had an attorney and I was on my own.

Meanwhile, I called and e-mailed any organization I could find that dealt with whistleblowers and First Amendment cases, those who claimed to be fighting excessive secrecy and executive branch abuses of power. I needed their support and expertise, yet in spite of the fact that my case embodied all these civil liberties, not a single organization lifted a finger to contact me, call me back, or offer any assistance. (While it was a hard blow and a tough pill to swallow at the time, this experience helped me a great deal a few years later, when I formed my own coalition, network and organization to deal with and help government whistleblowers.)

My relationship with my family had ceased to exist. For their own protection and security we had to cease all contacts until . . . well, no one could even begin to predict. Every minute of every day I felt the pang, void, and longing. There was a hole in me.

Matthew as well lost two of his closest friends after the "60 Minutes" piece aired, one of whom he'd known for fifty years. Mostly, we had been deserted by everyone we knew. We had to borrow to meet the payment schedule for my legal fees and were under terrific financial pressure. Up to this point, we seemed to have lost every battle; it felt as though every viable channel pursued had stalled, and that every door we'd knocked on, from Congress to the courts, had been slammed in our face.

During our 2003 Thanksgiving dinner, with only two of us at the table, I had only one thing to be thankful for: my husband had stood by me and taken every blow delivered with such vengeance by our so-called Justice Department, our premier "law enforcement" agency and most injudicious judiciary.

One Sunday afternoon in December, a week or so before Christmas in 2003, I received from an acquaintance an e-mail with a link to an article. The sender thought it would be of interest. She was right.

The article was a very thorough piece written by *New York Observer* reporter Gail Sheehy on the relentless time and energy spent by four 9/11 widows in New Jersey to pressure Congress and the 9/11 Commission to do what they should have been doing from the start: get out the facts and truth on the 9/11 attacks and our failures leading up to them; bring about accountability for those responsible (whether through criminal acts, intent or incompetence); and bring about real reform rather than the cosmetic fixes put in place since 9/11.

The story was effective and touching on many levels. Here were four housewives—young mothers, grieving widows—who had chosen to do something about injustice and fight against the powerful in Washington, instead of burying themselves in their grief and outrage.

According to the story, these women had taken on some powerful senators and congressmen. They opposed and successfully replaced as chairman of the 9/11 Commission the infamous Henry Kissinger. They were urging people with information to come forward and disclose it to the commissioners; the list went on. How impressive. I respected their courage, persistence and resolve; I applauded their style. I utterly agreed with their assessment of what had happened, what had to be known, and what needed to happen next. Above all, their story made me reconsider my previous decision not to pursue the 9/11 Commission after my brief, frustrating interaction with it.

I sat by the fire and reread the article several times. It made me feel more determined than ever to press on with my case. I wondered if they knew about the commissioners' response and attitude toward people with relevant information. I wondered what their reaction would be to the cases and issues I had encountered in the bureau that dealt with 9/11.

I would contact them directly and find out. I brought the phone to the kitchen table and dialed 411. I started with the group's leader, Kristen Breitweiser. The operator explained it was an unlisted number. I asked her to try a second name, Mindy Kleinberg, New Jersey. Yes, she had the number. I quickly wrote it down, hung up, and dialed again. I didn't know where to start or how to introduce myself. Mindy picked up on the third ring.

I told her my name and apologized for calling her on a Sunday. Then I went on autopilot and gave her a summary of my experience with the 9/11 Commission, the type of information involved, and my background.

She sounded truly appalled by what the 9/11 Commissioner had said to me. She almost screamed, "These bastards! They promised us, they gave us their word, that they would not turn away a single source, witness or document. I cannot believe this!" To my relief she was appreciative and extremely knowledgeable on various intelligence issues, cases and incidents related to the FBI and 9/11.

"I need to contact the other three, Kristen, Lorie and Patty, right away," she told me. "Will you be available later this afternoon? I would like to arrange for a conference call and have them ask you questions and hear what those bastards have done. Would that be okay?" Yes, surely. We exchanged our contact information and she said she would be in touch.

Two hours later, I had a conference call with Kristen, Lorie and Mindy. Mindy asked me to repeat to the others what I had told her earlier. They reacted in the same way: they found it inexcusable. "What you told us is in line with other calls and reports we've received from various former and current intelligence and law enforcement employees," Lorie said. We've had people from the CIA, FBI, FAA—you name it—contacting us and basically telling us of similar experiences with this commission."

Kristen, the leader, got straight to the point. "We need to bring public attention to this. Of course, that's assuming we'll get the goddamn
main media's attention; so far they've been *disastrous*. Before that, we
need to gather all those who have gone through an experience similar
to Sibel's and drag them with us into the commissioners' office—and let
them refuse to interview them if they dare!"

They wanted to know about the details. Most of those I could not
discuss, due to classification. They asked for names of other witnesses
related to my case; I preferred not to discuss them over the phone, especially after Sarshar had confirmed that mine was tapped.

Kristen suggested we meet right away.

We decided on the following Friday at two at the Hyatt Hotel in downtown Baltimore.

That evening I faxed them the letters and e-mail I had sent to the 9/11
Commission as well as the dates of the follow-up calls to their offices. I
told Matthew about the conversation and our plan to meet. He thought it
was a very good idea. I began to feel re-energized. I was glad I had made
the decision to contact the Jersey Moms. I knew I couldn't have done that
if I were still represented by attorneys.

In this instance, I had to use my own judgment and common sense;
to make a decision based on what I knew directly and perceived to be the
case with the other party and *just go with it*. This is how I had lived my life
before. From the day I began working for the bureau until a few months
earlier, when abandoned by my attorneys, I had lived and acted according to restrictions and nonsensical rules and regulations imposed by the
FBI, the Inspector General, Congress, my attorneys . . . there seemed
to be more and more of them, shutting me down. As of this day, after
talking with the Jersey Moms, I began a new stage in my battle—not just
my own but in others' too that soon I would end up joining. This was a
beginning, another new stage; in some ways, another turning point.

That Friday I arrived at the hotel early. Around fifteen minutes past the appointed hour, I noticed two women walking toward me: Mindy and Kristen. While each was rather different, both had certain features in common: deep and very dark wells under their eyes and facial lines that screamed exhaustion. That made three of us. The hollows under my eyes seemed to have become permanent. I liked these women right away; I sensed a kinship in our fighting a no-win war: Davids against Goliath.

We hugged each other and sat. I spoke for almost an hour, telling them all I could. They listened almost without blinking, took in everything I said, and stopped me to ask detailed questions.

Afterwards we talked about other potential witnesses who had either been turned away or were too afraid to have even contacted the commission. They asked me if I would be willing to join the fight to bring these cases to light. I told them, "Absolutely."

They asked whether I could get Sarshar to go to the commissioners. I would. They thought I had a better chance of getting in touch with former law enforcement and intelligence people, other whistleblowers. I agreed. We had about six months before the commissioners' so-called investigation came to an end. We needed to get as many people to come forward as possible. That was our plan.

After New Year's I contacted Sarshar. I had not heard from him since the previous January, when he had called to say that he had reported the case to the DOJ-IG in writing and had not heard back. He had been given the option of voluntary early retirement. He was thinking about it. His wife was not supportive of his taking a stand. She wanted him to walk away. Thinking of my mother—as well as most everybody else—I knew just how he felt.

I told him briefly about my meeting with the Jersey Moms. I asked him to contact the 9/11 Commission and ask to be interviewed. He knew a great deal.

He laughed. "Sibel, I contacted them last June. I wrote to them. They said they didn't need any more information, and that they had more than enough witnesses and documents to make the case and issue a report."

"What! Did you keep the letter, log the calls?"

"But of course; I worked for the bureau for over ten years, my friend!"

I asked him to meet with me and the Jersey Moms—to let them know. He explained that he had been threatened and harassed to keep his mouth shut. He didn't want any more problems from the FBI.

I called the Jersey Moms and told them what I had just learned, talking with Sarshar.

"We need to meet with him, right away!" Kristen screamed. "In fact, we need to have a reporter with us and have him go on record. Damn it, I want to go and puke all over these people—the commissioners' investigators."

"Slow down," I cautioned, "he's afraid. He's a timid man with no support from his wife. He has taken a lot of shit in the past two years from the FBI. You go tell him the word *reporter* and he'll move out of the state. Let me approach him and convince him slowly, okay?"

They agreed, but they also emphasized urgency. I asked them to give me a week.

I called Sarshar and left several messages. More than a week later, he called me back. (He didn't have the heart to say no so he was avoiding my calls instead.)

After an hour of persuasion, he agreed to meet with them. I asked when would be the earliest he could meet with us. He said the following Sunday, January 18.

"Okay, you got it, Sunday it is."

The moms would arrange for baby-sitters and get to DC for a late lunch on Sunday. They also called their friend, a female reporter who lived in New York City (whom I had met), and asked her to be present at the meeting. The reporter had to rearrange travel plans and catch the redeye to DC, but said she wouldn't miss it for anything. I would pick her up from Reagan National Airport, near my house.

That Saturday we ended up getting three inches of snow that turned to sleet, and by Sunday morning, a severe advisory was issued. The roads, even parts of the beltway, were covered with thick layers of ice.

Mindy's call woke me up at seven. She said the meeting had to be canceled and rescheduled. I asked her to hold while I checked my e-mails and voice mails. Sure enough, the reporter had left LA and would be in DC at eleven that morning.

I told Mindy, "Listen, it took me hours to persuade Sarshar; he can change his mind tomorrow. This woman reporter is on her way here. We have to have this meeting today."

She argued there was no way they could drive that far and if I didn't believe her, just go out and look for myself.

I had an idea. Putting her on hold, I went up to the bedroom and asked Matthew, "Can you be kind enough to drive Sarshar and me to New Jersey?"

He looked at me as though I had two heads. "You're kidding me! Have you seen the conditions out there?"

"Matthew, I'm begging you . . . What if it's only to Wilmington? That's only two hours away . . . Please . . ."

He sighed. "Okay, we'll go out there and try. If it's too bad we'll turn around and come back home. OK?"

I told Mindy about the plan. "Listen, get your ass down to Wilmington, it's only an hour and a half from where you girls live. You have a four-wheel drive, let's do this."

After two hours of back and forth calls between the girls and me and Sarshar, we were finally set to give this meeting a shot. Matthew and I drove forty-five minutes from where we live to pick up Sarshar. Everything was ice. We drove 25 miles per hour on a major highway; the beltway was almost deserted. We pulled up in front of Sarshar's house and before I even made it out of the car, he appeared and got in. Then we had to turn around and drive to Reagan Airport, where Matthew double-parked in front while I ran inside to find the reporter who had landed only minutes before.

I found her at the baggage carousel, having a major fit. The airline had lost her luggage. She was all over the flight attendant and the argument was going nowhere. We didn't have the luxury of time.

I pulled the attendant aside. "What's the best way we can resolve this? Can you track it and have it sent to this lady's place in NYC?"

"Wait here for a minute."

Five minutes later she was back; they had been able to trace the whereabouts of the luggage and placed instructions to have it onboard the first available flight to NYC. With that resolved we walked outside and waited for Matthew to reappear. Knowing her excellent but aggressive reporting style, I warned her. "Listen, go easy on Sarshar, understood? He's very nervous and unsure, don't freak him out; take it easy." She nodded.

Two hours later, as we were approaching Baltimore, the reporter tried to get Sarshar to talk by asking him some general questions. After a few minutes, Sarshar eased up and started to answer. The reporter made her next move: unwisely, she pulled out her tape recorder. "Can I record this conversation?" Sarshar vehemently shook his head no and retreated into his shell. For the remaining couple of hours we rode in silence.

When we pulled up in front of the Holiday Inn in Wilmington, I spotted Kristen, Mindy and Patty out front smoking. We parked and went inside. For the next three hours we sat around a large table in the hotel's dining room and talked. The reporter did not attempt to push the tape recorder again. The girls fired off hundreds of questions and took detailed notes, about the Iranian informant in particular, but also on many other issues and cases. I could tell Sarshar liked them and was comfortable.

In the end, the Jersey Moms told me they were going to contact the 9/11 Commission and set up a meeting regarding the turning away of witnesses. They asked me to participate. They also wanted to set up times for me and Sarshar to be interviewed. Considering Sarshar's justifiable apprehension, I suggested we set up a meeting with Senator Grassley's staff—all of us—to demand that they issue some sort of immunity for those witnesses and whistleblowers reluctant to testify before Congress and the commission.

This was just the beginning.

After the first *Washington Post* article on my case, a year and a half earlier, I had spent weeks fruitlessly trying to find contact information for the second FBI whistleblower cited in that article, John M. Cole, FBI Counterintelligence Operations Specialist in charge of Pakistan and Afghanistan. My (then) attorneys introduced me to Emmanuel (Manny) Johnson, a former veteran agent with the FBI counterterrorism division. After blowing the whistle and suffering cruel retaliation, Manny had resigned from his job at the FBI, set up his own private investigation firm, and once in a while performed investigative services for my attorneys. All he was able to find out was that Cole had resigned and left the city after tremendous pressure and attacks by the bureau following the *Post* article. He would let me know if he ever came across other agents from the FBI Washington Field Office familiar with my case. For over a year I did not hear from him.

One early afternoon near the end of January, I received a call from Manny. He wanted to arrange a meeting between me and a veteran counterintelligence special agent, recently retired from the FBI's Washington field office, who had firsthand information related to my case. I asked him for this agent's name and held my breath.

"Special Agent Gilbert Graham."

"You mean *the* Gil Graham, in charge of FBI's Counterintelligence unit on Turkey?!" The very same. "Do you know how important he is to my case? My God, one copy of every piece I translated related to DC operations was sent to him! He knows a lot!"

Manny laughed. "Of course; why do you think I'm calling you? I've known Graham for years. He contacted me a few weeks after the CBS piece aired and told me about his connection. It took me this long to persuade him to meet with you directly. He's under retaliation himself . . ."

I asked him to set up the meeting ASAP. We agreed on a coffeehouse in Alexandria. I got there ten minutes early. At the counter, I felt a hand on my shoulder, and there was Manny with his usual wide, sincere smile. African American, of medium height, his eyes always appeared to sparkle with unexplained joy. With his domelike belly and shaved head, he reminded me of Buddha.

Behind him stood a strikingly handsome African-American man with pronounced cheekbones, over six feet two, muscular build and broad shoulders, dressed impeccably in a pressed suit and a crisp shirt. Graham and I had never before met face to face. He was impressive to behold.

Once seated, I started telling Graham about my case. He raised his palm to stop me. He said he already knew everything there was, at least most of it. It was his turn to tell me about his case, what he had blown the whistle on, and the connection to my case and what I knew (cryptically, of course).

According to Graham, back in 1997 he and other agents involved in counterintelligence operations (in which I too had become involved) notified HQ about Turkish targets targeting certain elected officials. Through various bribery and blackmail operations, they had hooked these officials and were able to obtain classified information and, in some cases, favorable contracts and votes from them. At least four well-known elected officials were involved in this scheme.

The illegal activities did not end there. State Department bureaucrats and Pentagon officials were also hooked. The targets were provided with highly sensitive classified documents and information. Considering the targets' direct involvement in nuclear black market illegal arms sales and money laundering activities, this case, in Graham's assessment, had to be transferred from Counterintelligence (geared only to monitor, not investigate) to criminal and Counterterrorism operations. The agents also believed that they had enough proof, evidence and direct information to get the Department of Justice to launch a criminal investigation of the U.S. persons involved, and perhaps even appoint a special counsel–prosecutor to the case.

While I knew his story to be true, I hadn't known the grisly details.

Graham continued. "This was during the Clinton administration. The Justice Department, under Janet Reno, finally agreed to appoint counsel and move forward with our recommendations. There were some disagreements as to whether to pursue elected officials or appointed ones; they had finally settled on elected officials. But then we were hit by the scandals involving Clinton's dick, so there it went, down the tubes; the whole thing was put on hold and set aside while the entire country dealt with who gave whom a blow job!"

I interrupted him. "You mean *permanently*?"

He shook his head. "No, for a while. Then it seemed to get back on a track a little, but then came the elections. With the Clinton administration gone and the new administration in the process of taking over, we didn't hear anything back from the Justice Department. When we did, well, that outraged every single one of us, and led me to put my foot down. The Bush administration, AG Ashcroft, turned off the switch on the special prosecutor deal. Then, they chopped the operation into several pieces, with one of them going to Chicago. Finally, toward the end of 2001, they decided to close the criminal investigation angle. They shut down the DC operations and gave Chicago until January or February to get rid of the case and close it for good."

"So, what was their excuse with you?" I asked. "What happened to you and your report?"

"Basically, same thing that happened to you. They first asked me to shut up and stop pursuing this. Then, of course, the retaliation began. After a while I couldn't take it anymore; they pushed me to the point where I requested and filed for early retirement. Once that was done,

I filed a case in DC federal court, pro se; the only way I could bring out the case, and the most viable channel, was the EEO [Equal Employment Opportunity Commission]. Now they are going after my filings, a lot of it classified with a black marker. Considering what they did to you," he added, "and how afraid they are, I expect they'll invoke state secrets in my case too; once they get away with yours, they'll try it with my case. I believe your case is their 'experiment' case; if successful, they'll use it right and left."

I wanted to know if he would be willing to testify in court as my witness—if he would consider visiting the Senate with me and providing them with this explosive information. With twenty-two years under his belt, impeccable reputation and firsthand knowledge of what truly was involved in my case, I needed him on my side, prepared and ready to testify.

He sighed. "Sibel, that's the most important reason I wanted to meet with you. Forget about pushing this via Congress, IG and the courts. They'll eat you alive. There is no friggin' way they'll let even the tiniest part of this criminal conspiracy see the light of day. Do you understand? How can you even trust Congress? If they have shit on Grassley, Leahy, or whoever you think supports you, then they'll use it against them. Man, I tell you, they have lots of shit on a lot of people. For instance," he continued, "take your Judge Walton: How do you think they got him assigned to your case? Do you know what I did in the early nineties for the bureau? I ran background checks on federal judges. If we came up with shit—skeletons in their closets—the Justice Department kept it in their pantry to be used against them in the future or to get them to do what they want in certain cases—cases like yours, like mine."

I asked him again if he would be willing to talk with the appropriate people involved in my case.

"Look, I initially contacted the IG. They didn't want to hear about this case; no response from them."

"You mean even after they started on my case, they didn't ask you to go there and provide them with information on my issues?"

"No."

I asked him one more time.

He sighed. "Sibel, do you realize how dangerous this is? Do you realize how much danger you're in? Have you heard about the veteran CIA operative who came across a load of shit, similar to ours, and decided to get some congressional attention to it?"

"No."

"He disappeared for a while, and finally his body was pulled out of the river here in DC; his hands were tied behind his back. They ruled it as 'suicide.' Do you want to meet the same fate? Even more than our filthy government, you should be afraid of what the involved criminals—the targets of our CI operations—are capable of doing to you or your family. Those are some nasty people, worse than the Italian Mafioso; they happen to be very well connected, on top of that. With the immunity they have from our government, they'll take you out if you were to press on."

I told him that I thought the chances of them "taking me out" would be far greater before the information was made public; afterwards, it wouldn't do them any good. This was all the more reason to push and get this information out into the public.

Toward the end of our meeting, I was finally able to get a conditional consent from Graham. "Sibel, I will not volunteer any information. I won't walk into the corrupt Congress and hand them information; however, if you get them to subpoena me, or even formally request me to go there and answer their questions, I'll do it. I promise."

I couldn't ask for more. I would notify the DOJ-IG. I would let the Senate know. I would bring it up with the 9/11 Commission. I would urge them all to subpoena Gilbert Graham.

Before we parted, I asked him one more question. "Have you contacted the Nine Eleven Commission?"

He was thinking of doing that. Through sources, he had put the word out to the commission of his availability and desire to testify.

I would let the Jersey Moms know, and follow up.

Graham's parting words were that my life and my family's life were in serious danger: I had to watch out; and that the chances of our successfully bringing this out were slim to none.

Driving back home, I saw that my hands were shaking again, uncontrollably.

Soon after the ice storm meeting of January 18, the Jersey Moms began a flurry of calls to the commissioners' offices. I started to push the Senate Judiciary Committee about guaranteeing immunity for current government employees who were willing to testify before the 9/11 Commission. Congresspeople and the commission kicked it back and forth. Who would provide immunity for witnesses? Each claimed it was the other's responsibility.

I attended one meeting with the commissioners' investigators and chief of staff initiated by the Jersey Moms. After much browbeating, they finally pledged that not a single witness would be turned away. That time we emerged victorious. The Jersey Moms had threatened to go to the press.

On Wednesday, February 11, 2004, I appeared at the commissioners' office for my interview. Two of their investigators greeted me and asked me to follow them into the Sensitive Compartmented Information Facility. I tensed at the prospect of another claustrophobic, airless interrogation, but I was not about to give these so-called independent investigators another excuse to avoid knowing by refusing to go in, so I followed them.

One of them pulled out a digital recorder and we began. I gave them a detailed account of the blueprints case; the Iranian informant; "visas for money"; the link between certain actors in the nuclear market and terrorist-related entities, money laundering and illegal arms sales by certain foreign front organizations from countries considered our "allies"; and the forged signatures and tampering with documents related to detainees rounded up in New York and New Jersey by counterterrorism field agents.

I briefly told them about the involvement of certain elected and appointed officials—U.S. persons—with the target organizations, and named these individuals. When I mentioned one of those officials (an elected representative at the highest level), one investigator's face turned crimson and the other began to cough spasmodically. They seemed startled. I gave the name and number of the case files and their location. I provided them with the names of relevant witnesses with direct knowledge of these cases. I concluded my testimony with what I had told the IG and Congress; I asked them to subpoena these specific documents, audios and witnesses to verify everything I had provided.

The entire session took over two hours. I was exhausted and apprehensive that they had not asked a single question, not even one. What kind of an interview was that?

Sarshar's interview was scheduled for the next day. The entire session lasted about two hours, during which he provided detailed accounts of two very important cases. He had given them the relevant documents and the names and contact information for all pertinent witnesses, including the Iranian informant.

I was surprised that he had given out the name and address of the informant. Sarshar told me he had contacted the informant and told him about the 9/11 family members and the scheduled commission interview. The informant supported Sarshar's decision and was willing to provide all the explosive information, including taped phone conversations and documents, but only if subpoenaed. The bureau had taken the informant off its payroll—just as they had gotten rid of Sarshar and threatened the agents involved with retaliation if they didn't keep their mouths shut.

The next day, Friday, the girls and I took Sarshar to the Senate Judiciary Committee staff. They too thought the recent development regarding the Iranian informant was explosive. I agreed. We decided to drag Sarshar to the Senate and have him go on record one more time, with a separate entity, with that information.

We sat with the staff and spent the first fifteen minutes emphasizing the importance of Sarshar's information, urging them to provide him and other similar witnesses with immunity. They needed protection. Afterwards we left Sarshar to provide the staff with his account, to go into the SCIF if necessary. Before leaving, Kristen turned around and let them have it. "You f— this up and I'll make sure the entire media goes after your ass, you understand? We have been fighting for the truth and accountability for our husbands' deaths. We are tired of this bullshit attitude, we are tired of you guys in Congress not doing what you were elected to do. I'll come after you, I promise."

One of Grassley's staff turned red and blustered, "We won't have this attitude in here! You have no right to threaten us."

Halfway out and without even turning, Kristen shot back, "That was a warning, not a threat. You f— up and you'll see what a threat really is." With that she slammed the door. We both knew the futility of pushing Congress to do the right thing, to do what it is supposed to be doing. We'd been there, tried that.

During the three-month period between March and June 2004, I attended, along with the 9/11 family members, almost every single 9/11 Commission public hearing in Washington.

During one of these hearings, on March 24, just a day or two after then National Security Advisor Condoleezza Rice had issued a public statement saying that the administration had received no specific threat or warning prior to the September 11 attacks, I had hooked up with the girls and a few other 9/11 family members for a quick coffee during a break. They were seething over Rice's comments.

After the break we headed back to the hearing room at the Senate Dirksen building, took our seats, and waited for another infuriating round of dodgeball, otherwise known as Questions and Answers.

During the second break, I followed the girls outside, where we had to pass through a gauntlet of reporters stationed there to intercept commissioners and high-level government officials.

Kristen and Lorie stopped to chat with a few, so I continued on, until I heard Kristen's voice yelling, "Okay guys! In addition to these officials you need to hear from others, those who actually worked on the front lines. Here is one person you need to talk to, all of you: Sibel Edmonds."

I froze. What was she doing? Kristen and Lorie came over; one held my briefcase while the other pushed me in front of more than twenty reporters, all with lights and cameras. I had no notes, no prepared statements and hadn't given a thought what to say in a situation like this.

Someone yelled out a question; I somehow answered it, briefly; then another. I went into automatic mode and blindly (I couldn't see in the glare of the lights) began to answer questions for nearly ten minutes straight. Reporters closed around me. I managed to break away and almost ran outside, where I was stopped by Kyle, a 9/11 family members' supporter and activist within the 9/11 truth movement community. He had a cameraman with him and begged me to answer a few questions on camera. That session continued for another ten minutes. From the corner of my eye I saw Kristen; I caught up with her and gave her an earful for throwing me to the wolves so entirely unprepared.

Kristen listened quietly with a mischievous smile. "You did good, Sibel. It's about time for you to get in touch with the public. Today was the beginning." She was right. I had only one channel left that had not been thoroughly pursued: the court of public opinion.

The following morning, all that changed. I was in several major U.S. papers and others in the U.K. The episode kicked off a media frenzy that lasted almost two months. In the weeks to come I was interviewed by at least twenty radio shows, almost all of them independent and alternative, which are much less biased.

My favorite, Amy Goodman's "Democracy Now," with national syndication, did the first and by far best and most comprehensive interview during this period. I was nervous, as usual in those days. The cameraman yelled "go" and we were on. Goodman had done her homework and within the first two minutes I began to relax.

After a short break she welcomed another guest who was joining us, Mr. Dan Ellsberg. This completely threw me. I had read about Ellsberg's case when I lived in Turkey and greatly admired his courage and integrity, what he had stood up for, against all odds. He knew my struggle perhaps better than anyone. For me to be there with him, on the same show and receiving his compliments, was a rare honor. Ellsberg well knew the FBI and U.S. Department of Justice, what they could do to people who got in their way. He knew what it felt like to have his entire family threatened with prison or worse, to live day to day looking over your shoulder, never knowing what might happen next. He knew the American government.

After I got home I found my answering machine blinking. It was a message from Goodman's producer: Ellsberg had asked him to pass on his phone number to me. I wrote it down and called him. We spent the next three hours talking. At one point he even asked if he could put me on speakerphone so that his wife, Patricia, could join us. Of course!

Apart from my husband, Matthew, this was truly the first time since my dark journey began that anyone spent this much time in an effort to give me courage, to shore me up. For too long my confidence had been at an all-time low; here was someone who understood the pain I had experienced and the dilemma I faced; who wholeheartedly supported my decision to fight rather than quit. Those three precious hours with Dan and Patricia helped to fill that hole—that void—left by the friendships and family ties I had lost; it provided me with the surrogate warmth of my father, his love. He and Patricia would soon become close in a way I can only describe as family. Ellsberg was not only my champion but someone who showed up to stand by my side. Matthew and I are fortunate indeed; this rare, lucky friendship is one of the best things to come from the worst nightmare time in my life.

15

Gag Orders and
Classification

During the six-month period from October 2003 to April 2004
my own case, the IG report and my primary court claim, took a
backseat to the 9/11 Commission's investigations and hearings
and the whirlwind of a media campaign with 9/11 family members.

Release of the long-overdue IG report now seemed a far-fetched
fantasy. Congress had stalled, and the report lacked oversight. No new
date had been issued for its release, and we were given no status report.

In the meantime, I had found an attorney, Mark Zaid, who was on
standby in case of any "unexpected developments" in my primary court
claim. Until Walton ruled on the case—which he showed no signs of ever
doing—there could be no appeal to the higher courts.

Then, during the first week in April, I received an e-mail from a well-
known law firm, Motley-Rice, stating they were planning to subpoena
my deposition. The firm represented over one thousand 9/11 victims'
family members in a class action lawsuit against individuals, powerful
banks and charities behind the Al Qaeda terrorist financing network.

I forwarded the e-mail to my standby attorney and asked him to handle it. I made it clear that I would be more than willing to provide testimony and do anything I could to support the family members. According

to my attorney, Motley-Rice had to submit a copy of the subpoena to the FBI and the Justice Department; he expected too that the government would try to interfere with my deposition in "some way."

I thought it would be foolish for the government to interfere. Considering the family members' visibility and the nation's support of them, the media and public outrage would drown them! Again, I would be proved wrong.

Within days after the subpoena, attorneys from the FBI and Department of Justice filed an emergency request with the Walton Court to quash the deposition. Walton, true to form, immediately acted on the request and set up an emergency hearing for Monday, April 26, 2004. My attorney and the 9/11 family attorneys made sure to give the media a heads up.

In court, the government argued to quash my deposition based on the ultrasensitive nature of what I knew and the pending State Secrets Privilege invoked by the attorney general himself testifying to that. They brought up the fact that even my FOIA claim was ruled against by Judge Huvelle due to the top-secret and national security implications of what I knew and what my case involved.

Motley-Rice argued that they did not need to get into any secret or classified area for the purpose of this deposition, assuring the court that they would only ask for information that had already become public (such as letters by Senators Grassley and Leahy posted on Congress's own website).

Judge Walton turned to the government attorneys and asked them what they thought of the opposing party's point on "the Senate letters" being available and widely known public documents.

The government attorneys argued, paradoxically, that already being in public domain didn't make this information and these documents any less sensitive or less classified—or less covered by state secrets. There it was. Kafka could have written the script.

Walton granted the government's motion to quash the subpoena until June 14, to give him time to review both parties' arguments. He also asked the family members' attorneys to submit to him and to the government, in advance of the ruling on June 14, all the questions they planned to ask me during the deposition. Then, unexpectedly, he announced, "Since the pending Edmonds' State Secrets Privilege case has a direct bearing on this subpoena case, I will need this time to prepare for ruling on her case as well."

So, the puppet judge would shoot for a two-for-one deal: he would rule on both cases at once, the 9/11 family members' deposition and mine—and in less than two months.

The court session ended. The following day, the deposition case made it into papers all over the world, some of them front-page news. As expected, all the articles, radio shows, public forums and blogosphere were outraged by the government's effort to interfere with the 9/11 family members' lawsuit targeting the terrorists' financial network and backing. The family members were fuming, and many issued statements slamming the government. This started another round of intense interviews in both print and radio on me and my case, which lasted two full, frenzied weeks.

Matthew and I decided to take a much-needed break, a weeklong vacation, the third week of May. My body had only just started to relax when the idyll was rudely interrupted with an e-mail marked *urgent* from my attorney. *Call me right away; an unbelievable new development: your case is going to be on the front page of the* New York Times *tomorrow morning.* What had happened now? Did it have to do with Walton? Was it about the Motley-Rice deposition? Had the government issued an arrest warrant for me, for talking to the media? I had to find out. I called.

"You won't believe what these assholes did!" were the first words out of his mouth. "Nobody has ever seen anything like this! Holy shit, Sibel, now I'm afraid to even guess what it was you stumbled upon during your short tenure with the bureau! Oh, *man!*"

"Stop the bullshit, you're killing me. What happened?"

"The government issued a gag order to the entire Congress, girl—*that's* what happened!"

"What?!"

"The Justice Department—Mr. Fascist Ashcroft—issued an order to *retroactively classify* anything that has been said, written, any letters or statements to the media and public, by any member of the House and the Senate!"

"What the hell," I asked, "is retroactive classification?"

"When the government decides that something is classified, when that something has already become public," he explained. "For over two years, the letters by Senators Grassley and Leahy have been on their websites; these senators have talked about your case on TV, have issued statements to the newspapers. Now, two years after thousands of people have downloaded these letters from the Senate website, two years after millions have watched your CBS segment—which has aired twice—two years after millions have read the *Post* article and others with quotes by these senators . . . the government is saying, 'oops, we now consider all these letters and statements classified.' That's what."

I thought, *How could this be? How could they even attempt gagging the United States Congress?* I didn't think for even a second that Congress would let the executive branch get away with this. I assumed that Congress would fight back tooth and nail against this fascistic move; even schoolchildren knew about the separation of powers. Did the grown-ups?

"But they won't get away with this, right? . . . The Congress wouldn't allow them in a million years, right?"

"With this administration," he groaned, "with everything they've been doing in the past three years, I don't know what to expect, Sibel . . . will they fight this? I'm no longer so sure. . . . Senator Grassley has issued a strong statement that will appear in the *Times'* front-page article tomorrow. We'll see what he's got to say about this . . ."

I asked what I could or should do. He told me to expect a lot of requests for interviews.

"Go, sit down, and write your response, your formal statement. I'll add to that my own and release it to the media tomorrow. Send me your draft by this evening." He had to go, he said, to fend off reporters until he had something solid from me. There went my vacation.

I spent the entire day in front of the tiny screen of our notepad computer. I wanted to say so much, but I was dealing with court-ordered restrictions, privileges and classification. Thus bound and gagged, here was the best I could do.

Sibel Edmonds' Statement Re: DOJ Gagging the United States Congress
05/21/2004

Attorney General John Ashcroft, the Department of Justice, and the FBI have been engaged in covering up my reports and investigations into my allegations for over two years now: They have blocked the release of all documents related to my case that were requested under FOIA for over two years. They have asserted the rarely invoked State Secrets Privilege in my court proceedings. They have blocked the release of the DOJ-IG report of its investigations into my reports and allegations. They have quashed a subpoena for my deposition on information regarding 911. *And now they are gagging the United States Congress.*

They are not protecting the "national security" of the United States. On the contrary, they are endangering our national security by covering up facts and information related to criminal activities against this country and its citizens. To this date the American people have not heard the real facts of these criminal activities, nor of the involved semi-legit organizations, nor of the connected officials. The Department of Justice and this administration are fully aware that making this information public will bring about the question of accountability. And they do not want to be held accountable. It is for these reasons that I have been striving to get the Congress to hold its own public hearings regarding these issues. I no longer intend to go behind their secured-closed doors to testify. I intend to testify openly, publicly, and under oath.

I sent the statement to my attorney that night. The case did indeed make page one of the *New York Times*. Senator Grassley considered it "not a retroactive classification" but a "gag on Congress." Another Senate aide is quoted as saying, "I have never heard of a retroactive classification two years back . . . People are puzzled and, frankly, worried, because the effect here is to quash Congressional oversight. We don't even know what we can't talk about."

Instantly upon return, I started to organize an event around the June 14 hearing scheduled by Walton to rule on the subpoena. The least I could do was to not make it easy for the government. I was resolved to fight harder and scream louder; if the court wouldn't do it, if Congress had abdicated its responsibility, I would take it on myself to wake up the public and get them involved in the fight against *our* rights. This time I would stand my ground and fight with all I had. I had seen this before. I know what can happen.

I set out to hold a press conference on the steps of the district courthouse. I had never before held a press conference and had no idea how to go about doing it. I called Dan Ellsberg in California and asked him whether he would join me, to which he replied, "most definitely." With Ellsberg's commitment to stand by my side before the courthouse on June 14, determined to make a statement even if no one showed up, I began to prepare.

The day before Walton's hearing, I prepared the advisory and sent it to everyone I could. Then I met Ellsberg for lunch. (This was our first face-to-face meeting: we spent the entire day and into the night talking nonstop.) In the early afternoon, in the middle of our lunch, I saw that I had an urgent message from my attorney: just hours earlier, Walton decided to cancel the hearing.

I was overcome with rage. This was less than twenty hours' notice—Walton's fourth cancellation and fourth dirty trick. This had everything to do with my plans and preparations. It was well timed and well executed, and could only have been the result of knowing in advance what I was about to do. Of course they were reading my e-mails and listening to every phone conversation, so the idea here, clearly, was to teach me another lesson—this time in the art of humiliation. I would have to cancel my press conference on the steps of the court, notify everyone I had sent the advisory to, cause Ellsberg to waste a trip for nothing, humiliating and silencing him too (they knew he planned to make a statement as well); my hearing was canceled not only to ruin my plans but even more importantly, to circumvent media attention. This was red meat and they knew it. Walton's intention was to shut me down.

"So," my attorney asked, "I guess now you have to cancel your plans, right? You have to let everyone know that it's been canceled, right, Sibel?"

I felt tears welling up. I took a deep breath and tried to think straight, to collect my thoughts before answering. "F— them, I'm going to do it anyway. I'll have my press conference without the hearing. In fact, it will show the public how filthy this Walton and his corrupt court have been. I'm moving forward, hearing or no hearing. These bastards want to make their point and teach me; well, I think I'm going to turn the tables and teach them. I'll use their ammunition against them. Just wait and see. Make sure you're there at ten o'clock tomorrow."

Zaid sounded shocked. "Don't be ridiculous, Sibel. First of all, no one will show up from the press. I'm sure they'll check the docket and realize that it's been canceled. Second, you'll be humiliated standing there alone, with no media attention or public support, all by yourself reading from your statement like a fool. Just be a good girl and cancel this nonsense."

"NO," I sharply corrected him, "I'm going forward as planned. I need you there, by my side, tomorrow. You have to give them the legal implications and points as an attorney, as an expert, as my advisor."

"No way; there is no way I'm going to share this humiliation. I won't be there. Bye." He hung up.

I realized I had left Ellsberg alone at the table for nearly fifteen minutes. I returned and told him of the cancellation and my plans to move forward regardless.

His first word was "Bravo." Ellsberg wholeheartedly agreed. "What's the big deal if no one shows up, huh? What have you lost? It won't be humiliating; it will show your determination. I'll be there, right by your side. We'll read our statements to each other if no one else ends up showing up, okay?"

If I had any doubts, they were washed away in that instant. I fell in love with him all over again; his courage and activism inspired me.

The next day we arrived at the courthouse thirty minutes ahead of time. To our surprise, one by one, reporters started to show up. Others came too to lend their support—for solidarity. We ended up with a nice-sized crowd. Ellsberg delivered a very effective speech, eloquent and well argued. I read the following brief statement.

"For over two years the attorney general, John Ashcroft, has been relentlessly engaged in actions geared toward covering up my reports and investigations into my allegations. His actions against my case include *gagging* the United States Congress, *blocking* court proceedings on my case by invoking State Secrets Privilege, *quashing* a subpoena for my deposition on information regarding 9/11, *withholding* documents requested under the Freedom of Information Act, and *preventing* the release of the Inspector General's report of its investigations into my reports and allegations.

"John Ashcroft's actions are anti–freedom of speech and anti–due process. His actions are anti-transparency and anti-accountability. In short, John Ashcroft's actions are anti-Constitution and anti-democracy.

"To become an American Citizen, I took the citizenship oath. In taking this oath I pledged that I would support and defend the Constitution and laws of the United States of America against all enemies, foreign and *domestic*. Therefore, not only do I have the right to challenge John Ashcroft's anti-Constitution and Un-American actions, as an American citizen I am required to do so. So are you."

The next day, our press conference received small coverage in the mainstream media but the entire event was discussed on activists' blogs. Ellsberg and I were invited on several radio shows for joint interviews. All in all, the outcome of my first clumsily prepared press conference was a success.

Soon I started to receive offers of support and solidarity from various whistleblower, government watchdog and public interest nonprofit organizations, something I found bitterly amusing. Where were these groups when I most needed them? Strangely enough, I was helped, in a way, by seeing how they operate. In time, this understanding would become a catalyst for forming my own organization for whistleblowers.

On June 23, 2004, about ten days after our courthouse press conference, without any hearings or prior heads up, Judge Walton issued his ruling on the Motley-Rice subpoena. First, having receiving the law firm's forty-something questions in advance, the court allowed the government, after review, to strike out almost all of the questions. The Justice Department then invoked State Secrets Privilege for the second time in my case. This was followed by the judge conducting private, in camera, ex parte sessions with the government attorneys—expressly forbidding the other party to be present. No wonder then Judge Reggie Walton ruled against Motley-Rice, upheld the government's invocation of privilege and forbade the law firm from deposing me. Was anyone surprised?

From court documents we obtained the banned list of questions the law firm had prepared for my deposition: a list of straightforward questions with answers that can be obtained from public records. Almost all of them were stamped by the government as *covered by state secrets* and *classified*. Even more shocking was that a federal judge, however puppet, had agreed with these classifications and censorship—a gag order. Some examples:

When and where were you born?

Where did you go to school?

What did you focus your studies on in school?

What languages do you speak?

What is your proficiency in each of these languages?

In what capacity have you been employed by the United States government?

I was appalled at the legal maneuvers that defied our laws and rendered the Constitution irrelevant. Take question one for example: If *when* I was born—my birthday—is considered state secrets and classified, then how can I use my driver's license? If *where* I was born—my birthplace—is considered state secrets and classified, then how can I use my passport? Does it mean I can no longer leave this country, because showing my passport to officials constitutes a breach of security?

Take the two questions about school: If the colleges and universities I attended—all in the States—are considered state secrets and classified, then must I black them out from my resume? How am I to answer in a job interview? Must these schools now black me out of their yearbooks and records to preserve our national security?

Take the question about employment: If my job title and the nature of the work I performed are considered state secrets and classified, will the FBI have to throw all their full-time translators in jail if any of them ever printed and handed out business cards that describe them as FBI language specialists? If my languages are considered state secrets and classified, does it mean I can't even talk to my friends and family? What if somebody overheard? Would it constitute a breach?

How in the world could a judge allow this kind of nonsense? According to this ruling, my language, education background, family and birth history all were classified. In a way, they had classified *me*. I was now a Classified Woman.

This classification of *me* received scant coverage in the mainstream media, which appeared to be distancing itself from the case. One had to wonder. What were they being told? It made a terrible kind of sense, though, that a government willing to go to such lengths to gag, classify and invoke privileges would surely go the extra mile to make sure that the public never finds out.

On Tuesday, July 6, 2004, Judge Reggie Walton issued his ruling on my case. After sitting on it for two years, after four cancellations and postponements, his court had finally ruled on the first State Secrets Privilege case in the past five decades. As I had suspected he would, the judge dismissed my case, ruled against me, and as he had done with the 9/11 family members' subpoena, upheld the arcane State Secrets Privilege. He said he was satisfied with claims by Attorney General John Ashcroft and a senior FBI official that my civil lawsuit could disrupt diplomatic and business relations with certain foreign governments; however, Walton added, he couldn't "explain further" because any explanation would itself expose sensitive secrets!

In his decision, Judge Walton shamelessly acknowledged that dismissing a lawsuit before the facts of the case can be heard is "Draconian" and said he was throwing out the lawsuit "with great consternation."

This Bush-appointed puppet had ruled without a single hearing on my case. He had dismissed my case without giving me the right to discovery as mandated by law. He had obeyed and served the executive branch despite all the evidence and congressional verification. He had at once upheld state secrets and excluded my attorney and me, the plaintiff, from being present during ex parte, in camera sessions with the government attorneys by citing "necessary secrecy."

What happened to the rights guaranteed me under our Constitution?

Did Walton's ruling come as a shock? Absolutely not; but I was hit hard by the severity of this blow and its repercussions for the nation, the place I chose to make my home. Here was a precedent. A ruling had been handed down, not from the court but from the executive branch. There would be others to follow. And the media, so far, was quiet.

Matthew had taken this decision extremely hard. Uncharacteristically, he began to speak up—in public, and with me, surrounded by the press. Here is the statement he delivered on the day following the Walton court's ruling:

"John Ashcroft is attempting to silence Sibel, using every means at the government's disposal, and he has been ably assisted by Judge Walton, with the passive approval of the Congress; and with the specter of September 11 in the background allowing Ashcroft and the government to cry 'security' and frighten us all with the threat of new terrorist attacks. Judge Walton used this ploy in his somewhat less than legal statement in his ruling, that the court 'must be mindful, especially at a time when our nation's security is threatened by acts of terrorism.' The clear implication is that we must sacrifice our freedom for the sake of security. For those, including Judge Walton, who would accept that, I offer a quote from one of our nation's founding fathers, Benjamin Franklin, who so perceptively stated, 'They that can give up essential liberty to obtain a little temporary safety deserve neither liberty nor safety.'

"As Americans, it is all our duty to resist the forces that would take away our cherished freedom. It is our time to fight the battle; it is our time to join with those patriots who came before us in the defense of liberty. And we have in Sibel today one who is fighting the fight, who is an inspiration to us all; listen to what she has to say, and take heed."

Then—lo and behold—two days after the court's ruling, the Department of Justice Office of the Inspector General publicly announced that it had completed and issued its report on my case. Yet, according to the same announcement, the entire report, based on the Justice Department's order, was classified and would not be released to the public. John Ashcroft and the DOJ had blacked out the entire investigation and its findings—the report on my case!

I had been anticipating this report for exactly two years and four months. I had been told that I needed this so-called independent report's findings to vindicate me and expose criminal conduct and other wrongdoings by the FBI. I needed it for my case, but they told me I couldn't have it, that it was classified. The purpose of the IG report—any IG report—is for the public's right to know. Yet the Inspector General, having spent more than two years investigating, interviewing and reviewing my case, was not permitted to say why it was classified. That too was classified. I was living in *Catch-22*.

VI

ALL DOORS CLOSE

16

Commission Report

Despite all the back-to-back blows that my case and I had suffered, I was more than ever resolved to continue on. If government orders were intended to keep me gagged and classified, Walton's ruling had quite the opposite effect on me. I must have appeared like one of those boxers who kept being knocked down and bloodied in the ring, yet each time grabbing the ropes, forcing himself to his feet and continuing to throw little punches in the air. I refused to stay down, I refused to go away. I rejected the acceptance of defeat.

On July 23, 2004, the widely anticipated 9/11 Commission Report came out. The commission decided to release it first in DC before making it available in bookstores nationwide. So I went downtown and stood in line for an hour, then spent the rest of that day and night devouring its contents. First, however, I checked the index for my testimony as well as the testimonies of national security experts and whistleblowers such as Sarshar, Dick Stoltz and Gil Graham.

The commission had reduced my entire testimony to a short footnote, number 25 in chapter three. It read only, "refer to the Justice Department Inspector General Report." How convenient is that? The entire IG report was classified. There was no mention whatsoever of Sarshar's report; so, according to this Commission Report, there was no Iranian informant, since he never appears anywhere its findings. (Interestingly, though, the *Chicago Tribune* had just run an article on Sarshar's case:

when the Tribune reporter contacted the FBI director's office for confirmation, he was told, "Director Mueller was surprised that the commission never raised this particular issue with him during the hearing"! The FBI confirmed Sarshar's report and the Tribune ran the article as substantiated.)

According to the commission chairman, they had seen "every single document" and interviewed "every single relevant witness and authority." Thus to its members, this report was a resounding success: almost nothing had been redacted, classified or glossed over. Given the administration's renown for secrecy, this was puzzling if not downright suspect, and more than a little curious.

I know what I testified to in my three-plus-hour briefing, which was taped. The Commission Report mentions nothing, for instance, about "intentionally blocked translations by certain Middle Eastern translators, who also breached FBI security, as confirmed by the Senate Judiciary"; nothing regarding "adamant resistance to investigations of certain terrorist and criminal activities, refusing to transfer them to Counterterrorism from existing Counterintelligence investigations, solely based on the vague notion of protecting certain foreign relations"; nothing about "continued efforts to cover up certain highly specific information received prior to September 11, even now, years after nine eleven"; nothing about "knowingly allowing certain individuals—directly or indirectly related to terrorist activities—to leave the United States months after nine eleven without any interrogation and per the State Department's request." Why not? Didn't the commissioners consider any of that testimony "relevant"?

Nevertheless, all parties and all agencies readily accepted this report. Apparently, the president himself considered it "rosy"; the previous administration sighed with relief (having scored a minus 4, compared to this administration's minus 6 in the blame game); and the notorious attorney general, Ashcroft, left his state secrets guns in their holsters. All very puzzling and curious indeed, to see such a report, blessed by all those entrusted with our nation's security, so violently breached on their watch.

The whole point of the 9/11 Commission was to get all the facts, establish accountability for those who failed us due to their intentional or unintentional acts, and provide recommendations for real fixes and meaningful remedies. The commission had fulfilled none of those objectives. Entrusted by the 9/11 family members and their public supporters to report all the facts, the commissioners either refused to interview all relevant experts and witnesses or they censored the reports provided them by those with direct and firsthand information. Any way you look at it, both these acts are selective and intentional. Contrary to their pledge to establish accountability, the 9/11 commissioners refused to hold anyone accountable and lamely justified that by saying, "We don't want to point a finger at anyone." All those responsible remained in their positions or were promoted. As far as meaningful remedies and real reforms are concerned, the commission threw in senseless—and in some cases, detrimental—cosmetic and bureaucratic "solutions" that ended up making our government even more cumbersome and unable to respond to threats to national security. In the name of solutions and reforms, they forced down our throats exactly what led to the failure to protect our nation on 9/11: a highly bureaucratic, inefficient behemoth of malfunction—a dangerous machine.

So. I decided to write a comprehensive letter, to go on record with specific facts contradicting the 9/11 Commission Report's claims. The few people I spoke with warned me against doing that. This included my interim attorney and the directors of several government watchdog organizations. Their reasoning goes as follows. "The American media is in love with the commission and the report; everyone is praising it as the best thing since sliced bread. You will be the only person in the country to come out and criticize the widely adored commissioners and their report. They will lynch you with counterattacks." Not a single person was willing to support my stand. Ironically, in private, they said they agreed with me and that they found the commissioners' conclusions and recommendations a joke, but no one wanted to stick his or her neck out and express this in public. They were afraid.

I contacted the Jersey Moms. They were not happy with the report and felt terribly let down. Yet they were exhausted and discouraged, and they too didn't want to be the first ones out against the popular commissioners.

Nobody wanted to be the first vocal critic, to go against the popular tide. This was a major dilemma. I wrestled with the decision: Do what I strongly believe to be right, or go with the flow and stay away from controversy? I decided on the former. On July 31, I sat down and composed a nine-page letter to the commission's chairman, Thomas Kean. Once finished, I faxed and e-mailed the letter to each commissioner. Afterwards, I sent the letter out to every media, forum and blog I could think of. I disseminated the letter as widely as I could, then sat, buckled up, and waited for the attacks to begin. Here I was again—blowing the whistle in the line of fire!

In less than twenty-four hours, many major blogs, online publications and forums, nationally and internationally, picked up and published my nine-page letter to the 9/11 Commission. One major publication, *Asia Times*, published the entire letter. Though the mainstream media here in the States chose to completely ignore the letter and its galvanizing effect on grassroots activists, online media and forums, my telephone rang nonstop for weeks. Alternative radio and international publications were calling for interviews to discuss the letter.

Contrary to what I was told by so-called experts prior to releasing it, almost all coverage and every response to my letter was positive and supportive. Within days, I began to get e-mails from dozens of veteran experts from government intelligence, aviation and law enforcement communities. These patriots too had tried to provide the commission with evidence and reports related to the 9/11 attacks and had met with similar results: their testimonies had been refused or completely censored and omitted. Unlike me, whose tenure with the bureau was brief, these individuals each had served (or were still serving) these agencies for years—and many of them held high-level positions. They included several FBI counterterrorism agents, as well as experts from the former Federal Aviation Administration (FAA), all of whom had incredible stories to tell. The commissioners weren't interested; they hadn't the time or the resources, they said.

Within a week after sending out my letter to the 9/11 Commission, I had gathered a group of about twenty national security experts who had come forward to report security-related incompetence, wrongdoing, cover-ups or even, in some cases, criminal conduct. I created a separate e-mail list for our group and added to the list the other FBI veterans I had met the previous year, such as Gilbert Graham, Dr. Frederic Whitehurst (the first FBI whistleblower I'd ever met, who warned me my case would take years), and Manny Johnson. This list, this group, became what people began to refer to as Sibel's National Security Whistleblowers Coalition.

At the time I had no idea what this group could accomplish with their unity, solid reputations, expertise and, most importantly, their desire to bring about real and meaningful reforms within their diverse communities. I didn't yet know how to best utilize the power coming from the numbers, but I felt comradeship, and deep inside I knew these people would become an inseparable part of my future fight and activities. This was the first of several steps that brought about the formation of my organization, the National Security Whistleblowers Coalition (NSWBC). This group became the frontier for a coalition that grew to exceed one hundred members, all national security veterans: experts.

I spent all of August reviewing boxes of material, reports and files sent to me by these national security professionals. I'd spend hours on the phone with them. Some became very good friends with whom Matthew and I associated regularly. Bit by bit, the hole in me was being filled, by people whose stories and experience I shared, and whose lives and hearts touched mine.

One evening toward the end of August, sitting at my computer, I stopped at an unopened e-mail sent by one Cole J. M. Could this be John M. Cole, the FBI whistleblower for whom I'd been searching these past two years?

I clicked on the e-mail and there he was, asking me to call him.

I was ecstatic. For over two years I had been hoping, praying, for more people in the FBI familiar with my case to step forward, to join me in my quest to expose the crimes and cover-ups. I had not given up hope, and here was a man who could support my report: one of the FBI's top experts in espionage, in charge of counterintelligence operations for Afghanistan, Pakistan and India. His case was cited next to mine in the first exposé by the *Washington Post*, two months after I was fired. Thus far I had two credible witnesses: Gilbert Graham, the FBI agent in charge of FBI-WFO counterintelligence operations on Turkey; and, of course, Behrooz Sarshar, the FBI-WFO Farsi translator. Now, possibly, John M. Cole would add his name to the list.

That evening I spoke with Cole, who was very glad to hear from me. We spent nearly three hours discussing both our cases and strategies on where to go next.

Cole told me what went on in the FBI HQ during the summer of 2002, when my case became public. According to him, most people at headquarters were cheering for me. Everyone had known about Dickerson; it was well understood both at headquarters and the Washington field office that husband and wife were on the payroll of the target foreign entities active in the United States. This was an established fact.

Cole went even further by letting me know that he had firsthand knowledge of the Turkish networks involved in the nuclear black market and their penetration of several U.S. nuclear facilities and weapons labs. His unit had spent the entire mid-to-late 1990s monitoring this

Turkish group and their Israeli counterparts. He was aware of their far-reaching influence and connection to high-level State Department and Pentagon officials. He and I knew precisely which front companies and organizations in New Jersey, Chicago and DC were utilized for these illegal activities and other related operations involving narcotics and money laundering.

In addition, Cole explained, he had found out more on Major Douglas Dickerson. He said that although Dickerson had used his air force title as a cover, he was not listed in the U.S. Air Force personnel directory nationally or internationally. One of Cole's contacts, who worked with the U.S. Air Force Office of Inspector General, had told Cole that in the mid-1990s, while in Turkey working for Marc Grossman, then the U.S. ambassador to Turkey, Major Dickerson had come under investigation by the IG for possible espionage. According to this man, they found out that Dickerson had been receiving lavish gifts from foreign entities while in Turkey.

I was thunderstruck. I wanted to know if this air force man was willing to come forward and report this to Congress and DOJ-IG. Through my other sources I had already established that Douglas Dickerson was actually operating under some joint State Department and Pentagon operations. With this new piece of information from Cole, my sources had been proved right. Cole and I agreed that a high-level group within the Pentagon and State Department was working with and protecting Dickerson. I told him I already knew two of them: Douglas Feith and Marc Grossman. He agreed, and further, he confirmed.

After discussing the Dickersons and my case, Cole began to tell me about his experiences. It was incredible to listen to his accounts of all the other FBI translator cases involving espionage activities. I had thought Dickerson a rare and extraordinary instance, but after speaking with Cole for several hours, I heard tell of at least twelve established espionage cases involving FBI translators since the infamous Hanssen case.

When Cole had finished telling me one such story (with eerie parallels to mine, including a "kill the messenger" denouement), I asked him about his pursuing the Congress and Justice Department IG. He had sent letters and reports to both, and had called them many times to no avail. Not only that, he had contacted the IG office regarding my case—as a witness with direct information relevant to my case and other similar espionage cases within the bureau—also without result. I didn't find that surprising.

I inquired about other colleagues and friends from the FBI who might also come forward and join us. I believed that with Sarshar, the Iranian informant, me, Agent Gilbert Graham, and now John Cole, we had a good chance of pushing for an open public congressional hearing with all these witnesses on the stand to testify.

I told him about the 9/11 Commission Report—more of an Omission Report—and my now very public letter. (He had read it and agreed with my position.) Had he too approached them? To my surprise, he had. Cole had written to the commission and asked to be interviewed: he had documented evidence showing certain aspects of the 9/11 attacks involving the Pakistani military intelligence (ISI) and cases of FBI penetration by terrorist-related elements. Despite letters and numerous calls, the commission never responded or acknowledged him.

This last got my blood boiling. Writing a well-publicized letter was no longer enough. With Cole on board, along with a dozen or more others with similar experiences related to 9/11 and the Commission Report, it was time to take this to the next level.

I shared these thoughts with Cole. He wholeheartedly agreed. I suggested we organize an event, a press conference, to bring all these veteran national security experts, including Cole, together on one stage. We would argue against and denounce this fraudulent report being forced upon us as gospel. Cole said, "Count me in."

That evening, after talking with Cole, I began planning the logistics. We—the members on my list, my coalition—would stage our first national security whistleblowers press conference.

September 11 fell that year on a weekend, so I decided to schedule our event for the following Monday, September 13, 2004. I then issued an action alert to all the list members, urging them to join the conference and voice their position loudly and publicly. They were ecstatic, fired up and ready to go. All signed on to the petition, a two-page statement ending with a demand for congressional investigation of facts and cases omitted from the 9/11 Commission Report. I had less than three weeks to prepare.

Having secured a conference room (in the Steward Mott House, owned and operated by a nonprofit foundation), I found rooms and hosts for whistleblowers who had far to travel. I prepared a formal press advisory and called members of the press in advance. Without office or staff or any real experience—and with little-to-no money—I would nevertheless give it my best shot. Now, with these venerable experts joining the fight, I wouldn't let anything stop me.

The day had arrived and here we were, gathered together for the very first time. It was a sight that filled me with optimism and determination. Some I had never met in person; now I could put a face to those names, those cases. The feeling in the room was electric. Something would happen here today. Contrary to what I was told to expect, the room began to fill up with reporters from print media and TV networks. Toward the end, they couldn't even squeeze into the room; they were bending through the doorway.

I spoke first, making a few introductory remarks about what brought us all here; then, I read our joint petition.

Our statement began with a clarion call to address serious shortcomings in the report and its recommendations, urging Congress to "apply brakes" in their race to implement those recommendations. "It is not too late," the statement continued, "for Congress to break with the practice of limiting testimony to that from politicians and top-layer career bureaucrats—many with personal reputations to defend and institutional equities to protect." Instead, we implored, "use this unique opportunity to introduce salutary reform, an opportunity that must not be squandered by politically driven haste."

We believed that chief among the report's major flaws was omission. "We are aware of significant issues and cases that were duly reported to the commission by those of us with direct knowledge, but somehow escaped attention. Serious problems and shortcomings within government agencies likewise were reported to the commission but were not included in the report. The report simply does not get at key problems within the intelligence, aviation security, and law enforcement communities. The omission of such serious and applicable issues and information . . . casts doubt on the validity of many of its recommendations."

Moreover, we held, the commission in its report holds *no one accountable*, and thereby fails in its primary purpose. When calling for accountability, the statement continued, "we refer to intentional actions or inaction by individuals responsible for our national security, actions or inaction dictated by motives other than the security of the people of the United States." The report, we pointed out, deliberately ignored what all of the petition's signatories knew so well to be the case: that officials and civil servants were and still are negligent or derelict in their duties to the nation; and that if they are protected rather than held accountable, "the mind-set that enabled 9/11 will persist, no matter how many layers of bureaucracy are added, and no matter how much money is poured into the agencies. Character counts."

The statement described the whistleblowers' experience, of coming forward under duress and being retaliated against by government agencies. The commission, we explained, neither acknowledged what they, whistleblowers, had done nor faced up to the need to protect them against such forces.

While the commission *did* emphasize barriers to the flow of information as a primary cause for wasting opportunities to prevent 9/11, "it skipped a basic truth. Secrecy enforced by repression threatens national security as much as bureaucratic turf fights. It sustains vulnerability to terrorism caused by government breakdowns." Reforms, we insisted, "will be paper tigers without a safe channel for whistleblowers to keep them honest in practice. It is unrealistic to expect that government workers will defend the public, if they can't defend themselves." What the general public didn't or couldn't know, unfortunately, was that current whistleblower rights are a cruel trap. "The Whistleblower Protection Act has turned into an efficient way to finish whistleblowers off by endorsing termination." Legislative reform was needed to allow government workers access to jury trials, as Congress had done for corporate whistleblowers. The 9/11 Commission Report failed to address this flaw.

We argued against some of their fixes—for instance, an "intelligence czar" or haphazard increases in intelligence budgets, as needlessly adding layers of bureaucracy to an already overburdened, complex system.

Finally, we maintained that Congress "has not included the voices of the people working within the intelligence and broader national security communities who deal with the real issues and problems day after day and who possess the needed expertise and experience—in short, those who not only do the job but are conscientious enough to stick their necks out in pointing to the impediments they experience in trying to do it effectively."

"We the undersigned," I concluded, "who have worked within various government agencies (FBI, CIA, FAA, DIA, Customs) responsible for national security and public safety, call upon you in Congress to include the voices of those with firsthand knowledge and expertise in the important issues at hand. We stand ready to do our part."

Despite the large crowd, except for the clicking of cameras you could hear a pin drop. As soon as I finished reading, coalition members and a few 9/11 family members stood up and gave a lengthy ovation. I glanced at the reporters intently taking notes and knew this was a success—though short-lived, never translating into victory. Again, I had defied the timid experts. Others spoke, veteran agents and analysts; even the mainstream media couldn't help but be impressed. I was so proud of

them, these courageous people, who now had been labeled whistleblowers.

At the end of the conference, each of us carried our personal copy
of the 9/11 Commission Report over to the corner and ceremoniously
dumped it in the trash where it belonged.

The seeds of our movement, our future organization, were solidly
planted that day. When word of the conference got out, our membership doubled in less than six months. Even more whistleblowers were
out there, and we had no intention of going away.

I spent the next three months, from August until November, getting the
message out and trying to educate the public on the need for congressional oversight and accountability; though it's never an easy sell—broken systems that fail to protect, never-ending assaults on civil liberties,
State Secrets Privileges and classification, which no one ever wants to
hear about—I was doing all I could, utilizing all available channels. I was
speaking before all sorts of different groups and people willing to listen.

In September, the National Organization for Women (NOW) invited
me to New York to speak before an audience of members gathered for
an annual rally in Central Park. I gladly accepted. I thought it would be
a small event with an intimate group. When I got there, thousands were
gathered in the park waiting for the speakers, who in turn began to speak
about abortion, gay rights and equality. Suddenly I dreaded the prospect.
I wanted to turn around and run. I looked down at my two-page speech:
it was all about Ashcroft, gag orders, Congress, and lack of oversight and
accountability. I felt totally out of place, a misfit; I regretted not doing
my homework.

When they called my name, I almost dragged myself to the podium.
They had to lower the microphone all the way down, which only added to
my sense of smallness. Here I was this tiny person, self-conscious and
inexperienced; however silly it may seem now, at the time I was filled
with terror.

I started my speech, voice barely audible, lacking all confidence with badly strained nerves. The audience, in the thousands, began to scream "Louder!" and "Speak up! We can't hear you!" I coughed and started over, forcing myself to project—it felt like I was yelling at the top of my lungs. Somehow with every sentence, every point on how I had been gagged, my fury at the government and passion to fight back grew to a point where I could no longer contain it, which in turn gave conviction to my voice and expression. Soon the crowd joined in with cheers, forcing me to pause for their heartfelt ovations. Their warmth and support gave me courage.

By the time I had finished, with the crowd in wild applause, my anxieties had totally disappeared. Far from disaster, this speech had become one of the most successful public endeavors I had ever taken on. I had connected with them, inflamed their passion. I never experienced that before. I loved it.

The NOW event was followed by several others in September. I was invited by the New England Translators Association to go to Boston and speak before a group of professional career translators and interpreters. For two hours after the speech they asked me question after question. Many had thought about joining the CIA or FBI as translators; now they realized that those agencies might not be the best place to work. Some worked with courts on criminal cases as live interpreters, and understood very well the implication of blocking translations or intentional mistranslation. My message was getting through. Whatever doubts I may have had, time and again my audience proved me wrong: they were very informed and interested. Their questions were entirely relevant and well thought out; furthermore, I ended up asking them a great deal of questions, and learning more from their answers.

Also in September a coalition of veteran intelligence officers, the Sam Adams Foundation, presented me with their 2004 Sam Adams Courage Award. I had spent days preparing my speech. I decided to focus on endangered civil liberties, those rights guaranteed under our Constitution.

I spoke of growing up in Turkey and Iran, where such rights never existed. For the first time in public, I spoke about the torture of my father for reading certain books and talking about equality and workers' rights. I told them about the censorship I had experienced firsthand for writing an essay about the lack of freedom of the press. I warned the audience about the alarming situations we were now living under and so readily accepting in the name of national security—the price we were paying for some abstract war against the concept of terrorism. I explained about the classification imposed on me and my case, and how all three branches of government had failed in preventing these unconstitutional assaults on our rights.

At the end of my speech, noting their enthusiastic applause, I came to another realization. What I was doing here was preaching to the choir. These people were already informed; all were active in the fight. The question I was struggling to find an answer to was, how do I reach others who are not informed? How do we get through to those who readily have accepted the despotism being marketed to them as security? How?

I would spend a lot of time during this period and in the years to come trying to find an answer to those questions—unsuccessfully. With the complete failure of the mainstream media to cover these vital issues, I would not find a way to reach out to the rest. The uninformed remain in the dark.

The time spent on activism and other national security whistleblower cases was therapeutic. It took my mind off my miseries. As October arrived, I needed to focus on my case. The deadline to appeal the Walton ruling was fast approaching and couldn't wait. I had less than three months to file a comprehensive appeal with the appellate court.

I knew that Mark Zaid, my attorney, was not keen on fighting this case. He had not won many—if any—cases dealing with national security whistleblowers or the State Secrets Privilege. To strategically prepare and present this case well before the appellate court would take time, resources and dedication. My interim attorney didn't seem to have any of those, and I could not afford new high-priced attorneys.

During the Sam Adams Award conference, a dark-haired petite woman in her thirties had walked over and introduced herself: Ann Beeson, with the ACLU New York Legal division. She congratulated me on all my efforts and in gathering others to form a coalition. Ann wanted to know if I were planning to appeal the case, because if so, the ACLU would be interested in helping. This made me snap at her, rather rudely. I told her all about my past experience begging for their help—how they had made me wait for months for an answer, only to turn me down. None of their attorneys were interested. Then I pointed my finger and said, "I'm disgusted with all these organizations who preach one thing then do another—who only approach people and help them if those people are surrounded by publicity."

Ann kept her cool. She apologized for my hardship and for not providing the needed support, adding that "This time you will be dealing with the New York office, our headquarters, and me."

I ignored her attempts to mend fences and walked. Later that day she even tried again, to which I nastily replied, "These whistleblowers all need legal help, and they won't welcome an organization that has not extended help to them. In fact, if I see anyone from your organization, I'll have them removed." Again, Ann didn't lose her calm. Deep inside, I admired her strength and control. She appeared to be a very strong woman, self-assured and articulate.

About three weeks after my first fiery interaction with Ann, a good friend and supporter called to inform me that the director of the ACLU Legal division, Anthony Romero, wanted to talk with me about my case. My response was nearly the same I'd given Ann. "If he wants to talk with me, he'll call me."

Within minutes, I received a call directly from Romero. He patiently listened, apologized for the ACLU, and then got down to it. Now, he said, they were set and determined to represent me, the State Secrets Privilege case, with all they had and without sparing any resources. He said he knew how dangerous this privilege was and the implications of its effect on all of us, not just me. He sounded sincere, genuine.

After he told me that the ACLU was creating a division for national security whistleblower cases, he had me convinced. I agreed to be represented by the ACLU in the appellate court, and from there to the Supreme Court, if it came to that.

The lead attorney, he said, who would be handling my case with her team was Ann Beeson.

I couldn't have been more startled and surprised. Romero explained how passionate she was about my case, about the abuse of the State Secrets doctrine. It sounded promising.

Ann and I exchanged e-mails and discussed, among other things, my interim attorneys Mark Zaid and Eric Seiff, a friend and one of the best criminal attorneys in New York, who would be given the courtesy of opting to leave or remain on the case. We arranged a time to meet in DC, where I also met her assistant, Melissa Goodman. Eric came along to make sure things went smoothly. At the end of our meeting, both Eric and Ann seemed pleased, and the ACLU had taken my case officially. All were ready to fight. During the next few months, I made several trips to New York to meet with Ann and her team. I was introduced to Ann's other assistant attorney, Ben Wizner, a capable, competent, intelligent attorney with an equally great personality. They too made regular trips to DC for meetings, events and preparations for the appeal.

It didn't take long for me to realize how fortunate indeed I was to have the ACLU, particularly this team, representing me. Without a doubt they believed in the cause; they felt genuinely passionate. I had the best team possible, the best attorneys a person could hope for.

When your basic rights are attacked and destroyed, it changes your perspective. The world never looks the same after that. In the past, before my case began, I was among those who dismissed the ACLU as liberal ideologues with certain extreme views. They often appeared to be on the wrong side of protected speech, as with child pornography and other troubling cases. Yet, after what I went through during this dark period in America following the 9/11 attacks—to say nothing of such widespread abuses as torture, undeclared detainees in secret CIA prisons, extraordinary rendition, NSA eavesdropping, and more and more invocations of the State Secrets Privilege that precious few even know about—the ACLU showed up to fight, not only for me but for everyone whose rights are guaranteed by our Constitution.

We—my new team and I—spent all of November and December 2004 preparing to file with the appellate court. The ACLU decided to gather amicus briefs from relevant government watchdog organizations and associations: that is, have them sign up as supporters with stakes in my case to be brought before the court. We were successful in recruiting such organizations as Project on Government Oversight (POGO), the American Library Association and their various chapters, several anti-secrecy organizations and others to join our appeal. All had a dog in this fight.

We also planned to hold a major press conference on the day of our filing in DC that would include other national security whistleblowers who suffered or continued to suffer similar abuses by the government: my coalition members.

On Friday, January 14, 2005, I received a call from a New York Times reporter, who wanted to know my response to the newly released Inspector General's report. This was news to me. Had they declassified it? When had it been released? Apparently, the report had been issued only hours earlier, that day. I immediately called Ann.

I couldn't find anything on the IG's website; they hadn't posted it. Ann called back to tell me the IG had not declassified the report: instead, they had rewritten it and issued their "unclassified" version. Most of their findings remained classified. Ann would get a copy and send it to me ASAP.

I waited next to my fax machine for over two hours without moving. In fact I had been waiting two years. Congress, after all, had promised me a public hearing on release of this report. So I continued to count the seconds with no small anxiety. Had they whitewashed the case? Did they issue lies and slander? Would it be a solid report, vindicating me and my case? Meanwhile, the phone wouldn't stop ringing. Every reporter I knew, every TV network, called for my response. They invited me on their shows. I was unable to comment or give them a quote until I'd read the entire report several times.

That afternoon around three, Ann sent me the IG report. She sounded overjoyed: while the report was short on information, it did in fact vindicate me one hundred percent, finding that "my claims were supported by other witnesses, documents and evidence."

At first I was relieved; then I immediately began to wonder how much information they had omitted. I printed out the thirty-page report and sat with my pink Hi-Liter, reading through it at least three times.

The DOJ Inspector General's report concluded that I was fired for reporting serious security breaches and misconduct in the FBI's translation program.

Their investigation found that "many of Edmonds' claims were supported, that the FBI did not take them seriously enough, and that her allegations were, in fact, the most significant factor in the FBI's decision to terminate her services."

The report's summary criticized the agency for not investigating my allegations more thoroughly, comparing the FBI's mishandling of my allegations to the mishandling of the case involving former FBI counterintelligence agent Robert Hanssen, who pled guilty to spying for the Soviet Union. The summary states, "Edmonds' claims raised serious concerns that, if true, could potentially have extremely damaging consequences for the FBI."

Furthermore, the Inspector General stated, "By terminating Edmonds' services, in large [part] because of her allegations of misconduct, the FBI's actions also may have the effect of discouraging others from raising concerns."

Highlights from the long-awaited IG report include:

"Finally rather than investigate Edmonds' allegations vigorously and thoroughly, the FBI concluded that she was a disruption and terminated her contract" (p. 11);

"In sum, we believe the FBI's initial inquiries in response to Edmonds' allegations were seriously deficient" (p. 24);

"The FBI should not discourage employees or contractors from raising good-faith allegations of misconduct or mismanagement" (p. 31);

"In light of the need for FBI vigilance about security issues, as demonstrated by the Hanssen case, we believe the FBI should have investigated these serious allegations more thoroughly" (p. 34).

Their findings surprised me. In almost all such cases, IG reports do one of two things: slander the whistleblower unjustly, or whitewash the case by characterizing their findings as "inconclusive." I guessed with all the prior investigations made public by the Senate Judiciary Committee, the IG had a difficult time doing either.

I thought this called for celebration. I believed that now, with a report like this, my appeal would be a slam dunk. All the judges had to do was read it. How indeed could the FBI counter this in court? With the Senate letters and this IG report, as well as witnesses I had gathered—Cole, Graham and Sarshar—I considered my court case won. Furthermore, Congress could now hold public hearings; it had what it needed to proceed with my case. Little I knew.

Upon release of the IG report, my attorneys Ann Beeson and Mark Zaid issued strong statements to the press condemning the government's actions, specifically, the attorney general for hiding behind the State Secrets Privilege and the FBI for my unlawful firing, calling the denial of my rights to a day in court "a mockery of national security and the Constitution."

Following release of the report, I rode another media wave, or rather, an interview roller coaster. From CNN to MSNBC, the Washington Post to the Boston Globe, everyone seemed interested. Yet, the media still refused to ask the real questions: Why was the State Secrets Privilege invoked in the first place? Who were the targets involved in espionage, including high-level government insiders? Who were the Dickersons, and who did they work for? The media—that is, the mainstream media in the United States—never asked these questions, never sought an answer through investigative work. Never.

I followed up with the Senate Judiciary the week after release of the IG's report. To my dismay, no one returned my calls. I made another round of calls—again, to no avail. Were they scared? Were they warned to stay away from my case? What was the reason for silence?

I refused to be discouraged. If Congress wouldn't act, I had to find a way to change their position, by force, if necessary. I created a website and an online petition to garner public support: the public had the right to know. This was about congressional oversight and accountability for the executive branch. I launched my petition, and my online supporters joined the campaign to gather signatures.

On January 26, 2005, about two weeks after the report, the ACLU held its press conference. It was well attended by the coalition and received decent media coverage. The speakers discussed the unprecedented level of secrecy imposed by the Bush administration to quash dissent and gag truth tellers. Ann Beeson gave an overview of the State Secrets Privilege, its justified and unjustified uses. I talked for five minutes or so, urging other present and perhaps future whistleblowers to join our movement, and emphasized the Congress's abdication of its responsibility and all that implies; the consequences.

By the end of January I had hit a wall. I was worn out, exhausted. I couldn't really sleep, didn't really eat, and neglected every other aspect of my life. Still, I couldn't pause, I couldn't stop. I had to keep pushing forward.

I remember one interview in particular. Sheila Weller (who became a good friend) from Glamour asked me, "When do you let off steam? When do you ever cry? You seem to be always in control. Nobody has seen you sad or crying. Do you ever get depressed? Do you cry?"

"Let me give you this analogy," I explained. "You know when you're driving and this tiny piece of gravel flies from a big truck and hits your windshield? That little tiny piece can create a small crack; a tiny one that's hard to see. Yet, it's enough to eventually crack the entire windshield. It won't remain a tiny crack; it will expand and destroy the entire windshield." I paused to see if she was getting it. "I feel if I stop, even if it is for a short while—if I let myself pour out, cry—I'll go crashing down. It will work just like that small gravel. I can't let myself stop or get depressed or cry. I'm afraid if I did, I would never be able to recover. Maybe, maybe one day, when everything is over, I'll go somewhere, maybe on top of a high mountain where no one is around, and scream my lungs out; sob and cry my eyes out. But not now; I can't do it now. Do you understand?"

That's how I felt. I couldn't let myself pause or stop; I had to keep on fighting.

Our hearing before three appellate court judges was scheduled for the morning of April 21, 2005. We had the names of the assigned judges, and according to my attorneys, we couldn't have hit a worse panel if we tried. Judges Douglas H. Ginsburg, David B. Sentelle and Karen L. Henderson all were Reagan appointees and almost always sided with classification and government secrecy.

Yet, my attorneys felt positive. More than enough organizations joined the amicus brief in support of our case. Media coverage, though not a lot, all had been positive. In addition to our legal team, we had other supportive civil liberties attorneys providing us with advice and assistance. Overall, things seemed to be going well.

On April 20, one day before our hearing in the appellate court, the ACLU organized a small press conference and roundtable discussion on my case and the abuse of the state secrets doctrine. The panel included well-known scholars and legal experts from such organizations as the Center for Constitutional Rights and the First Amendment Center. The U.S. media, to some degree (though not a lot), had started to pay attention to this arcane, common law–based privilege being used as a tool to quash legitimate cases and to cover up executive branch wrongdoings and, in certain cases, criminal activities. Interestingly, though, the majority of reporters and camera crews present were foreign: the room was filled primarily with German, French, British and Russian journalists. The mainstream U.S. media was conspicuously absent. I found this sad.

After we wrapped up the conference, on the way out I was stopped by two documentary filmmakers from France who had been pestering me about their new project, a film about me and the State Secrets Privilege. They were persistent about wanting to interview me and all the relevant witnesses pertaining to my case, and I had repeatedly refused to accept. I simply hadn't the time or energy and kept brushing them off. The older of the two, Mathieu, wouldn't take no for an answer. (The younger one, Jean, who handled the camera, seemed to be the quiet type.) He began to bargain.

"How about only two hours?"

I declined and held up my hand for him to stop. "No, I don't have any desire to be in a film, period. I've got to go."

As I walked away, he followed me out and brilliantly pushed my button. "But think about it, you'll do a service to all these other whistleblowers. You are the leader of this pack, national security whistleblowers. If your case is publicized, it would be good for all these other whistleblowers who have been abused like you . . ."

That last stopped me in my tracks. He had a point; this could be a great opportunity to shine a spotlight on the saga of national security whistleblowers. This guy was good—really good. I turned around and walked back. "All right then, let's make a deal."

He smiled. He knew he was very close. "I like deals, let's make one."

I couldn't help but smile back. "Here is the deal: for this project of yours, you'll cover my coalition's various events and congressional rallies. You will also interview several of my coalition members—at least five or six national security whistleblowers. In return, I will spend time with you; I'll let you interview me, not for two hours but for thirty minutes, and I'll ask my attorneys and other relevant witnesses to speak with you. Deal?"

"Deal, but as far as that thirty-minute rule goes, we'll see. I think I'll change your mind on that, but I'll take the thirty minutes."

This happened to be a very good decision. Not only did they interview many of my initial members, but Mathieu, with a background in investigative journalism, spent nearly two years uncovering facts and more witnesses relevant to my state secrets case. The pair made several trips to the States and were always there filming during my expanding coalition's congressional testimonies, rallies and media events. They came to follow me everywhere; and what's more, Mathieu and Jean became trusted friends.

17

Appellate Court

On the day before our appellate court hearing, I went to lunch with my ACLU team, Ann, Ben, and Melissa, along with a few others. The mood was upbeat. We were wired, anticipating the upcoming hearing, and bubbling over with plans. Ann felt confident and was fully prepared. In addition to Ben and Melissa, she would have Art Spitzer, their DC chapter attorney, present at the plaintiff's table. Zaid and Seiff also would be there, seated behind the primary team. The press advisory had been released, and the ACLU communication and PR division expected a good press turnout. Everything was ready and going smoothly so far. The feeling wouldn't even last through lunch.

Just as we were ordering coffee and dessert, Ann's pager went off; seconds later, Ben and Melissa's cell phones also started to ring. Ann looked at the pager with a frown. "It says *emergency*."

Melissa instantly added, "Mine too. It says *extremely urgent*. I'll go out and call HQ." Melissa left, almost running.

"I can't think what it could be," Ann said. "This is weird."

"Could it be that the judges postponed the hearing? I wouldn't be surprised—it would be consistent with their track record; canceling hearings with less than twenty-four hours' notice when they see potential media coverage."

Everyone turned to me. No one said a word, but I knew they were thinking precisely the same thing. I could see it in their faces and felt a knot in my stomach. I had been here before, many times. I tried to reassure myself that this time would be different. After all, I thought, we have the big guns: the ACLU and its tiger-like attorneys, numerous organizations that had signed on in support, and plenty of media attention. Could they defeat all this too? I wondered.

Melissa rushed in, near to bursting with this latest development. We held our breaths.

"Oh my God," she began, "you won't believe what the court did. I have never seen or heard of anything like this before."

"Come on Melissa, what the hell is it?" Ann demanded.

With tears welling up, she delivered the news. "The court—our appellate judges—just released an order, only a few minutes ago. They're *barring* all reporters and the public from the court hearing tomorrow. Except for the plaintiff and defendant attorneys, no one else can be inside; no one!"

Ann looked shocked. "What! Based on what? What kind of reasons did they cite for this outrageous order?"

"That's another weird, unprecedented point," Melissa replied. "No reason cited! They didn't provide any explana—"

Art Spitzer interrupted. "They can't do this. This is against the law. Unless they provide precedent or a legit reason, they cannot take away the freedom of the press. This is a very high-profile case!"

Ann was thinking. I could tell her pragmatic, critical faculty had kicked into high gear: she was already looking to counterattack. "Okay people," she began. "We need to tackle this immediately. We have less than twenty-four hours to do something. We'll start contacting all the media organizations, companies and associations and will get them to fight along with us. It won't be too difficult, since they'll be pissed big time being barred like this. Even those who didn't plan to cover the hearing will not swallow this; this is about their rights too. They have some pride . . ."

During the next thirty minutes my team continued to strategize and distribute To Do items and assign tasks to its members. They were appalled. They hadn't expected this. As I sat watching, I thought, *Welcome to my world*. At least now I had them with me; I was grateful.

I left the Washington Hotel and walked the streets aimlessly for almost an hour, then took the metro back home. By that time I already had several e-mails waiting, updates from the ACLU: the draft press release, the media's intention to file a claim against this unprecedented order, the organizations' pledge to join the battle . . .

I also had a voice mail from my good friend Ellsberg; despite chronic pain and a long trip from Berkeley, he would be out in front of the courthouse early the next day. Talk about support! I had other voice mails too from people wishing me luck.

I opened some wine and took it out to the patio, where I sat and calculated: in over three years now, since my battle had begun, I hadn't gone a day without a fight. Not one. How much longer could I last?

That night I couldn't sleep, nor even shut my eyes. By four in the morning I was showering, and by six, all dressed and ready. I sat in the kitchen waiting for Matthew to wake up.

My husband wanted to make a big breakfast but even the thought of food made me sick. I drank two coffees instead. He asked if I had prepared a statement. I shook my head no.

We drove to the DC courthouse in fitting rain—as was typical for every one of my canceled court date appearances before the press. Matthew dropped me at the courthouse entrance then went to find a parking spot. The cameras were already set up out front, and a dozen or so reporters were there, mostly from alternative media and the foreign press, along with fifty or so people; friends and supporters. Ellsberg too. I walked up and gave him a big hug. I was so glad to have him there, his support.

Beeson and the rest of the team had not yet arrived. I ducked under Dan's umbrella and waited anxiously. A man whom I'd never before met walked up and said he was a supporter from Kansas and had driven all night to get here—for solidarity. That was so touching. Here I was, surrounded by love and support.

Several reporters asked for comments. I told them I had nothing yet and asked them to wait until the hearing was concluded—*if there ends up being one*, I thought. I didn't know a thing about our status. I had to wait for Ann and the rest of the crew to find out.

At last the team arrived: Ann, Ben, Melissa and Art Spitzer. I asked Ann about the status. We would go inside, she said, to a private room designated for the plaintiffs, where we could discuss the case until called for the hearing. Once in the room, we were told that the court had not yet responded to the claim filed by the coalition of major newspapers and reporters. They hadn't responded to our request for an explanation either. We had to sit and wait.

I was bewildered. We had less than thirty minutes to the hearing. How could they wait to the last minute? The reporters and supporters too looked disgusted, but we had no other choice.

A few minutes later, word came down: "No Response." The court—our appellate judges—had rejected the reporters' claim out of hand; no reason or justification was provided. The same went for our request: no reason was provided for the exclusion of the public and reporters from my now CLOSED hearing.

What else could we do to counter this? My attorneys shook their heads: nothing. I asked if we would just stand there and take it. They had no reply. I started pacing, until finally we were called to the hearing room. There was one case ahead of us and we were asked to take a seat in the back and wait.

Their hearing took almost two hours. I looked at my watch every five minutes, fidgeting. I turned around and saw that every row had filled up, with many from the mainstream media. Many others had gathered outside the room, waiting to see what would develop.

Finally, the hearing for those ahead of us concluded. As their attorneys began packing up to leave, Judge Ginsburg, the lead judge, motioned to one of the court security guards. He whispered something to the guard, then leaned over to Judge Sentelle and whispered something in his ear. I wondered what they were cooking up. I didn't have to wait to find out.

When the other group's attorneys had left, Judge Ginsburg made his announcement.

"We now are going to ask everyone in this room, except for the plaintiff and defendant attorneys, to leave this courtroom. As of now, this courtroom is in closed session. Guards, please escort everyone out."

Some of the reporters stood to leave on their own, while others waited to be escorted out. A few had to be removed by force, shouting appropriate slogans such as, "Where is our Constitution?" and "This is no justice!"

I watched the courtroom empty of all my friends, supporters and a handful of reporters. I almost broke down and cried as the guard approached my husband. He was my partner; he was affected by all this as much as I; he was my rock. I asked Ann to do something. She shook her head and said he had to follow the order. The guard escorted my husband out. In my lap I made a tight fist and dug my nails into my palm until I drew blood. With so much rage and frustration bottled up inside me, I had to poke holes in myself to let some out before I exploded.

The three judges sat and waited for my attorney to take her stand before them. Ginsburg, with his white goatee, smirked during the entire time. Sentelle, the ruddy fat judge, always deferred to Ginsburg for his cues; and Henderson, the scrawny-looking judge, remained silent throughout, and stared into space as if stoned.

According to the appellate hearing protocol, the plaintiff's attorney goes first, followed by the defendant's attorney, and finally, a Q & A session. Each party would be allowed precisely five minutes to deliver a statement, and then answer any judge's questions to clarify points.

Beeson went first and presented our case, arguing against state secrets on the grounds that it was meant to be invoked to exclude specific evidence, documents or information—not to disallow the entire case from proceeding in court, as had happened with mine. Furthermore, referring to all the already public records and documents (such as congressional letters, the IG report, and hundreds of articles), she made it clear to the judges that to argue my case I didn't even need to seek anything classified for use as evidence.

None of the judges were having it. Ginsburg asked an irrelevant question, suggesting another venue for my case—that we engage in arbitration with the FBI directly. (Ann calmly explained why that could not be done.) Sentelle cracked wise to some FBI attorneys in the room, evoking forced and phony laughter. I stared unamused, waiting for them to move on.

Now it was the defendants' turn. The Justice Department and the FBI had more than a dozen top-flight attorneys between them, which was overkill. Our party consisted of six, including me. As we waited for their attorney to take his stand, Ginsburg cleared his throat and spoke into the mike.

"Now we have to ask the plaintiff and her attorneys to leave the room. Due to the sensitivity and secrecy involved in the case, we have decided to exclude you from the hearing room while the government presents and argues its case."

We all froze in place. What in the world was happening? This was unheard of: the plaintiff and her attorneys being excluded from the court hearing, forbidden to hear the defendants' argument? How were we supposed to argue against what we didn't even know? How were we going to respond to something we were not allowed to hear? Even Kafka would have been shocked.

I turned to Ann. "I am not leaving. This is absurd. Let's stay and fight this. We shouldn't allow this to happen. We can't let them get away with this. I am not leaving." I was shaking, my whole body was shaking.

Ann put her arm around my shoulder and leaned very close and whispered, "Sibel, you're right. I know. I know this is ridiculous. However, we have to obey the judges at this point. This isn't over yet. They are not going to rule today. We have plenty of time to address this, tackle this later. Now, we have to be respectful and comply. Otherwise they'll have us arrested."

I looked up in disbelief. "They are the ones who should be arrested. These judges are criminals; they are butchering our Constitution and rights!"

Patiently and gently, Ann led me out of the room; the rest of our team followed. Art's face was red. I could see smoke coming out of his ears. Three court security guards accompanied us, asking that we remain in the hall, in case the judges decided to bring us back in for questions. Once outside the courtroom, I watched the guard shut the doors, then turn and stand at attention before them, as though guarding against any eavesdropping. I was trembling violently now, ready to scream; I was close to breaking down.

We waited in the hall for almost fifteen minutes while the defendants in the courtroom fed the judges anything they pleased, unopposed, unchallenged. I couldn't stand still and kept pacing the hall.

At the end of our wait, the court clerk appeared to notify us that the session, the hearing, was concluded. We now could leave. It was over. My one and only hearing—from which I, myself, was excluded—was at an end.

As we walked to the elevators, I was trying to think of what to say to the press. They were waiting. How was I to deliver a statement without stammering, breaking down and crying? How was I to handle the rage, frustration and crushing sense of defeat before that crowd?

Ann stopped me before we stepped out. "Sibel, I know you're angry. I'm angry too; we all are. But please, *please* don't say anything negative about the judges up there. You don't want to piss them off. This is not over yet. They still have to rule. You don't want to antagonize them at this point. Try to set a positive tone; be mild."

"Screw those judges," I snapped. "They don't belong on the bench. I am not going to lie about this. I am not going to help them cover this up. The public has the right to know about what's happening inside these courtrooms. They have the right to know about these judges. I didn't do it in Walton's case; I regret that . . ."

Ann tried to persuade me. I walked away fast, out of the building. There were so many people standing in the rain looking drenched and bedraggled, waiting for me. There were reporters too, and a couple of TV cameras. I stepped forward and positioned myself before a dozen microphones. I tried to breathe; I couldn't. I stood silently and took a minute or two to force back the sob in my throat and regain my voice. Matthew came and stood next to me, and held an umbrella over my head.

I began to speak. I explained what had happened inside. I put forth the implications of what had taken place. I remember pausing, reflecting on just who was before me, then telling them, "If you think this is all about me, if you think this is all about one whistleblower's case, you are wrong! This is about you too. This is about all of us, our rights. The implications of this will affect all of you, not only me. If they can get away so easily with invoking a ridiculous privilege like this, they will not stop with this case. They are going to invoke this time after time; whenever they want to cover up their own criminal acts, whenever they want to leave you all in the dark . . ."

I had no idea how soon I would be proved right in that prediction. After my case, the administration began to invoke state secrets right and left. In the coming years they would invoke it many times. It didn't end with that administration: the trend would continue with the next administration, full force.

As I was speaking, I noticed Congresswoman Carolyn Maloney, representative from New York, walking toward me. She came and stood beside me. I stepped aside and offered her the mike. First she hugged me; then she delivered a powerful speech on the injustice and transparent abuses heaped on me and my case, made all the more egregious since my vindication. The reporters kept writing, cameras kept flashing in our faces. I recognized my new French partners, Mathieu and Jean, filming the scene, capturing that moment in the rain. They were soaked. They had been there since eight that morning.

Then Ann delivered a statement, ever succinct and articulate, followed by Dan Ellsberg, who gave a passionate speech. I couldn't stay a minute longer. My legs were giving out. I hadn't eaten for more than a day, and with all the feelings I fought so hard to repress, I didn't have an ounce of energy left.

I left them all without saying a word. I had to go. As I walked to our car, refusing to stay under Matthew's umbrella, the raindrops soaked my hair and face. No one could see I was crying.

Less than three weeks later, on May 6, 2005, the appellate court issued its decision, consisting of a single line: *Uphold the lower court's decision and the State Secrets Privilege.* They did not cite a reason. They did not write an opinion, and gave no further explanation.

After seeing their attitude and what went on at my hearing, how could I have expected anything more from those judges? My ACLU attorneys were disappointed but not surprised. They promised this would not be the end of my case. They would take this to the highest court of the land, the U.S. Supreme Court.

18

Another Turning Point

May through October 2005 was consumed with intense activity. I now spent nearly every waking hour in four different channels of work.

I continued to collect signatures, via my website, on my petition to Congress. So far I had over ten thousand people signed on. Additionally, I had gathered pledges of support from more than two dozen organizations and public policy groups. I posted all pertinent articles and updates, and spent time every evening responding to supporters or anyone requesting more information on my case.

I continued my public speaking and media campaign on whistleblower issues and relevant civil liberties cases. In any given week I would have four or five radio interviews, most of them local and/or alternative stations. I tried to write regularly and publish short op-ed pieces.

I spent much of this time working with the coalition. The NSWBC had doubled in size and now had nearly fifty national security whistleblower members. We had been taking on the Congress and were trying to make our voice in the media louder and more often heard. During the previous March, I had come in contact with a man who would become a catalyst in raising our coalition's profile and taking it to the next level. William (Bill) Weaver was an associate professor of political science and an associate in the Center for Law and Border Studies at the University of Texas at El Paso. He specialized in executive branch secrecy policy, governmental abuse, and law and bureaucracy.

I had stumbled on a paper Bill had written, the best and most comprehensive piece ever on the State Secrets Privilege, and decided to contact him. He was happy to hear from me (he had cited my case in his paper), and when I told him about others in the coalition and our activities targeting the Congress, he seemed interested. He joined us in our congressional briefing and rallies, and spent time helping me research and investigate potential members. Bill encouraged me to take the next step and structure the coalition, to define its objectives and mission, create a web presence, turn it into an organization and even draft model legislation for meaningful whistleblower protection. His expertise, advice and overall support were indispensable. He became a mentor and best friend. Unlike many, Bill is all about action, he gets things done.

Finally, there was the upcoming Supreme Court filing that capped my attention and energy. My attorneys planned to file the petition with the Court by the end of summer, and a lot of work had to be done. I knew this was my last stop as far as the courts were concerned. My FOIA case was lost, to secrecy and classification. This, my primary case, had already lost in the hands of Judge Walton and was thrown out on appeal by a kangaroo court.

The IG's report had neither brought accountability nor needed reforms in the FBI. From what I heard, things continued as usual, and the translation unit remained a mess. Feghali had even been promoted to now supervise the Arabic department. Bryan too was promoted, to a high-level position in HQ. Frields and Watson are happily retired and secured cushy positions at Booz Allen Hamilton, a private firm. No one in Congress was willing or brave enough to take up my case and hold public hearings. I had not totally given up, however, and continued to collect more public support to petition them; yet the prospects seemed slim to none. Clearly, mine was not the only case that lacked congressional oversight. I had by now become well aware of many other critical cases in which responsibility on the part of Congress was nowhere to be found. Their reluctance is legendary.

The spectacular failure of the executive branch and its investigative bodies, along with the notorious absence of congressional vigilance, left me with one last channel.

Beeson and her team were hard at work through all of June and July 2005. Filing a claim with the Supreme Court is so very different from any other court filings, and the rules of argument unlike anything before the lower courts. Prior to my case, Ann had argued twice before the Supreme Court—and one of those cases she won. I had no doubt I was in most capable hands.

Just as in my appeal, my legal team decided to gather other parties to join our case through filing amicus briefs. This time around, we also had the support of organizations and groups filing briefs on their exclusion from my earlier hearing before the appellate court—that included the media.

We were presenting the Supreme Court with two questions: (1) whether the court of appeals erred in affirming dismissal of a retaliatory termination case by an FBI whistleblower based on the State Secrets Privilege prior to any discovery or consideration of nonprivileged evidence; and (2) whether, consistent with the First and Fifth Amendments, the court of appeals erred in excluding the press and public, sua sponte ("of one's own will"), from an appellate proceeding without case-specific findings demonstrating the necessity of closure.

My attorneys were preparing a well-articulated argument on the misuse of the State Secrets Privilege in my case and on the confusion of the lower courts in dealing with this arcane tool. How could the courts dismiss without granting discovery—without a single witness testifying, a single document entered into evidence, or a single oral argument? Where in our Constitution did our founding fathers give the federal government the right to take away a citizen's right to petition the courts and receive a fair trial?

The government's case was simple: due to national security–related reasons, I had no First Amendment rights. Moreover, due to certain state secrets with effects on so-called national security, I had to be stripped of my Fourth and Fifth Amendment rights. I was not their only victim; more and more American citizens were being gagged and stripped of their rights.

I couldn't help asking myself, where had we gone wrong to get to this point? Had we—meaning *we the people*—forsaken checks and balances in one fell swoop, through fear? This was all being done in the name of national security. Our guaranteed rights were no longer guaranteed, but conditional. How could the other two branches, our courts and Congress, allow the executive branch such sway, to go unchecked, unchallenged? Saddest of all, what had become of our fourth branch, the media? Why were they all lying down?

The facts were grim: our government had begun to torture and sodomize its detainees in the name of national security; our executive branch was engaged in kidnapping people from all over the world and imprisoning them in secret locations—this too in the name of national security; our intelligence agencies had turned against its own citizens by utilizing technology to illegally spy on them—again, for reasons of national security.

These were some of many reasons I had to pursue the Supreme Court as tenaciously as I could. My case was one way to protect other Americans from going through similar injustices and abuses. Too many others have suffered at the hands of a government whose power is absolute; once wielded, there's no end to invoking state secrets.

I had lost so much already. Gone were my family ties and heritage, my house in Turkey, my privacy . . . and more. The Supreme Court was my last chance. I put everything I had, all my hope and expectations, into this one last battle.

In the middle of June 2005, I received a call from *Vanity Fair* reporter David Rose, who called to let me know that his feature article on my case was scheduled to come out in the first week of August, less than two months.

I had met Rose the previous fall. He had called me from England to introduce himself and to let me know that he had taken an interest in my case and battle against the "odd privilege." He was a respected independent reporter, a seasoned and savvy investigative journalist with impeccable credentials.

David spent over six months investigating and interviewing relevant witnesses, including several high-level people inside the FBI, Congress and the Justice Department with firsthand knowledge of my case. Further, he had uncovered certain facts and reasons as to why, in my case, state secrets had been invoked. I expected a groundbreaking article.

After speaking with him, I immediately called my ACLU attorneys to notify them: the piece in *Vanity Fair* would hit the stands the first week of August. We decided to time our Supreme Court filing accordingly.

The ten-page feature, titled "An Inconvenient Patriot," was revelatory and explosive. David had beautifully woven together many of the facts, revelations, history and emotional aspects of my case. He had succeeded in unearthing one major case that my own case and one of the FBI counterintelligence projects involved. In so doing, it was revealed that one of the most powerful men in the United States, the Speaker of the House, the heavyweight representative from Chicago, Dennis Hastert, had been receiving large sums in bribes from certain Turkish people and organizations in the United States who happened to be the targets of FBI wiretap investigations.

Rose connected the dots, quoting one FBI counterintelligence official who confirmed Chicago as the hub of an international criminal network with direct ties to Congress. The bribery scandal, it turned out, involved elected officials in both parties. Initially, there had been internal pressure from the bureau to appoint a special prosecutor to take on the case; but as soon as word got out, colleagues were steered away from investigating elected politicians and turned their focus instead on appointed officials. My wiretap translations threatened to expose them. Ashcroft and the Department of Justice reacted as they did to ensure that none of this came out.

As Rose reports in the article,

Some of the calls reportedly contained what sounded like references to large-scale drug shipments and other crimes. To a person who knew nothing about their context, the details were confusing and it wasn't always clear what might be significant. One name, however, apparently stood out—a man the Turkish callers often referred to by the nickname "Denny boy." It was the Republican congressman from Illinois and Speaker of the House, Dennis Hastert. According to some of the wiretaps, the F.B.I.'s targets had arranged for tens of thousands of dollars to be paid to Hastert's campaign funds in small checks. Under Federal Election Commission rules, donations of less than $200 are not required to be itemized in public filings.

An examination of Hastert's federal filings shows that the level of un-itemized payments his campaigns received over many years was relatively high. Between April 1996 and December 2002, un-itemized personal donations to the Hastert for Congress Committee amounted to $483,000. In contrast, un-itemized contributions in the same period to the committee run on behalf of the House majority leader, Tom Delay, Republican of Texas, were only $99,000.

The lengthy and comprehensive article went on to provide a more detailed account of Hastert's campaign donations and his flip-flop voting record in Congress on issues involving Turkey. Rose quoted current and former FBI officials and senior congressional staff familiar with my case, testimonies, and even the classified IG report.

The reaction in the mainstream press was not just muted, it was stunningly silent. Even though the Justice Department, the FBI and Hastert's office did not and would not return reporters' calls seeking comments, none issued a single denial. Puzzlingly—and disturbingly—that didn't seem to matter, because the mainstream media apparently wasn't interested. They hadn't covered the article. In contrast, the online communities and international press treated the story like a bombshell. The piece was picked up by thousands of websites and forums within a week of its release.

My attorneys filed the Cert Petition with the Supreme Court a day after the Rose piece came out, on August 4, 2005. From this point on, we would sit and wait.

In the first half of fall 2005, as I waited for the Supreme Court's decision, I focused all my energy and attention on various activities and events dealing with our now formalized coalition, the National Security Whistleblowers Coalition. We had successfully launched the organization's website. We now had over a dozen partner organizations, more than fifty whistleblower members, and one of the top experts on relevant legislative and legal issues as senior advisor and on our board of directors.

This anxiety-filled period of waiting to hear from the Court was filled with frenetic activity. Rallies, briefings and the first-ever national security whistleblowers conference all helped to reduce ongoing stress and grief.

Thus occupied almost 24/7 with whistleblower issues and meeting after meeting with congressional staff, the clock, in the meantime, kept ticking on my case. The anxiously awaited news reached me on Monday, November 28, with a phone call. As soon as I picked up, I could hear it in her voice. It was Ann.

"Sibel . . . I am so sorry ..." A pain shot up from my guts to my throat. All I could do was blink and try to swallow. "We just found out. The Supreme Court decided not to take our case. This nonsense State Secrets

Privilege won another round . . ."

When I regained my voice, I asked her almost in a whisper, "Did they say why? Did they give any reason?"

Ann sighed. "No, not a single word. I know how painful this must be for you; I am so sorry, Sibel. I am so sorry for our country."

I began to shake and couldn't stop my voice from trembling. "What can we do about this? Is there anything that can be done? Is it all over, one hundred percent?"

Another deep sigh. "As far as the courts are concerned, yes. It is all over, this was the last stop. It's such nonsense—with all the congressional confirmation and the amazing IG report confirming your reports and vindicating you. But as far as the Congress goes, now it is even more urgent that they address your case . . ."

Tears had already started rolling down my face, salty drops on my lips; I needed air. "I have to go, Ann. You did your best; I know I had the best legal team . . . you were great . . ." and I just hung up. I began to sob; a loud, guttural sob. I hunched on the floor and sobbed nonstop, my body a bundle of pain, as though everything were pouring out at once: the longing for my dad, the hole and the loneliness that was the absence of my family, the shocks endured from relentless, cruel government attacks for the past four years, the exhaustion of never-ending defeat . . .

I sobbed on the floor for hours until I was numb. Then I just sat staring at nothing, in a timeless void, exhausted. It was over. I recalled the reporter who asked me how I managed in the face of all the blows and pain. I remembered my small stone, hitting the glass and forming a crack that would grow until the object shattered. I said I could never let that happen.

Well, the stone hit my shield. The fatal crack had formed, and it was expanding.

The months following the Supreme Court's rejection of my case remain a blur. I had experienced my first depression that came with the death of my father and gone through its stages; yet this one was manifestly different. I would lie days in a row in bed under the covers, not sobbing or crying or thinking of anything in particular, just numb and totally blank. Then I would suddenly go into a manic phase, combing through boxes and shoving into garbage bags every document, letter and file I could get my hands on having anything to do with my case: there were thousands of them, seemingly everywhere. Then I would set these overstuffed bags out front, to be taken out with the trash. I wanted everything to be erased, every scrap of my four-year battle. I wanted them gone from my life. My husband, without my knowledge, rescued those bags and tucked them in our attic.

I kept my home phones unplugged and did not return any calls. I only attended to a few previous NSWBC commitments without knowing or even caring why.

In December, during Christmas, I attempted to go back to Turkey for a visit: face the threat of arrest, even death, and get it over with. Was this an unconscious suicide attempt? I plotted it secretly, which might well be an answer; I didn't want Matthew to find out and talk sense into me. In the end, I couldn't do it; I packed my suitcase, left a note for my husband and departed to the airport, only to park a mile away and watch my plane take off without me.

I refused to talk about my case—with Matthew, with anyone, period. Matthew tried very hard. Anytime he mentioned a new piece of news, dealing with civil liberties, for example, or a whistleblower case, I'd stop him. "I don't give a damn," I'd tell him, "no point."

Purging my life of every reminder was not enough to alter the atmosphere of my bleak house and the depressing air that filled it. I wanted it gone as well. My feelings were non-negotiable; I put it to Matthew in absolute terms. "I want to sell this house and move. I don't want to live in this house." He had no say—for the first time in our thirteen-year partnership. I still wonder how he put up with it all, my determined attempt to eradicate our past; how he patiently bowed to my cold steel resolve.

Together we had built so much.

By February, I had contacted a real estate agent and put our furnished house on the market. The only thing I wanted were the photo albums, along with a few essential items. I donated every one of my suits, every stitch of clothing worn to the court events and congressional testimonies. No matter how many times they went to the cleaners, I'd never be able to remove the smell of defeat and disillusionment.

My mother's bitter statements rang in my ears; they kept on playing in my head. *Do you think this country is any different from Turkey or Iran when it comes to the government? Haven't you learned from your father's experience?* And perhaps most damning of all, her wretched analogy—*you are swimming against Niagara Falls!* Experience proved her right. I was naïve, a Pollyanna, ignoring clear defeat, outmatched by my foes and pretending I could ever beat them. I swallowed the bitter pill. How could anyone bring justice to such protected criminals, backed as they are by such interests? Was I insane to think I could? Yet how I tried!

In the worst depths of my rage and despair, my husband quietly talked to me. He had planned a trip to a Caribbean island for the two of us, a perfect getaway. No TV, no computers, no radio or news. Our deal was not to discuss anything related to my all-consuming struggle of the past four years—some trick!—but that was the plan. It lasted until the fourth day, when Matthew, understandably and deeply concerned, turned to me with empathy. "I know how hard it is for you, how hard it's been," he began. "It's been hard on me too. I know you think you lost—lost everything—but you are wrong, Sibel. You accomplished a lot; I just can't stand to see you not seeing this ..."

"Yeah well too bad, futile," I snapped, clenching my fist. "Wasted four long years and lost everything—almost everything. And you know what? In the end, no one gives a shit, people don't care. They are too busy with their lives, like I was before this. As far as the government goes, this government is worse than a monarchy; at least with a monarchy you don't have any expectations or illusions . . . I don't want to talk about it. You promised . . ."

He didn't back off. "You're wrong. People do care; *some* do. You went beyond your own case, Sibel ..." He talked about some things I managed to accomplish. I didn't want to hear it. I cut him off.

"Frankly, I'm sorry that I gave hope to all these whistleblowers ..." I continued with my defeatist rant; I grew more and more manic. "Remember that so-called saint, the revered Democrat, Representative Henry Waxman? What happened? I went inside a SCIF for only, God, like my what, tenth SCIF session . . . I went in there with his top people, and they said they wanted to know, know everything about Dennis Hastert and the rest of the corrupt cabal—and what happened? In the middle of my testimony, his chief legal advisor stops me, interrupts to ask, 'Before you go any further, were there any Democrats involved in this?' to which I replied, 'Yes, a few.' And then he gets up and says, 'We have to stop here and not go any further. We don't want to know. Not at this point. We'll wait for the IG report and after that contact you to come again.' Aha! *That's* the way it works!"

I paused to catch my breath. "I wish you would have stopped me instead of encouraging me to keep pushing. My mother was right, this damn government is no different than the rest—it is nothing but a grand illusion!"

I went inside the cottage and grabbed another beer. My heart was pounding frantically. I was angry now, *very* angry. I guessed this was another stage. I'd gone from inconsolable sobbing to nonstop crying to total numbness to sleeping and hiding to discarding reminders and taking flight in my mind and now this: to raw, unexpurgated anger. I didn't want to dump it all on him, not here, not now, but Matthew had started it, he opened the floodgate. His optimism and hope enraged me. How could he? Was he blind or just stupid? He maintained the illusion I once believed in, the eternal vigilance crap, the light at the end of the tunnel dream; white knights defeating the forces of evil.

I raved at him and told him all that. I accused him of being blind and naïve. I demanded that he wake up and smell reality. I poured out four years of bottled-up anger until I ran out of words, exhausted. Now what? What was left in me? I wondered.

Matthew listened serenely, in part relieved, and glad—I'm sure—to see me worked up and wired rather than so utterly devoid of feeling. He was frustrated too for not being able to reach me, to make me see what he saw. At the end of my tirade, he spoke gently, with insistence. "I'm sorry, I know I promised not to talk about this . . . I only wanted to make you realize that not all was loss . . . they [testimonies, briefings, interviews, rallies, et al.] were not for nothing. They touched some people; they affected some; they woke up some of them. Some whistleblowers decided to come forward after seeing your efforts and reading about you; some will do the same in the future. There may be other people and organizations paying attention to these cases and issues you don't know of." He got up from his chair and faced me. "Maybe your legal case is now over, in the courts. But I see a movement you've started. That one is just beginning. That's all."

I didn't believe him. Rather, I didn't *want* to believe him. I was afraid to hope. I'd made up my mind to put it behind me, to end it, and I didn't want him planting doubts. I was determined to move on, as far as I could from the filth of politics, DC: the *real* sin city. I had plans and all sorts of things to take care of: a house to sell, a city to choose, a job to obtain. In a few months' time, I kept telling myself, nobody would even remember this saga. No one really cares to know, let alone fight for these issues.

"Ms. Edmonds," the strange voice on the phone almost pleaded, after I had tried to cut him off, "my name is Larry Siems. I'm not with the news. I'm with PEN Foundation in New York. You were one of the nominees for our 2006 PEN Newman First Amendment Award."

Oh. I did remember receiving a notification letter a few months back. My name had been put forth by the National Coalition Against Censorship (NCAC), a coalition of top-notch civil liberties organizations, as a nominee for this prestigious award. Though honored, I'd dismissed it as highly unlikely, considering who'd won it in the past. I didn't think I had the slightest chance.

"Right, I apologize for the mix-up," I told him dismissively. "So, who won this year?"

He gave a quiet chuckle. "Well, that's why I'm calling you, Ms. Edmonds. Our committee, our panel of judges, has selected you as the winner of this year's PEN Newman First Amendment Award. You are the winner."

I was speechless. I remained silent for what must've been minutes, letting this news sink in. These organizations in NCAC, the PEN Foundation, its staff and juries, all of whom were familiar with my case, had recognized my struggle—my relentless battle—as not only that of one lone whistleblower but a battle for freedom of speech itself, our first and most precious guaranteed right.

In a voice now nearly a whisper, I managed to stammer how honored I was, confessing to this stranger how I'd decided no one cared and how futile it all was. Suddenly this voice sounded small. *My God . . .*

Larry told me to expect follow-up calls and e-mails from the foundation. Their annual award gala was scheduled for April 18, about a month away. I thanked him again, hung up, and sat there awhile, as if in a dream. My father had spent his entire life fighting for this most important, essential right: the right of free speech. That my battle now was recognized as such felt akin to victory. I would have given anything to bring him back, if only to share this moment, an impossible wish. I knew in that very same moment, however, how fortunate I was to have a person, a life partner, who lived this with me, every high and low, each pain, each tiny victory. And victory it was. With that thought I reached for the phone and dialed.

Matthew answered on the first ring. "Hi and how are you doing to-day?"

"Matthew . . ." and suddenly I burst into tears.

He panicked. "What's wrong? Where are you? What happened?"

I grabbed hold of myself, almost embarrassed. "I received a call from the PEN Foundation. Remember that letter from a few months back? . . ."

He would be home in an hour, he said. "This calls for a celebration. I'll pick up a bottle of champagne on the way . . ."

An hour later, Matthew came home, and after giving me a long hug, dragged me to our home office. "Wait, first I want to show you something." He sat me in front of the computer and pulled up a chair. Then he went to Google and under Search typed *State Secrets Privilege* and hit Enter. The search result brought up over 100,000 hits. Matthew turned to me. "Remember four years ago, when we found out about Ashcroft invoking the State Secrets Privilege in your case? Remember how we searched under Google to find out what the heck it was about?" I nodded and he went on. "Remember we got less than ten hits? Look at it now: over one hundred thousand. Almost all of it on you—your fight, your battle; you and your case put this out in the public domain. Your relentless pursuit, your refusal to give up and your public outcry was picked up by tens of thousands of people, forums and websites."

Next he typed *Sibel Edmonds* in the search box and hit Enter. This search brought up over 400,000 hits. Matthew turned to me again. "Nearly half a million, Sibel. You said 'it was for nothing, it didn't make a difference, no one cares' but the results, the facts, say otherwise. There are tens of thousands of people who have been publishing everything you've been writing, everything you've ever said; they have documented all the court filings, articles, letters, you name it. You owe these people, you have to keep up the fight. It's not over, not yet."

He was right. I may have lost the court battles, the battle in getting Congress to do what it should have done, as its duty to the nation, and the attempt to shake up the media to stand up and do its job. I may have lost my birth country and all my family relations there; but I had not lost all the battles. Maybe some—however few, however little—I had won, and others still continued; none of them mine alone.

On April 18, 2006, the evening of the PEN Award gala, I couldn't relax. I was worried about the appropriateness of the short acceptance speech I had already rewritten several times. I was nervous about standing in a spotlight before such a distinguished crowd in so formal a setting, reading this brief statement. Reflecting on the award itself, I was overwhelmed with its significance, and that it had been bestowed on me.

ABC's Diane Sawyer hosted the award. After the introduction, the screens came on and a beautifully executed six-minute film on my case began to play. I was surprised. No one had told me they had produced this touching film; it meant so much. There was Congresswoman Carolyn Maloney, offering her passionate testimonial from the screen, ". . . she not only was a strong advocate for her own case, but she became a strong advocate for the public policy, for the greater good." Then Senator Lautenberg, our organization's only advocate in the Senate, whose staff also helped to draft comprehensive legislation to protect whistleblowers, added to the film his gracious remarks.

The voice-over was done by Sawyer, who went on to describe how a large marble piece of the U.S. Supreme Court building had broken off and shattered into pieces on the very day the judges there rejected hearing my case.

And finally, there he was, Paul Newman himself, on my 2006 PEN Newman First Amendment Award film, delivering one of my all-time favorite quotes.

"I'm Paul Newman. For the past fourteen years we've been honoring courageous Americans who have defended their First Amendment rights against overwhelming odds, and in so doing, affirmed the protection of the First Amendment for all of us. Sibel Edmonds adds luster to this distinguished group of honorees with her refusal to back down from her confrontation with the FBI. In his straight-talking way, President Harry Truman said: When even one American, who has done nothing wrong, is forced by fear to shut his mouth, then all Americans are in peril. Sibel Edmonds would not let an intimidating FBI shut her mouth, and as a result, suffered grievous consequences, but she has persevered and we are better off for her sacrifices."

Diane Sawyer announced my name as I made my way through the maze of tables to the stage, clutching the piece of paper with my brief acceptance speech.

Once there, in the spotlight, gazing into the darkened full room, I wished that my father, Dan Ellsberg, Bill Weaver, and every single member of the NSWBC were there to share that moment. I felt a surge of energy, confidence and determination—something I thought had been lost forever. All anxiety and nervousness began to melt as I started to speak. I thanked the National Coalition Against Censorship and PEN. I accepted the award on behalf of all our whistleblowers at NSWBC and continued with the following.,

"Standing up to despotism and tyranny has always been considered illegal by those in power, and dangerous to those who would expose them. Today we are facing despots who use 'national security' to push everything under a blanket of secrecy; to gag and call it a privilege; to detain without having to show a cause; and to torture yet believe it's fully justified.

"We must be vigilant and fight back, for our freedom is under assault—not from terrorists—for they only attack us, not our freedom, and they can never prevail. No, the attacks on our freedom are from within, from our very own government; and unless we recognize these attacks for what they are, and stand up, and speak out—no, shout out—against those in government who are attempting to silence the brave few who are warning us, then we are doomed to wake up one sad morning and wonder when and where our freedom died."

There came a thunder of applause; people stood up and kept applauding for what seemed a very long time. I knew they were applauding not only for me but for those who had fought the bloody fight for the past four years; those who had stood up for our rights and freedom, despite the severe consequences brought on them by the now despotic state.

As I descended from the stage, I found myself face to face with Verboud, my French director friend. He put his hand on my arm and said, "This is where our documentary ends. We started with Sibel the FBI whistleblower; then Sibel the gagged and classified woman; and that was followed by Sibel the whistleblower coalition leader and organizer. Today, Sibel has been recognized and awarded by other activists on the broader front where the fight is for freedom. This is the beginning of your 'next stage.' I want to congratulate you again . . . you have given up so much; you deserve this and so much more. Your fight has not ended."

From the time I was a kid, I always liked to step out of myself and look at my life from above; to pretend I'm a camera, capturing a snapshot, mainly of turning points: those discrete, ethereal choices that determine what we become and where we go.

I had almost given up. I had decided that my little voice and small raised fists didn't count—that I could kick and scream and fight all I could and it wouldn't make a difference in the end. I was ready to move on and become the "uninvolved" citizen again; live my day-to-day life and tune out the alarms. One decision by one organization, followed by a phone call, changed all that; it became a turning point. It put me back on course, not as a fighter for one case, not a whistleblower for her cause, but as a fighter for our most sacrosanct right: our freedom. In a moment of despair, I had nearly forgotten Jefferson's priceless words, that the price of freedom is eternal vigilance. I would continue this fight for as long as it took; that may be my lifetime. I will do so as a loving human, as my father's daughter, as a woman, and as a citizen of a nation that promised and guaranteed my freedom.

19

Vietnam and Motherhood

The announcement came over the speakers, an update of our ETA by the pilot. In less than two hours, my long trip home from Hanoi, Vietnam, was going to end. Well almost, since I had one more flight from Los Angeles to DC, another excruciating five hours. That was nothing compared to the fourteen hours I'd already spent in the air.

I readjusted the baby carrier and pressed my nose on top of my almost five-month-old daughter's head. Breathing in her scent and listening to her steady breathing, I locked my arms around her tiny sleeping body wrapped tightly against me. I was taking her home for the very first time. Many first times were waiting for her: her first time in the United States, her first real home, first real nursery, first winter . . . I was excited for her, excited and nervous. I was nervous for me too. This was my coming back home after spending almost eight months abroad in Vietnam, after being away in many ways and going through the changes that accompany first-time motherhood.

I had spent almost all of 2008 abroad, most of it in Vietnam. I spent considerable time exploring the country north to south, visiting orphanages and ethnic minority schools, interviewing and documenting nonprofit organizations with a focus on children there, while waiting impatiently to be matched with my child to be. The amazing second half of my journey started with meeting my daughter, Ela, and from that point my life revolved around her. First I had to go through three months of paperwork and procedures by the Vietnamese government required for international adoption. During this period, I spent every single day at the orphanage feeding, holding and forming my attachment to her and, inevitably, bonding with the rest of the children there and their Vietnamese caregivers. After Ela was officially released to my custody, we went through equally arduous procedures to have the adoption approved by the U.S. government and obtain her entry visa into the States.

This time away from home served as therapy. I badly needed the healing time to detoxify myself from the pessimism and cynicism that had naturally settled in. Body and mind demanded it.

In 2006, following the Supreme Court saga and the PEN/Newman Award, my entire focus had been to seek hearings and legislation on congressional oversight and accountability, excessive secrecy and, of course, meaningful protections for whistleblowers. My days were filled with meetings, alliances with other watchdog groups, networking, rallies; the list goes on.

I wanted something positive—something good—to come out of my case that would benefit others. I was determined to use my network to get Congress to act, to fulfill its role of oversight and accountability. We needed more than words. We needed sound legislation. We were long overdue for laws with teeth that would truly provide protection for those seeking to tell the truth about what their government is up to. We lacked the mechanisms to enforce accountability.

Arousing passion is no easy task. A malaise had settled in, a "you can't rock the boat" attitude among my coalition members and friends. Who could blame them? I know well what exhaustion will do, and the battles are never-ending. I also knew that I was in a unique position; my experience had armed me, in a way. If anyone could get them to rise from their weariness, from flagging in the midst of a fight, it was me. And to-gether, drawing strength from one another, we did it. We were united in a single cause: Get Congress to act.

As we pounded on the doors of congressional offices, the executive branch was hard at work behind the scenes holding private meetings with congressional leaders on better ways and stronger laws to silence and punish government whistleblowers. As always, their tactic was to use the fear factor and throw a blanket over crimes under the guise of "national security." The executive branch considered those who exposed such crimes as traitors. How dare they let the public know! The admin-istration wanted tougher laws against government whistleblowers, and they proposed tougher punishment as well: the kind suited for spies and those engaged in sedition. What's more, they didn't meet with much re-sistance or disagreement from their audience in Congress.

We ended up gathering a handful of supporters in the House (no re-sponse from either party in the Senate). Our supporters were leaders of the appropriate House committees and subcommittees yet were in the Democratic Minority. The most ambitious and outspoken was Congress-man Henry Waxman, who headed the Government Reform Committee.

What we wanted, what we asked for, was to have public hearings on our cases, put these public testimonies and witnesses into congressio-nal records and transcripts, and let Americans see and hear what their government is doing to them on their behalf, with their tax money, and with zero accountability. For that we needed new laws that would be en-forced. Our handful of minority supporters seemed to wholeheartedly agree, and promised to back our initiatives.

We set to work. That entailed a blizzard of activity over months. We were facing three fronts in our hearings and legislation campaign: the main players within the congressional majority who opposed the entire thing outright; the midlevel power holders who pushed for a one-sided compromise (thereby watering the whole thing down); and a handful who appeared to be fighting for the entire deal: actual whistleblower protection laws.

In the end, we got absolutely nothing. We were told repeatedly that as long as the Republican majority remained in Congress we had no chance whatsoever. They told us that unless that status changed in the coming congressional elections of 2006, there would be no hearings and, of course, no legislation. Thus, we waited. The elections were two months away.

On the evening of November 7, 2006, I was one of many national security whistleblowers who sat behind her desktop, online, anticipating the results. Many of us stayed up until late in the night counting, anticipating, and hoping. As now we know, the Democrats won, and became the majority in both House and Senate. We thought we had won; we celebrated online—prematurely. Our list of witnesses (that included my name) and our organized case documentations were ready for our long-anticipated January and February 2007 dreams for a hearing. Now, we felt, nothing could stop us. Our day in court had arrived, courtesy of the Democrats.

The month of January came and went without a single notification, e-mail or phone call from our "handful of congressional angels," one of whom who had become the chairman of the Committee on Oversight and Government Reform. In February, we started to call. No one was returning them. I called and e-mailed our formerly fiery and supportive staff members from Henry Waxman's office many times. I received no response. We tried for another two months, and to our genuine shock, we—the coalition organizations and whistleblowers guaranteed support—went unacknowledged. The new majority Democrats, including our "handful" of backers, didn't even want to hear about the hearings they had promised us. They would not have anything to do with the proposed legislation that they themselves helped us put together. The new majority had filled up the seats of the old one, and except for that capital D, would continue to a tee the practice of their predecessors.

We had lost—again. We all had learned a lesson, but the lesson didn't leave us with even one channel left to pursue. This exactly mirrored my own past experience. The system put in place by our founders, the separation of powers among the three branches—the system of checks and balances—had been tampered with and permanently corrupted. We were a constitutional democracy in name only. Where was the rule of law? This was more than about a single issue or problem affecting some activists; this was a cancer metastasizing and decaying the nation at its core, and the people didn't even know about it.

By June 2007, almost all national security whistleblower activities and campaigns had ended. After all, what was left to pursue? Our members were disillusioned, exhausted and utterly disgusted, and I topped that list.

The federal courts kept on ruling pro-secrecy and pro-government cover-ups, and continued issuing anti-accountability and anti-whistleblower rulings. The federal government, emboldened by these court compliances and congressional inaction, only increased the level of abuse, unwarranted excessive classification, and retaliation against whistleblowers. Without real media scrutiny and true investigative journalism, Congress remained as an extension of the executive branch with one task to perform: stamping its approval of every proposed action-abuse by the federal government and almost all budget increase requests by them.

Many of these whistleblowers, like me, had already fought the long fight within the executive branch agencies and channels and in federal courts. Our pursuit of real congressional action was the last stop. The Congress was driven by two major factors: money (the power of lobbying), and the media (re-elections and PR). We were not lobbyists; neither did we have access to deep pockets to purchase the needed action. Our cause was the public cause—typically free of deep-pockets backing.

The second equally powerful factor depended solely on mainstream media: reporters, networks and major print outlets. That factor too had been long absent in calls for oversight and accountability. They enabled Dennis Hastert to run for another term right after the *Vanity Fair* exposé, which was never denied or contested. They blacked out every report and source on the Hastert case and others. Similarly, it was intentional censorship and hold by the media that kept from the public the NSA illegal eavesdropping until after the presidential election. Volumes and numerous documentaries could be made on this one topic alone.

I had arrived at a point of pause and reflection. After spending six years in the fight—the one based on eternal vigilance—and putting every other aspect of my life on hold, I had hit a dead end, or what seemed to be a stalemate. Who had I become? Where was I going? What did I want from life?

I couldn't undo the past; nor could I recover the deep financial losses from pursuing fugitive justice. I could not erase the time gap in the course of my career. Most importantly, I could not go back to being who I was before these things happened, my unclassified self. That person no longer existed.

What about the future? Even more, the now that takes me there? Weren't there paths to be hewn and forged? Didn't I have those choices? What were they—the choices I truly wanted and actually could take? When would be the right time?

The answers to some of those questions were right here before me, and one I didn't need to look for too hard. It was in me, and one of my truest, strongest desires in life. It was there in my work and activism history, in the orphanages from Turkey to Russia; in the hundreds of hours in Juvenile court to the subjects I chose for my education. The answer was in every spare room in my house—in every place I'd lived in the last fifteen years: the one set up as a nursery, for the children I wanted to have.

I had always wanted to adopt, and hoped to adopt not just once but several times. That process would have begun in 1999, but my father's death put that plan on hold. And then came 9/11. All of which had brought me up to now. It was crisp and clear before me; the path to the future I wanted, always: my very own nest and family.

Once that hit me, I didn't lose a single minute. I started to research international adoption, the countries involved, agencies and requirements, adoption and immigration laws. In less than a month I had decided on the country and had chosen Vietnam for reasons important to me. I had put together a blueprint on exactly how to do this. I was ready.

By October 2007, I had completed everything, received my home study report, and had gotten approval from the Vietnamese government. I was now officially on the waiting list for U.S. families in the queue to be matched with orphan Vietnamese children. Ordinarily, adoptive families wait long months or even years to receive the referral for their child, owing to a byzantine bureaucratic process; well, not me. I was going to do it in a different way, as I had always envisioned doing it.

My plan—which goes against what the experts recommended—was to pack my suitcases and head for Vietnam, and get to know the country and its culture while I waited for my referral. Once I received that referral, I planned to spend every hour that I could with my child, in the orphanage, while the paperwork and procedures were completed. Most people—including some close to me—considered this course a dangerous one, difficult and burdensome and, to a certain degree, foolish.

I had my reasons. First, I had to know my child-to-be's heritage and culture: that was an important part of who he or she was and would remain. Second, I was well aware of the importance of early bonding in the case of institutionalized children. Spending five or six months or more after the matching (during which that child is considered mine) *away* from that child while he or she resides in an orphanage was out of the question. If allowed, I would spend every minute of that waiting time in the orphanage with her or him. I would do everything within my power to be there with my child.

So, with this plan in hand, I prepared for the journey.

After exploring the country and much of its culture, spending time in exotic and often heartbreaking locales, I arrived at my final destination in Vietnam: the tiny and beautiful, breezy palm-fringed coastal city of Phan Thiet in Bin Thuan province. I had made my reservations at a quaint hotel with suite-like rooms to accommodate long-term living arrangements with a baby. My unit had a small kitchenette and a bit of separation between the sleeping area and living room. It opened up to the beautiful Mui Ne beach, where I could sit on my patio and watch the traditional Vietnamese fishing boats at work. I even had a TV with satellite I intended to ignore (I did).

Immediately after settling in, I started to explore. I visited the orphanage where my child referral was expected to come almost daily; because orphanages in Vietnam have an open-door policy I could go there, spend time with the children, help out, and get to know and become friends with the caregivers. I also arranged to teach English in a church-sponsored charity organization as a volunteer. I started making friends—people with whom I expect to remain friends for the rest of my life. And I waited and waited, impatiently, for that call: to inform me of my referral, and to meet my child to be.

Waiting was not easy; not at all. With the clock ticking on the adoption window, and with August fast approaching, my anxiety was starting to mount. By the end of July, I was grimly looking for deals on flights back home. I had thirty-one days left, and the prospect didn't seem good. By August 4, I had my reservations in place and dimming hopes to deal with. It was out of my hands; twenty-seven more days of waiting.

Then, on August 8, the call at last came through: my referral. All I could make out in the haze of excitement was *baby girl, three weeks old, six pounds, relinquished* (i.e., not abandoned, meaning that the biological mother and/or father, formally and legally, had relinquished parental rights to the orphanage and, thus, the Vietnamese government). I sprang out of the hotel unit, ran to one of the managers, Phi, gave him a tight hug, and jumping up and down, babbled that I needed a motor bike to zoom me to the orphanage, fifteen minutes away. In less time than that I was in front of the door, pacing madly, waiting for the agency representative to show up. She arrived ten minutes later, which felt like an eon, and together we entered the place I had visited at least twenty times in two months.

I stood right behind her while she talked with one of the caregivers and showed her the paper with my daughter's—yes, my *daughter*'s—name. The caregiver walked to one of the small rooms where they kept six or so cribs with newborns. My heart was pounding. We followed her inside. She leaned over one of the cribs and picked up a teeny tiny baby bundled in red swaddle. I couldn't yet see her face; finally, the caregiver turned around and came to us. My representative took the baby and brought her up to me, and I reached out. Everything else after that is a complete blur. All I remember is holding my child in my arms and staring at her face, her jet black alert eyes, ruby red heart-shaped lips and a tiny nose on the tiniest baby face I'd ever seen. I held her closer to my chest, leaned over and kissed her for the very first time. I gazed in her shiny black eyes that were holding mine, and felt so very complete, so content.

From that day on, and for the next two months, I spent every day at the orphanage with my daughter, Ela. The orphanage staff and local government agencies were extremely accommodating, even though this was certainly not the usual protocol. After the first few days, my constant presence became a norm. I was part of that institution. I became one of the children's caregivers, the only family they'd ever known. For the next two months, the place became my home, and everyone there felt like family.

With less than fifteen minutes to go before landing, I maneuvered within the confines of my seatbelt and cramped seating area. I changed Ela's diaper and prepared her formula for feeding during our descent, which helps babies with the painful ear pressure. Meanwhile, anticipation of my homecoming was rapidly turning into acute anxiety bordering on a panic attack. I wasn't sure why.

For the last eight months I had been completely cut off from news and relationships; occasional e-mails to family and my regular phone calls with Matthew were the extent of my "being in touch." Sure, I couldn't escape the mania surrounding the presidential race and Barack Obama's victory. Unfortunately for me, Obama's presidency was no cause to celebrate. Certainly he "looked and talked" better than his opponents, but that was where differences ended. I had dealt with Obama's Senate office, and we as national security whistleblowers also had "tried" to work with his office—all to no avail. He was as anti-whistleblower, anti-transparency and anti-accountability as they come, along with many of his colleagues there, including Senator Hillary Rodham Clinton. They had made it clear to me and to all of us. Then there is Senator Obama's record, which speaks for itself. Whether on NSA illegal eavesdropping or the FBI's outrageous and frightening abuses of civil liberties, Obama was no different than his rival in the campaign, John McCain, or even George W. Bush. Last but not least were Obama's ties to and selection of infamous Illinois–Chicago figures about whom, thanks to my work with the FBI, I knew a great deal, and none of it was pretty. All that and more put me in a tiny minority who saw through the front, the mask, the phony lip service; and that gave me no reason for "hope" or any high regard for his other slogan, "change." My optimism had peaked with the 2006 elections; having seen the result—the toxic status quo—it now had reached an all-time low.

After our smooth landing and clearing through Customs and Immigration, with Ela wrapped around me in her carrier along with four suitcases, a diaper bag, a computer case and my handbag, we entered one of the domestic terminals at LAX for the next and last leg of our long trip home. After our check-in at the ticket counter we proceeded to the security gates. Once there, in a slow-moving, overcrowded line, I was taken aback: here were more than *fifty* TSA security officers—in uniform, with badges and a military police demeanor. They were loudly issuing orders to passengers in harsh and humiliating fashion. Some were busy patting and groping a randomly selected unfortunate few. Another had grabbed and violently emptied a woman's handbag in plain full view, which contained her birth control, tampons, makeup and other dangerous items.

Now it was my turn to pass through the scan. With Ela (now sleeping) attached to me I tried, with some difficulty, to remove my shoes and place them on the belt. Luckily, the female officer allowed me to go through without first detaching the carrier; but then she stopped me on the other side, and with the help of her colleague, began the pat-down with a loudly beeping handheld device.

As I sat on a bench and struggled again with my shoes, I noticed my palms were sweaty and both hands were trembling. This was one of many sorry points that our response to 9/11 had brought us to: a fear-driven police-like state. No wonder I was shaking. I had seen this before, in Turkey and Iran, and countless other places without the rule of law; no small reason for pessimism.

Now here I was, home in my country, and this was the state of the nation. All communications were monitored and stored by the police, intelligence, the military, or all three. All passengers were treated and searched as suspects, as criminals, and possibly terrorists. The terrible list goes on.

On our way home to Alexandria in a taxi from DC, on that damp and bone-chilling winter night, I gazed at the Capitol across the river, at the Lincoln Memorial and the Pentagon fortress.

The scenery and mood took me back. The years of constant surveillance and threats, my legal ordeals and desertion by family and friends, all had taken their toll; I remembered almost taking that flight to Turkey and shuddered. Almost all of my battles were losses. Over there, across the river, were the winners, the rulers; here in this taxi, with a brand-new baby daughter, still, I remained a classified woman.

20

Three Journeys
Converge

Aone, concluded. In some ways, it was a relief to go back to be-fter spending almost a year away, I was back and into a new life. The long chapter that had been my case was over, finished and ing me; but just who was this person? For the first few months, I didn't give it much thought; instead, I spent almost all my time with my daughter, enveloped in this intimate, warm cocoon of motherhood.

Without TV, satellite or cable, I was able to keep chaos mostly at bay. Once in a while, though, late at night, with Ela sound asleep, I would sit quietly at my desktop and quickly scan news and commentaries. Usually this would end with a disgusted shake of my head or wannabe detached shrug.

Our new president—the President of Change—appeared to be follow-ing in the footsteps of his predecessor. The new administration invoked the State Secrets Privilege three times in its first 100 days: *Al Haramain Islamic Foundation v. Obama*; *Mohammed v. Jeppesen Dataplan*; and *Jewel v. NSA*. The president continued the illegal wiretapping of Americans and pledged to shield and protect the participating telecom industry. Also—distressingly—this was the same president who quickly backped-aled on his promise to shut down the Guantanamo Bay detention facility.

Instead, he chose to revive the Bush-style military commission, albeit with a cosmetic tweak.

Tellingly, too, he instantly reversed his earlier stand on protection for government whistleblowers. This new White House was creating several new "czars" a week; the civilian death toll of our war in Afghanistan was climbing; the Patriot Act had a new guardian angel; the list goes on and on.

Clearly—at least to me—all of us were being led deeper into darkness. I tried to shake it off. I was no longer a case. At that time, I wasn't looking for a fight. I was grateful for Ela and the rest of my family. As long as I stayed in my warm cocoon, I would be safe and unaffected. Or so I thought.

In early March 2009, coming back from a short trip to Florida, I had a horrific confrontation with the airport security, specifically, one TSA badge-woman. It began with her demand that I remove my baby carrier (I'd already gone through without triggering any alarms; her arbitrary stop and search was unreasonable), and from there things escalated to a dreadful point. Supervisors and airport police were called in, we missed our flight, and in the meantime they refused to show me the rules, which they insisted were classified. This badge-woman possessed "unlimited discretion," she claimed, and that "there are no rules." What's more, she insisted, "we don't have to answer your questions." Clearly, this tiny woman with a baby posed a security threat: I had dared to question my rights and the rules of a government screening its citizens. I dared them to arrest me. I could feel Matthew's pleading exasperated eyes but I wasn't going down without a fight. I wasn't prepared to hand over my rights, not then, not now. I was adamant.

I noticed too as events were unfolding, how people rushed past us, scurrying to their gates. They gave me quick little glances, making sure to avoid any eye contact; maybe this reality—this new encroachment on their freedom to move about—was too close to the bone, too much for them to see. A few brave souls actually slowed down to whisper such things as, "This is disgusting" or "They have no right to treat people like this" or even "This is a shame."

At this point, I didn't want to be on a flight. We would rent a car and drive twenty hours back home. The two police officers escorting us out tried to commiserate, apologizing for "these TSA guys" whom they claimed, armed with guns and badges, were "high with a sense of power."

The first few hours of our long drive back home were spent in miserable silence. I simmered, more with fear than rage—not only of what we had become as a nation, but even more, where we were headed. All of this—the police state climate and practices—were way too familiar.

I turned to Matthew, driving on my left, and in a calm and measured voice said, "I won't let my daughter grow up in a police state and under these circumstances. I won't let her go through experiences like this. I won't let her go through what I did when I was a child. I won't let it happen."

To my surprise, he agreed. "This is not my country anymore," he told me with terrible sadness in his voice. "This is not my government. This place is now as foreign as any other foreign country to me. We the people must fight against all of this, but there doesn't seem to be enough of us who are willing to fight . . ."

We talked about other countries. Australia? No. It too has been catering to our nation's illegitimate demands, participating in our perpetual wars abroad, deserting its innocent citizens held with no probable cause in America's detention center, and participating in our intelligence operations. Western Europe? Definitely not: same old same old. New Zealand? Perhaps; not hawkish, not militarized, free and dignified air transportation procedures, not part of the global intelligence operations, excellent health care system, very good public education . . . a definite possibility. The question remained: At what point do we say enough is enough? At what point do we give up on our beloved country? What would we consider to be the turning point? We left that to time, and I knew the clock was ticking. It had been, in fact, ever since 9/11, since I went to work for the FBI.

With all I had gone through up to this point, I faced the need to speak up; to write. I wanted to share my observations of our police state status and precisely to what degree our media is complicit. I had firsthand knowledge of notorious incidents that were blacked out not only here, in our news, but abroad. Entire stories were killed in their tracks. The tentacles of our government's censorship extend far and wide, and I wondered how many others knew about it. I needed to know where others stood, and accordingly, where we were headed. I had to know if there was any hope of stopping and reversing these trends, and if not, I had to find out when and where I'd go next, if only to save my daughter. She didn't have to live as I once did. I thought I'd escaped that life, that I'd finally put it behind . . .

Now starting a personal blog seemed urgent. I could share my experience and observations of the escalating police state, the proliferation of badge-men and badge-women in our malls and cities and airports and hubs with their frightening weapons and dogs. I could inform others of noxious new developments and their real-life implications despite the media's blackout. I could list the already numerous changes brought about by President Obama, illustrating how all have been changes for the worse—at least so far; and to also show to what extent the partisan divide is political theater—dangerous antics, to be sure, but nevertheless a distraction from what both parties always never want you to know.

So I began my novice venture into the blogosphere. I set up a simple page under the "blogspot.com" free Google platform, named it 123 Real Change, and every few days or so posted an article or analysis; without a splash, without advertising it, and without any readers at first. To my amazement, within a few weeks, my small and almost invisible new site had been found by a few hundred weekly visitors, commenting with sincere and astute observations.

The sorry state of our nation, its ever-increasing number of wars and ever-worsening status of civil liberties, provided me with more topics than I could cover in a lifetime. Since taking office in January 2009, the president who duped the nation as a candidate for change has indeed manically brought about changes—most of them for the worse.

The persecution of whistleblowers has only escalated: now they are *prosecuted* for telling the truth. Far from protecting government whistle-blowers as promised, the Obama administration has amassed the worst record in U.S. history for persecuting, prosecuting and jailing govern-ment whistleblowers and truth tellers. This president's Department of Justice has *twisted the 1917 Espionage Act to press criminal charges in five instances of alleged national security leaks:* more such prosecutions than have occurred in all previous administrations combined, going all the way back to the founders.

The assault on the First Amendment has reached unprecedented lev-els. The government, via the Pentagon, now takes books off shelves and actually *burns* them. The reason? Sorry, that's classified. We aren't even allowed to know why.

Secrecy and gag orders too have reached new highs. President Obama has invoked baseless, unconstitutional executive secrecy to quash legal inquiries into hushed-up activity more often than any of his predeces-sors, including, famously, George Bush. This president's almost reflex-ive invocations of state secrets already has resulted in shutting down lawsuits involving the National Security Agency's (then) illegal wiretap-ping, extraordinary rendition, assassinations and illegal torture.

Under the present administration, not only government whistle-blowers but hundreds if not thousands of peaceful American activists and truth tellers have been subject to government witch hunts, surveil-lance and arrests. Recently, too, the FBI has launched a series of raids and issued grand jury subpoenas targeting dozens of antiwar activists. Thousands of protesters have been arrested for exercising their First Amendment right to speak out.

President Obama has initiated a covert assassination program as well, allocating to himself the power to include Americans on that list. Indeed, several United States citizens, including their children, have been assassinated abroad.

Contrary to his campaign pledge, President Obama not only granted amnesty to those involved in enacting and implementing illegal wiretapping of every American citizen's communications, he went further, to even sanction and expand these police state practices. The president is now preparing for the next assault: on Internet users and independent reporters and bloggers.

America's illegal, unjustified invocations of war more than quadrupled in the current term. Our commander in chief has expanded our war fronts to Libya, Yemen, Somalia and Pakistan; more are under way.

Toward the end of July 2009, less than two weeks before our departure for New Zealand (yes, I'd been doing some research for a suitable place we might go if and when things got worse), I received an unusual e-mail from a man named David Krikorian. In it, he briefly described his case as a candidate from Ohio who had run against incumbent Republican Representative Jean Schmidt. Schmidt, who was intensely favored by the Turkish lobby and its numerous networks, was a recipient of their generous contributions and support. He now was a party in a legal battle, a case pending before the Ohio Elections Commission, in which Ohio's Republican U.S. Congresswoman Jean Schmidt had filed a complaint against Krikorian, who, Schmidt had charged, distributed false statements about her during the previous year's campaign. Krikorian and his attorneys were planning to depose me.

I quickly ran an Internet search on *Schmidt v. Krikorian*. Schmidt alleged that Krikorian—who announced plans to run against Schmidt again, as a Democrat, in 2010—libeled her in campaign ads, claiming she had taken "blood money" as campaign donations from Turkish interest groups. Schmidt, as co-chairwoman of the Congressional Turkish Caucus, had received more than $10,000 from the Turkish Coalition

USA PAC since taking office in 2005, and had recently taken a trip to Turkey—sponsored by the Turkish Coalition of America—valued at more than $10,000. At issue in the initial *Schmidt v. Krikorian* case was the century-long debate over whether the extermination of some 1.5 million ethnic Armenians during World War I would be declared a "genocide" by the American government.

I immediately called Krikorian and we had a brief discussion, during which he provided general outlines of his case, the reasons he and his attorneys were seeking my deposition, and the timing of their upcoming legal filings. I found him sincere, likeable and articulate, and I knew exactly what he was up against. I knew only too well how Turkish-American operatives bought and managed elected representatives and candidates.

I was up-front with Krikorian. First, I let him know that although I was intimately familiar with some of the lobby groups and operatives involved, I had no direct information on Jean Schmidt. (Schmidt had gotten into Congress several years after I was fired from the bureau.) Next, I warned him what he was up against, a fact about which he was very well aware. And finally, I told him about my upcoming trip in less than two weeks, which was problematic with their case filings and hearing dates; and that I needed to consult with my attorney as to whether I would be able to testify in their case, considering the Justice Department's position in previous cases. Krikorian understood and said he and his attorneys would have a meeting and take the appropriate action.

Then I contacted Steve Kohn at the National Whistleblowers Center. I explained the case and situation, and asked for his legal advice. Steve told me that "based on FBI employment and classification rules, we have to submit their formal subpoena to the DOJ and ask them to clear your deposition." I told him about their deadline and my upcoming trip, to which he replied they would ask the DOJ for expedited clearance, that they were "obligated to respond and act accordingly."

I provided Krikorian and his team with the information I had gotten from Steve. They would prepare a subpoena for my deposition in forty-eight hours or less. My attorney then would submit it to the Justice Department for clearance.

Two days later, my attorney's office received Krikorian's subpoena for my deposition: the date was set for Saturday, August 8, at 10 A.M., exactly twenty-four hours before my departure to New Zealand. As required, the Krikorian legal team had included the major points and areas on which they were planning to question me. This was to be an "open to the media deposition." The subpoena stated I would testify that during the time I was employed by the FBI, I obtained evidence that (1) "The Government of Turkey had illegally infiltrated and influenced various U.S. government institutions and officials, including the Department of State, the Department of Defense and individual members of the United States Congress"; (2) "The Government of Turkey had engaged in practices and policies that were inimical to American interests and had in fact resulted in both the direct and indirect loss of American lives"; and (3) "Turkish American cultural and business groups conduct operations with direct and indirect support from the Government of Turkey."

My attorney submitted the subpoena together with their letter notifying the Justice Department. The FBI responded immediately by objecting to the request. In return, my attorneys sent a two-page letter to both the FBI and DOJ stating that the objections raised so far by the agency were not sufficient to block me from "truthfully answering questions while under oath pursuant to a lawful subpoena" on Saturday morning, August 8, in Washington, DC, as scheduled. The letter also requested that they be provided with a copy of my employment agreement, "as this document may impact on Ms. Edmonds' ability to testify"; and that "if the documents are not received by close of business today we will interpret this failure as a release of the government's right to suppress Ms. Edmonds' ability to truthfully answer questions while under oath pursuant to a lawful subpoena." The letter continued,

"In any event, consistent with my understanding of the Agency's prepublication clearance rules, oral disclosure, including oral testimony, is permitted without prior review. Consistent with the Agency's pre-publication rules, Ms. Edmonds will attempt, to the best of her ability, not [to] disclose classified information. However, Ms. Edmonds' recollection and judgment as to what information may be subject to lawful non-disclosure would, at best, be imperfect. As such, the FBI has at least three avenues available to guard against such inadvertent disclosure: 1) file a request for a protective order with the body that issued the subpoena; 2) file a motion to quash the deposition; and 3) dispatch legal counsel to the deposition capable of rais[ing] appropriate objections."

My attorney also issued a public statement to the press that strongly accused the FBI and DOJ of attempting "censorship" and trying to "silence a whistleblower." Of course, almost no one in the mainstream media picked up these publicly announced developments or press releases.

Interestingly—and alarmingly—my (by now) more visible blog was mysteriously suspended and taken down by Google. All of a sudden, as I started to counter the media blackout by posting recent developments and the notice of my deposition, my website disappeared from the Internet. After dozens of e-mails and inquiries, I was told by Google that my site was taken down due to anonymous complaints filed on its content. They would not say who these "complainers" were or what they had shown as "inappropriate" content. Google appeared to be using U.S. government–style classification and censorship, and just as with the government, there was not a thing I could do to overcome it in time to make what was happening public.

With the clock ticking and less than forty-eight hours to the scheduled deposition, the Justice Department and the FBI went into a sudden and mysterious silent mode. They did not file any motion to quash the subpoena, and they did not issue further threats or response of any kind. Just silence. Soon, on the day of the deposition, we would find out if their attorneys would be present. Meanwhile, we could see that the government had been quite successful in keeping the media at bay.

On Saturday, August 8, I met with the attorneys, as scheduled, at

Steve Kohn's law office in Georgetown. True to form, with the exception of a handful of activist bloggers and alternative news media, not a single reporter from the mainstream media was present. No government legal representative showed up for the deposition. I was free to provide my testimony under oath—for the first time in eight years trying. I had fought long years for just this opportunity.

I spent over four hours in a conference room with my attorneys, David Krikorian and his attorney, Bruce Fein (the attorney who represented Jean Schmidt), a court stenographer, a videographer, and a few legal aids and assistants for the parties involved. Fein acting as Schmidt's legal counsel spoke volumes in itself, as evidenced by the expansive and protective ring formed around Schmidt by powerful and shady Turkish operatives and lobbyists. Fein had been a crusty beltway foreign agent and lobbyist himself for nearly two decades. I knew him as an errand boy for the FBI's criminal and counterintelligence targets. I refused to be intimidated by the likes of him.

For four straight hours and with only one brief break, I answered questions for both parties under oath. I told the truth and held back very little, since only very little of my case could be arguably classified. I would never jeopardize an ongoing investigation, informant's identity or sensitive intelligence-gathering methods. By the same token, I would never hold back in exposing criminal operations against my country, espionage, political corruption and related cover-ups. They asked and I answered: on record, under oath.

The deposition included criminal allegations against specifically named members of Congress; among those I named as part of a broad criminal conspiracy were Representatives Dennis Hastert, Dan Burton, Roy Blunt, Bob Livingston, Stephen Solarz and Tom Lantos, as well as an unnamed, still-serving congresswoman who had been secretly videotaped, for blackmail purposes, during an affair.

Those high-ranking officials from the Bush administration named in my testimony as part of the criminal conspiracy on behalf of agents of the Government of Turkey included Douglas Feith, Paul Wolfowitz, Marc Grossman and others. I discussed covert "activities" by Turkish entities "that would involve trying to obtain very sensitive, highly classified U.S. intelligence information, weapons technology information, classified congressional records ... recruiting key U.S. individuals with access to highly sensitive information, blackmailing, bribery."

At the end of the intense four-hour session, the video and transcript of my deposition became a public document. In over two hundred pages of transcript, the public at long last would have the true account of blackmail, bribery, espionage, infiltration and criminal conspiracy by current and former members of the U.S. Congress, high-ranking State and Defense Department officials, and agents of the Government of Turkey. This was far from a complete report, since I was only able to provide answers sought by the Krikorian legal team, which pertained specifically to the area of illegal foreign lobbying activities, bribery, corruption and activities related to espionage cases that were already public. My testimony was certainly not the whole story, but the first under oath and in public; it was the only one—so far. Predictably, the media, collectively, censored and blacked out the deposition and all it contained.

Yet, as disheartening as all this seems, a flicker of hope for real change refused to be snuffed out. As Samuel Adams put it over two centuries ago, "It does not require a majority to prevail, but rather an irate, tireless minority keen to set brush fires in people's mind." Thus it boiled down, at least for me, to the question of how to inform others, how to set brush fires in their minds. Not necessarily the majority, but just enough outraged people who then would work tirelessly to bring about needed changes. The answer as to "how" was sitting before me: the Internet, of course.

In less than a few months, the little blog diary I had started in May 2009 had kindled that flicker of hope, and in time turned into a decent-sized flame. It was my starting point. It was where I rushed to at the end of my deposition session in the case of *Krikorian v. Schmidt*; I was intent on fanning it into a full-blast fire.

Having gone through being blocked and taken down by Google, I immediately went about finding a decent hosting company, setting up a "real" website, and putting together a plan to make this website a place for the sorely needed irate minority to help bring about those changes. I named the site Boiling Frogs Post: a sly reference to the legend (whether or not true) that if you put a frog in a pot of water and slowly, by degrees, gradually increase the temperature, the frog just sits there and never tries to jump out—until it's cooked, as the water boils. Here, the creeping implementation of police state practices that systematically deprive us of our rights one by one is the water; the increasingly desensitized American public, powerless in a bubbling cauldron of fear, is the frog. Some of us need to jump out—now.

My website was really taking off. Within the first few months I received an e-mail from a reader that contained a powerful, brilliantly executed cartoon related to my latest article. The author kindly complimented my work, encouraged my efforts, and offered the attachment as a complimentary addition. I checked out his name on the Web: Paul Jamiol, a nationally and internationally recognized cartoonist. Here he was, one of my regular readers, an activist and obviously a fellow supporter. Another e-mail from Jamiol with a brilliant toon followed within a week and another after that. Paul Jamiol became Boiling Frogs Post's editorial cartoonist with regular weekly presentations. His work made the website shine, and was cheered and welcomed by our expanding readership.

During this initial stage with the website, I also wanted to have a podcast program, interviews with those silenced or ignored by the government and media, as well as relevant audio and multimedia links for news, information and discussion—particularly on topics long censored by the mainstream and quasi alternatives alike.

With little familiarity and zero expertise in hosting a talk show or interview forum, I needed a partner with savvy and skills, someone like-minded, independent, whom I could trust. I racked my brains. Finally,

Matthew came to me and said, "Forget about the details of how you'd arrange, learn, and execute a podcast interview program for Boiling Frogs. First, answer one question: If you could have anyone as a partner for a weekly radio-podcast show—and I mean anyone—who would you pick?" Almost instantly, I replied, "Peter B. Collins."

I'd known Peter since 2004. He was one of the first three alternative radio talk show hosts who had braved inviting me on for a lengthy, comprehensive interview. He has integrity and a tenacious adherence to ethics; fiercely independent, impossible to manipulate or sway in any way. He was my people.

Matthew asked, "Why don't you call and ask Peter B. Collins? Just ask him. If he says no, then you'll know . . ." Good idea.

I called Peter, and his enthusiastic yes came without pause or hesitation. He came on board as a partner.

Slowly but surely we added to the roster, with independent authors and analysts contributing articles and editorials to Boiling Frogs Post. We did not shy from controversy nor did we shun taboo topics. Whether the facts on Afghanistan and our escalating wars, the Israel lobby or the CIA's role in such criminal activities as narcotics and more, we tackled our topics without any external or internally imposed barriers. Our audience has come to expect nothing less.

Boiling Frogs Post is complementary to and, in many ways, an extension of my National Security Whistleblowers Coalition. How many mainstream publications can claim to have over one hundred experts and sources from key intelligence and law enforcement agencies, each of whom, in turn, have their own network of government insiders and sources? (Answer: None.) The website also provides a platform for whistleblower issues and cases, and acts as a trusted channel for anonymous disclosure by those still inside government agencies.

By summer 2011, a new partner came aboard. Known for his brilliant and independent video report production from Japan, Canadian reporter James Corbett joined Boiling Frogs Post and we began a weekly series of investigative video reports on such issues as the CIA, the nuclear black market, Afghan heroin, Eurasia and the new Silk Road Project. These groundbreaking, original productions brought large international audiences to our site.

For clear and obvious reasons, as far as funding went, Boiling Frogs Post would rely solely on its readers' support and contributions. This is non-negotiable. There simply is no other way to remain independent. Another written-in-stone pledge for Boiling Frogs Post is the resolve to remain completely nonpartisan. This too is non-negotiable. The political news and activism landscape is littered and poisoned with partisanship—of the most toxic variety—and with that comes bias, bickering and attacks, distraction, futility, divisiveness; none of which have positive consequences. Partisanship acts as a cloak over truth and real causes; it is the single most effective way for the establishment to divide and rule—and therefore win. It is a sure way for the people—the majority—to lose.

My first objective is to help shed light and to inform. My other objective is to unite: to unite the irate minority in needed numbers. Partisanship stands in the way of both; and my ultimate objective—to bring about necessary change, whether gradually from within or drastically from outside—conflicts with the establishment's partisan divisiveness. As proven once again with Barack Obama's presidency, partisanship acts as an illusion of difference: when there is one establishment presented in two colors, red or blue, in two brands. Scratch the surface and see.

I held onto my pledges. My partners at Boiling Frogs Post happen to be my most trusted friends. Our readership and support has been steadily (albeit slowly) growing. Together we share the same objectives: inform, unite, and change.

In 1988, before I left Turkey for the United States, I had taken the required university entry exam. Everything was based on this score. This was how the public system operated. I could list my preferred subject areas along with five or six universities around the country, prioritized and ranked according to my preference, but ultimately my score would determine my fate, to which of these places I would go. In spite of my mother's warnings and threats, induced by the country's political climate of fear, the life-threatening risks all journalists faced, and our particular family's history, my top two choices were journalism schools at two universities, both in Istanbul. I could have had either one, but I didn't want to choose between my family and my passion. I didn't want to live in a nation and climate where people faced choices like that. So I left.

Twenty-four years later, after a nearly decade-long Kafkaesque journey, here I am, back to my original passion: journalism, reporting and exposing the truth, and working to inform and unite enough people to bring about needed "real" changes. Somehow my three life journeys had prepared and armed me with everything I needed for this new role. My linguistic abilities; firsthand knowledge and experience of consequences associated with U.S. foreign policies abroad; a long list of intelligence, law enforcement and congressional connections and sources obtained through my whistleblowing case; being an active party in several court and congressional cases in fighting for civil liberties, justice and accountability—all had come together in one place, and in a position where they could be put to good use toward a common cause. This is not a new journey but the continuation of three: converging, moving forward, out of darkness into light.

Epilogue

Even today, in early 2012, more than a decade since the start of my Orwellian journey that began with the FBI, I write these final words of a classified woman, not knowing if my story will ever see the light of day. In view of our present state of clampdown, all the legal experts tell me to expect more censorship, gag orders and retaliation against this book-to-be. Undeterred by their forecasts, I have written with one driving purpose: to shed light on the expanding darkness that slowly, by degrees, devours our liberties. Secrecy hates the light. Where power succeeds, darkness prevails. Their war is against us, if we dare to speak out; we get classified, banished, or worse. I am not naïve. I know the realities on the ground—only too well. Yet, if you are reading this, all is not lost.

My story is all our fight, every one of us. Otherwise, why bother writing? It is still my battle, yes, in many ways, but now I'm bringing it to you. This is about censorship and your right to hold government and power accountable for what it does in your name. It's a war against cover-up and smothering truth in untold secret places. Once you see the dark side—whether catching a glimpse or being locked behind one of its infinite doors—you cannot go back, put it behind or pretend it never existed. You can try, but it doesn't work. I tried to run away, to forget. I even tried self-induced amnesia; as happens with any trauma, though, it comes back, with interest, often disguised and in unpredictable ways. It never goes away. It can stalk you. In my case, I had come to a realization, an awakening, a moment of truth; I had to make a decision: How willing was I and to what lengths would I go to face this trauma and fear—to try to uncover its sources and perhaps find ways to conquer it? To what degree was I willing to seek the help of others?

When my life unpredictably veered into darkness, I was faced with those existential questions. In the beginning, I certainly did ponder running away, to quietly resign from the FBI, return to my previous life and work and never look back. At one point (more than one, in fact), I seriously considered dropping every course of action: every legal and congressional battle, and carry on with my life filled with fear—knowing, even, that this would probably continue for as long as I lived. In the end, though, a decision had been reached. I would face it, and tackle its sources as best as I could. I did, in fact, seek the help of others. That was the main purpose of my whistleblowers organization; and collectively, we tried to vanquish the darkness and its sources. Yet, during those crucial first few years, there didn't seem to be enough of us. Precious few who had experienced this dark side were willing to come forward or even to acknowledge it. Relaying what we knew, informing others, and alerting the majority however we could at that time seemed next to impossible.

Things seem to have changed. Many more have come to see, experience, or be touched by the darkness that envelops our freedom. People are more aware, which is heartening: the more we know, the better our chances to conquer it, to reclaim what is lost or threatened. It will always be an uphill battle, of that there can be no doubt, but none of us should ever give up hope; too much is at stake, the price of silence too steep. Of this darkness, many have been touched; some have had the merest glimpse while others have been drowned. Whether facing prosecution, jailed, harassed and scorned, gagged, censored, spied on and threatened, or persecuted in secret prisons, those who know the darkness also know it is here—and expanding. Some know by now that going to the polls is an exercise in futility. The media too operates in darkness. Our choices are not a choice. A few know—and that number is growing—that even at this late hour, it is not too late to cry out, to inform, unite and fight for true changes: against fear and the power of darkness. They are the irate minority. They are growing. And I am with them, have been, and always will be.

Acknowledgments

Stephen Kohn and the National Whistleblowers Center—you became the catalyst to take on this project and the myriad obstacles in the way of its publication. Thank you for keeping me motivated and for all your support for this book. Without your support I might never have brought it to completion.

Rita Rosenkranz, my agent—thank you for believing in me and for lending me your support in challenging the establishment, convention and tradition to bring this book to publication.

Michael Wilde, my editor—You are the best editor a person could have. You gave far more than your stellar editorial skills to this book. You took on this enormous task with passion and as a kindred soul. Thank you for all your work and support.

Paul Jamiol and Linda Habib—I am fortunate to have your never-ending support, advice and guidance, but it's your friendship that I treasure most. Thank you.

Matthew, my husband and partner—you rode this dark storm with me; and you are still here, standing by my side. I know you will be there to ride other storms surely to come, right by my side. You are the one person to whom I owe the greatest thanks. I am grateful to have you as my life partner.

My father—for teaching me the things that count the most in life: love, truth, fairness and the willingness to seek and fight for them. You are my conscience, in my heart and spirit, always.

My vigilant activist supporters—during the last ten years, you have put me back on my feet every time I was brought to my knees. Your endless support and belief in me has kept me going. I may not have responded to your many thousands of letters but I assure you I have read every one, and some more than once. I thank you all from the bottom of my heart.